THE
MILLIONAIRE

THE SURPRISING

SECRETS OF
NEXT

AMERICA'S WEALTHY
DOOR

Thomas J. Stanley, Ph.D.
William D. Danko, Ph.D.

POCKET BOOKS
New York   London   Toronto   Sydney   Singapore

POCKET BOOKS, a division of Simon & Schuster, Inc.
1230 Avenue of the Americas, New York, NY 10020

Copyright © 1996 by Thomas J. Stanley and William D. Danko

Published by arrangement with Longstreet Press, Inc.

All rights reserved, including the right to reproduce
this book or portions thereof in any form whatsoever.
For information address Longstreet Press, Inc.,
2140 Newmarket Parkway, Suite 122, Marietta, GA 30067

ISBN: 0-7434-2037-3

First Pocket Books mass market paperback printing December 2000

10 9 8 7 6 5 4

POCKET and colophon are registered trademarks of
Simon & Schuster, Inc.

Printed in the U.S.A.

For Janet, Sarah, and Brad—a million Christmases,
a trillion Fourth of Julys
—T. J. Stanley

For my loving wife, Connie, and my dear children,
Christy, Todd, and David
—W. D. Danko

CONTENTS

TABLES

THE

MILLIONAIRE

THE SURPRISING

SECRETS OF

NEXT

AMERICA'S WEALTHY

DOOR

INTRODUCTION

Twenty years ago we began studying how people become wealthy. Initially, we did it just as you might imagine, by surveying people in so-called upscale neighborhoods across the country. In time, we discovered something odd. Many people who live in expensive homes and drive luxury cars do not actually have much wealth. Then, we discovered something even odder: Many people who have a great deal of wealth do not even live in upscale neighborhoods.

That small insight changed our lives. It led one of us, Tom Stanley, out of an academic career, inspired him to write three books on marketing to the affluent in America, and made him an advisor to corporations that provide products and services to the affluent. In addition, he conducted research about the affluent for seven of the top ten financial service corporations in America. Between us, we have conducted hundreds of seminars on the topic of targeting the wealthy.

Why are so many people interested in what we have to say? Because we have discovered who the wealthy really are and who they are not. And, most important, we have determined how ordinary people can become wealthy.

What is so profound about these discoveries? Just this: Most people have it all wrong about wealth in America. Wealth is not the same as income. If you make a good income each year and spend it all, you are not getting wealthier. You are just living high. Wealth is what you accumulate, not what you spend.

How do you become wealthy? Here, too, most people have it wrong. It is seldom luck or inheritance or advanced degrees or even intelligence that enables people to amass fortunes. Wealth is more often the result of a lifestyle of hard work, perseverance, planning, and, most of all, self-discipline.

How come I am not wealthy?

Many people ask this question of themselves all the time. Often they are hard-working, well-educated, high-income people. Why, then, are so few affluent?

MILLIONAIRES AND YOU

There has never been more personal wealth in America than there is today (over $22 trillion in 1996). Yet most Americans are not wealthy. Nearly one-half of our wealth is owned by 3.5 percent of our households. Most of the other households don't even come close. By "other households," we are not referring to economic dropouts. Most of these millions of households are composed of people who earn moderate, even high, incomes. More than twenty-five million households in the United States have annual incomes in excess of $50,000; more than seven million have annual incomes over $100,000. But in spite of being "good income" earners, too many of these people have small levels of accumulated wealth. Many live from paycheck to paycheck. These are the people who will benefit most from this book.

The median (typical) household in America has a net worth of less than $15,000, excluding home equity. Factor out equity in motor vehicles, furniture, and such, and guess what? More often than not the household has zero financial assets, such as stocks and bonds. How long could the average American household survive economically without a monthly check from an employer? Perhaps a month or two in most cases. Even those in the top quintile are not really wealthy. Their median household net worth is less than $150,000. Excluding home equity, the median net worth for this group falls to less than $60,000. And what about our senior citizens? Without Social Security benefits, almost one-half of Americans over sixty-five would live in poverty.

Only a minority of Americans have even the most conventional types of financial assets. Only about 15 percent of American households have a money market deposit account; 22 percent, a certificate of deposit; 4.2 percent, a money market fund; 3.4 percent, corporate or municipal bonds; fewer than 25 percent, stocks and mutual funds; 8.4 percent, rental property; 18.1 percent, U.S. Savings Bonds; and 23 percent, IRA or KEOGH accounts.

But 65 percent of the households have equity in their own home, and more than 85 percent own one or more motor vehicles. Cars tend to depreciate rapidly. Financial assets tend to appreciate.

The millionaires we discuss in this book are financially independent. They could maintain their current lifestyle for years and years without earning even one month's pay. The large majority of these millionaires are not the descendants of the Rockefellers or Vanderbilts. More than 80 percent are ordinary people who have accumulated their wealth in one generation. They did it slowly, steadily, without signing a multimillion-dollar contract with the Yankees, without winning the lottery, without becoming the next Mick Jagger. Windfalls make great headlines, but such occurrences are rare. In the course of an adult's lifetime, the probability of becoming wealthy via such paths is lower than one in four thousand. Contrast these odds with the proportion of American households (3.5 per one hundred) in the $1 million and over net worth category.

THE SEVEN FACTORS

Who becomes wealthy? Usually the wealthy individual is a businessman who has lived in the same town for all of his adult life. This person owns a small factory, a chain of stores, or a service company. He has married once and remains married. He lives next door to people with a fraction of his wealth. He is a compulsive saver and investor. And he has made his money on his own. *Eighty percent of America's millionaires are first-generation rich.*

Affluent people typically follow a lifestyle conducive to accumulating money. In the course of our investigations, we discovered seven common denominators among those who successfully build wealth.

1. They live well below their means.

2. They allocate their time, energy, and money efficiently, in ways conducive to building wealth.

3. They believe that financial independence is more important than displaying high social status.

4. Their parents did not provide economic outpatient care.

5. **Their adult children are economically self-sufficient.**

6. **They are proficient in targeting market opportunities.**

7. **They chose the right occupation.**

In *The Millionaire Next Door*, you will study these seven characteristics of the wealthy. We hope you will learn how to develop them in yourself.

THE RESEARCH

The research for *The Millionaire Next Door* is the most comprehensive ever conducted on who the wealthy are in America—and how they got that way. Much of this research was developed from the most recent survey we conducted that, in turn, was developed from studies we had conducted over the previous twenty years. These studies included personal and focus group interviews with more than five hundred millionaires and surveys of more than eleven thousand high–net worth and/or high-income respondents.

More than one thousand people responded to our latest survey,* which was conducted from May 1995 through January 1996. It asked each respondent about his or her attitudes and behaviors regarding a wide variety of wealth-related issues. Each participant in our study answered 249 questions. These questions addressed topics ranging from household budget planning or lack of it to financial fears and worries, and from methods of bargaining when purchasing automobiles to the categories of financial gifts, or "acts of

*For details on how we targeted respondents for our survey, see Appendix 1.

kindness," wealthy people give to their adult children. Several sections of the questionnaire asked respondents to indicate the most they ever spent for motor vehicles, wristwatches, suits, shoes, vacations, and the like. This study was the most ambitious and thorough we have ever undertaken. No other study has focused on the key factors that explain how people become wealthy in one generation. Nor has a study revealed why many people, even most of those with high incomes, never accumulate even a modest amount of wealth.

In addition to our survey, we gained considerable insight into the millionaire next door from other research. We spent hundreds of hours conducting and analyzing in-depth interviews with self-made millionaires. We also interviewed many of their advisors, such as CPAs and other professional experts. These experts were very helpful in our exploration of the issues underlying the accumulation of wealth.

What have we discovered in all of our research? Mainly, that building wealth takes discipline, sacrifice, and hard work. Do you really want to become financially independent? Are you and your family willing to reorient your lifestyle to achieve this goal? Many will likely conclude they are not. If you are willing to make the necessary trade-offs of your time, energy, and consumption habits, however, you can begin building wealth and achieving financial independence. *The Millionaire Next Door* will start you on this journey.

MEET THE MILLIONAIRE NEXT DOOR

These people cannot be millionaires! They don't look like millionaires, they don't dress like millionaires, they don't eat like millionaires, they don't act like millionaires—they don't even have millionaire names. Where are the millionaires who look like millionaires?

The person who said this was a vice president of a trust department. He made these comments following a focus group interview and dinner that we hosted for ten first-generation millionaires. His view of millionaires is shared by most people who are not wealthy. They think millionaires own expensive clothes, watches, and other status artifacts. We have found this is not the case.

As a matter of fact, our trust officer friend spends significantly more for his suits than the typical American millionaire. He also wears a $5,000 watch. We know from our surveys that the majority of millionaires never spent even one-tenth of $5,000 for a watch. Our friend also drives a current-model imported luxury car. Most millionaires are not driving this year's model. Only a minority drive a foreign motor vehicle. An even smaller minority drive foreign luxury cars. Our trust officer leases, while only a minority of millionaires ever lease their motor vehicles.

But ask the typical American adult this question: Who looks more like a millionaire? Would it be our friend, the trust officer, or one of the people who participated in our interview? We would wager that most people by a wide margin would pick the trust officer. But looks can be deceiving.

This concept is perhaps best expressed by those wise and wealthy Texans who refer to our trust officer's type as

Big Hat No Cattle

We first heard this expression from a thirty-five-year-old Texan. He owned a very successful business that rebuilt large diesel engines. But he drove a ten-year-old car and wore jeans and a buckskin shirt. He lived in a modest house in a lower-middle-class area. His neighbors were postal clerks, firemen, and mechanics.

After he substantiated his financial success with actual numbers, this Texan told us:

[My] business does not look pretty. I don't play the part . . . don't act it. . . . When my British partners first met me, they thought I was one of our truck drivers. . . . They looked all over my office, looked at everyone but me. Then the senior guy of the group said, "Oh, we forgot we were in Texas!" I don't own big hats, but I have a lot of cattle.

PORTRAIT OF A MILLIONAIRE

Who is the prototypical American millionaire? What would he tell you about himself?*

*Our profile of the typical millionaire is based on studies of millionaire households, not individuals. It is, therefore, impossible in most cases to say with certainty whether our typical millionaire is a he or

◆ I am a fifty-seven-year-old male, married with three children. About 70 percent of us earn 80 percent or more of our household's income.

◆ About one in five of us is retired. About two-thirds of us who are working are self-employed. *Interestingly, self-employed people make up less than 20 percent of the workers in America but account for two-thirds of the millionaires.* Also, three out of four of us who are self-employed consider ourselves to be entrepreneurs. Most of the others are self-employed professionals, such as doctors and accountants.

◆ Many of the types of businesses we are in could be classified as dull-normal. We are welding contractors, auctioneers, rice farmers, owners of mobile-home parks, pest controllers, coin and stamp dealers, and paving contractors.

◆ About half of our wives do not work outside the home. The number-one occupation for those wives who do work is teacher.

◆ Our household's total annual realized (taxable) income is $131,000 (median, or 50th percentile), while our average income is $247,000. Note that those of us who have incomes in the $500,000 to $999,999 category (8 percent) and the $1 million or more category (5 percent) skew the average upward.

◆ We have an average household net worth of $3.7 million. Of course, some of our cohorts have accumulated much

she. Nevertheless, because 95 percent of millionaire households are composed of married couples, and because in 70 percent of these cases the male head of the household contributes at least 80 percent of the income, we will usually refer to the typical American millionaire as "he" in this book.

more. Nearly 6 percent have a net worth of over $10 million. Again, these people skew our average upward. The typical (median, or 50th percentile) millionaire household has a net worth of $1.6 million.

◆ On average, our total annual realized income is less than 7 percent of our wealth. In other words, we live on less than 7 percent of our wealth.

◆ Most of us (97 percent) are homeowners. We live in homes currently valued at an average of $320,000. About half of us have occupied the same home for more than twenty years. Thus, we have enjoyed significant increases in the value of our homes.

◆ Most of us have never felt at a disadvantage because we did not receive any inheritance. About 80 percent of us are first-generation affluent.

◆ We live well below our means. We wear inexpensive suits and drive American-made cars. Only a minority of us drive the current-model-year automobile. Only a minority ever lease our motor vehicles.

◆ Most of our wives are planners and meticulous budgeters. In fact, only 18 percent of us disagreed with the statement "Charity begins at home." Most of us will tell you that our wives are a lot more conservative with money than we are.

◆ We have a "go-to-hell fund." In other words, we have accumulated enough wealth to live without working for ten or more years. Thus, those of us with a net worth of $1.6 million could live comfortably for more than twelve years. Actually, we could live longer than that, since we save at least 15 percent of our earned income.

◆ We have more than six and one-half times the level of wealth of our nonmillionaire neighbors, but, in our neighborhood, these nonmillionaires outnumber us better than three to one. Could it be that they have chosen to trade wealth for acquiring high-status material possessions?

◆ As a group, we are fairly well educated. Only about one in five are not college graduates. Many of us hold advanced degrees. Eighteen percent have master's degrees, 8 percent law degrees, 6 percent medical degrees, and 6 percent Ph.D.s.

◆ Only 17 percent of us or our spouses ever attended a private elementary or private high school. But 55 percent of our children are currently attending or have attended private schools.

◆ As a group, we believe that education is extremely important for ourselves, our children, and our grandchildren. We spend heavily for the educations of our offspring.

◆ About two-thirds of us work between forty-five and fifty-five hours per week.

◆ We are fastidious investors. On average, we invest nearly 20 percent of our household realized income each year. Most of us invest at least 15 percent. Seventy-nine percent of us have at least one account with a brokerage company. But we make our own investment decisions.

◆ We hold nearly 20 percent of our household's wealth in transaction securities such as publicly traded stocks and mutual funds. But we rarely sell our equity investments. We hold even more in our pension plans. On average, 21 percent of our household's wealth is in our private businesses.

◆ As a group, we feel that our daughters are financially handicapped in comparison to our sons. Men seem to make much more money even within the same occupational categories. That is why most of us would not hesitate to share some of our wealth with our daughters. Our sons, and men in general, have the deck of economic cards stacked in their favor. They should not need subsidies from their parents.

◆ What would be the ideal occupations for our sons and daughters? There are about 3.5 millionaire households like ours. Our numbers are growing much faster than the general population. Our kids should consider providing affluent people with some valuable service. Overall, our most trusted financial advisors are our accountants. Our attorneys are also very important. So we recommend accounting and law to our children. Tax advisors and estate-planning experts will be in big demand over the next fifteen years.

◆ I am a tightwad. That's one of the main reasons I completed a long questionnaire for a crispy $1 bill. Why else would I spend two or three hours being personally interviewed by these authors? They paid me $100, $200, or $250. Oh, they made me another offer—to donate in my name the money I earned for my interview to my favorite charity. But I told them, "I am my favorite charity."

"WEALTHY" DEFINED

Ask the average American to define the term *wealthy*. Most would give the same definition found in *Webster's*. Wealthy to them refers to people who have an abundance of material possessions.

We define wealthy differently. We do not define wealthy, affluent, or rich in terms of material possessions. Many people who display a high-consumption lifestyle have little or no investments, appreciable assets, income-producing assets, common stocks, bonds, private businesses, oil/gas rights, or timber land. Conversely, those people whom we define as being wealthy get much more pleasure from owning substantial amounts of appreciable assets than from displaying a high-consumption lifestyle.

THE NOMINAL DEFINITION OF WEALTHY

One way we determine whether someone is wealthy or not is based on net worth—"cattle," not "chattel." Net worth is defined as the current value of one's assets less liabilities (exclude the principle in trust accounts). In this book we define the threshold level of being wealthy as having a net worth of $1 million or more. Based on this definition, only 3.5 million (3.5 percent) of the 100 million households in America are considered wealthy. About 95 percent of millionaires in America have a net worth of between $1 million and $10 million. Much of the discussion in this book centers on this segment of the population. Why the focus on this group? Because this level of wealth can be attained in one generation. It can be attained by many Americans.

How Wealthy Should You Be?

Another way of defining whether or not a person, household, or family is wealthy is based on one's expected level of net worth. A person's income and age are strong determinants of how much that person should be worth. In other words, the higher one's income, the higher one's net worth is expected to be (assuming one is working and not retired). Similarly, the longer one is generating income, the more likely one will accumulate more and more wealth. So higher-income people who are older should have accumulated more wealth than lower-income producers who are younger.

For most people in America with annual realized incomes of $50,000 or more and for most people twenty-five to sixty-five years of age, there is a corresponding expected level of wealth. Those who are significantly above this level can be considered wealthy in relation to others in their income/age cohort.

You may ask: How can someone be considered wealthy if, for example, he is worth only $460,000? After all, he's not a millionaire. Charles Bobbins is a forty-one-year-old fireman. His wife is a secretary. They have a combined annual income of $55,000. According to our research findings, Mr. Bobbins should have a net worth of approximately $225,500. But he is worth much more than others in his income/age category. Mr. and Mrs. Bobbins have been able to accumulate an above-average amount of net worth. Thus, they apparently know how to live on a fireman's and secretary's income and still save and invest a good bit. They likely have a low-consumption lifestyle. And given this lifestyle, Mr. Bobbins could sustain himself and his family for ten years without working. Within their income and age categories, the Bobbinses are wealthy.

The Bobbinses are quite different from John J. Ashton, M.D., age fifty-six, who has an annual income of approximately $560,000. How much is Dr. Ashton worth? Is he wealthy? According to one definition, he is, since his net worth is $1.1 million. But he is not wealthy according to our other definition. Given his age and income, he should be worth more than $3 million.

With his high-consumption lifestyle, how long do you think Dr. Ashton could sustain himself and his family if he were no longer employed? Perhaps for two, at most three, years.

How to Determine If You're Wealthy

Whatever your age, whatever your income, how much should you be worth right now? From years of surveying various high-income/high–net worth people, we have developed several multivariate-based wealth equations. A simple rule of thumb, however, is more than adequate in computing one's expected net worth.

Multiply your age times your realized pretax annual household income from all sources except inheritances. Divide by ten. This, less any inherited wealth, is what your net worth should be.

For example, if Mr. Anthony O. Duncan is forty-one years old, makes $143,000 a year, and has investments that return another $12,000, he would multiply $155,000 by forty-one. That equals $6,355,000. Dividing by ten, his net worth should be $635,500. If Ms. Lucy R. Frankel is sixty-one and has a total annual realized income of $235,000, her net worth should be $1,433,500.

Given your age and income, how does your net worth match up? Where do you stand along the wealth continuum? If you are in the top quartile for wealth accumulation, you are a **PAW,** or **prodigious accumulator of wealth**. If you are in the bottom quartile, you are a **UAW,** or **under accumulator of wealth**. Are you a **PAW,** a **UAW,** or just an **AAW (average accumulator of wealth)**?

We have developed another simple rule. To be well positioned in the PAW category, you should be worth twice the level of wealth expected. In other words, Mr. Duncan's net worth/wealth should be approximately twice the expected value or more for his income/age cohort, or $635,500 multiplied by two equals $1,271,000. If Mr. Duncan's net worth is approximately $1.27 million or more, he is a prodigious accumulator of wealth. Conversely, what if his level of wealth is one-half or less than expected for all those in his income/age category? Mr. Duncan would be classified as a UAW if his level of wealth were $317,750 or less (or one-half of $635,500).

PAWs versus UAWs

PAWs are builders of wealth—that is, they are the best at building net worth compared to others in their income/age category. PAWs typically have a minimum of four times the wealth accumulated by UAWs. Contrasting the characteristics of PAWs and UAWs is one of the most revealing parts of the research we have conducted over the past twenty years.

A good example of the difference between PAWs and UAWs is revealed in two case studies. Mr. Miller "Bubba" Richards, age fifty, is the proprietor of a mobile-home dealership. His total household income last year was $90,200.

Mr. Richards's net worth, as computed via the wealth equation, is expected to be $451,000. But "Bubba" is a PAW. His actual net worth is $1.1 million.

His counterpart is James H. Ford II. Mr. Ford, age fifty-one, is an attorney. His income last year was $92,330, slightly more than Mr. Richards's. What is Mr. Ford's actual net worth? His expected level of wealth? Mr. Ford's actual net worth is $226,511, while his expected level of wealth (again computed from the wealth equation) is $470,883. Mr. Ford, by our definition, is an under accumulator of wealth. Mr. Ford spent seven years in college. How can he possibly have less wealth than a mobile-home dealer? In fact, Mr. Richards has nearly five times the net worth of Mr. Ford. And remember, both are in the same income/age cohort. In trying to answer the above question, ask yourself two simpler questions:

- ◆ How much money does it take to maintain the upper-middle-class lifestyle of an attorney and his family?

- ◆ How much money is required to maintain the middle-class or even blue-collar lifestyle of a mobile-home dealer and his family?

Clearly, Mr. Ford, the attorney, must spend significantly more of his household's income to maintain and display his family's higher upper-middle-class lifestyle. What make of motor vehicle is congruent with the status of an attorney? Foreign luxury, no doubt. Who needs to wear a different high-quality suit to work each day? Who needs to join one or more country clubs? Who needs expensive Tiffany silverware and serving trays?

Mr. Ford, the UAW, has a higher propensity to spend than do the members of the PAW group. UAWs tend to live above their means; they emphasize consumption. And they tend to de-emphasize many of the key factors that underlie wealth building.

YOU OR YOUR ANCESTORS?

Most of America's millionaires are first-generation rich. How is it possible for people from modest backgrounds to become millionaires in one generation? Why is it that so many people with similar socioeconomic backgrounds never accumulate even modest amounts of wealth?

Most people who become millionaires have confidence in their own abilities. They do not spend time worrying about whether or not their parents were wealthy. They do not believe that one must be born wealthy. Conversely, people of modest backgrounds who believe that only the wealthy produce millionaires are predetermined to remain non-affluent. Have you always thought that most millionaires are born with silver spoons in their mouths? If so, consider the following facts that our research uncovered about American millionaires:

◆ Only 19 percent receive any income or wealth of any kind from a trust fund or an estate.

◆ Fewer than 20 percent inherited 10 percent or more of their wealth.

◆ More than half never received as much as $1 in inheritance.

◆ Fewer than 25 percent ever received "an act of kindness" of $10,000 or more from their parents, grandparents, or other relatives.

◆ Ninety-one percent never received, as a gift, as much as $1 of the ownership of a family business.

◆ Nearly half never received any college tuition from their parents or other relatives.

◆ Fewer than 10 percent believe they will ever receive an inheritance in the future.

America continues to hold great prospects for those who wish to accumulate wealth in one generation. In fact, America has always been a land of opportunity for those who believe in the fluid nature of our nation's social system and economy.

More than one hundred years ago the same was true. In *The American Economy*, Stanley Lebergott reviews a study conducted in 1892 of the 4,047 American millionaires. He reports that 84 percent "were nouveau riche, having reached the top without the benefit of inherited wealth."

BRITANNIA RULES?

Just before the American Revolution, most of this nation's wealth was held by landowners. More than half the land was owned by people who either were born in England or were born in America of English parents. Is more than half of this nation's wealth now of English origin? No. One of the major myths concerning wealth in this country relates to ethnic origin. Too many people think that America's affluent pop-

TABLE 1-1

THE TOP TEN ANCESTRY GROUPS OF AMERICAN MILLIONAIRES

Ancestry Group/ Ethnic Origin: Head of Household[1]	Percent of All U.S. Households	Number of Millionaire Households[2]	Percent of Millionaire Household Population	Rank: Percent of Millionaire Household Population	Concentration Ratio: % All Millionaire Households/ % All Households	Percent of Ancestry Group That Are Millionaire Households	Rank: Percent of Ancestry Group That Are Millionaire Households
ENGLISH	10.3	732,837	21.1	1st	2.06	7.71	4th
GERMAN	19.5	595,171	17.3	2nd	0.89	3.32	9th
IRISH	9.6	429,559	12.5	3rd	1.30	4.88	7th
SCOTTISH	1.7	322,255	9.3	4th	5.47	20.8	2nd
RUSSIAN	1.1	219,437	6.4	5th	5.82	22.0	1st
ITALIAN	4.8	174,929	5.1	6th	0.94	4.00	8th
FRENCH	2.5	128,350	3.7	7th	1.48	5.50	6th
DUTCH	1.6	102,818	3.0	8th	1.88	7.23	5th
NATIVE AMERICAN	4.9	89,707	2.6	9th	0.53	1.99	10th
HUNGARIAN	0.5	67,625	2.0	10th	4.00	15.1	3rd

[1]Head of Household refers to the adult within the household who responded to the survey. Respondents self-designated themselves as the person in their household who was responsible for making financial decisions.

[2]Millionaire households are those that have a net worth of $1M or more.

ulation is composed predominantly of direct descendants of the *Mayflower* voyagers.

Let's examine this assumption objectively. What if "country of origin" were the major factor in explaining variation in wealth? We would expect that more than half of America's millionaire population would be of English ancestry. This is not the case (see Table 1-1). In our most recent national survey of millionaires, we asked the respondents to designate their country of origin/ancestry/ethnic origin. The results may surprise you.

Those designating "English" as their ethnic origin accounted for 21.1 percent of the millionaire population. People of English origin account for 10.3 percent of the United States household population in general. Thus, American millionaires of English origin are more prevalent than expected, given their numbers in the entire U.S. population (10.3 percent versus 21.1 percent). In other words, this group has a millionaire concentration ratio of 2.06 (21.1 percent of all millionaire households divided by 10.3 percent of all households headed by persons of English origin), meaning that people of English origin are about twice as likely to head households in the millionaire category than would be expected from their portion of all households in America.

And yet, what percentage of the English ancestry group in America is in the millionaire category? Would you expect the English group to rank first? In fact, it ranks fourth. According to our research, 7.71 percent of all households in the English category have a net worth of $1 million or more. Three other ancestry groups have significantly higher concentrations of millionaires.

How can it be possible that the English ancestry group does not have the highest concentration of millionaire households? After all, they were among the first Europeans to arrive in the New World. They were on the ground floor to take economic advantage in this land of opportunity. In 1790 Colonial America, more than two-thirds of households were headed by a self-employed person. *In America, the achievements of the current generation are more a factor in explaining wealth accumulation than what has taken place in the past.* Again, most American millionaires today (about 80 percent) are first-generation rich. Typically, the fortunes built by these people will be completely dissipated by the second or third generation. The American economy is a fluid one. There are many people today who are on their way to becoming wealthy. And there are many others who are spending their way out of the affluent category.

WINNING ANCESTRY GROUPS

If the English ancestry group does not have the highest concentration of millionaire households, then which group does? The Russian ancestry group ranks first, the Scottish ranks second, and the Hungarian ranks third. Although the Russian ancestry group accounts for only about 1.1 percent of all households in America, it accounts for 6.4 percent of all millionaire households. We estimate that approximately 22 of every 100 households headed by someone of Russian ancestry has a net worth of $1 million or more. This is in sharp contrast to the English ancestry group, in which only 7.71 in 100 of its members are in the millionaire league. How much wealth does this Russian American millionaire group have in total? We estimate approximately $1.1 trillion, or nearly 5 percent of all the personal wealth in America today!

How can one explain the economic productivity of Russian Americans? In general, most American millionaires are manager-owners of businesses. Russians in disproportionate numbers are manager-owners of businesses. Further, this entrepreneurial spirit seems to translate from one generation of Russians to the next.

The Hungarian ancestry group also is entrepreneurially inclined. This group accounts for only 0.5 percent of all households in this country. Yet it makes up 2 percent of the millionaire households. Contrast this with the German ancestry group, which accounts for nearly one in five households (19.5 percent) in this country. Only 17.3 percent of all millionaire households are headed by persons of German ancestry, and only about 3.3 percent of German households are in the millionaire league.

THRIFTY SCOTS

The Scottish ancestry group makes up only 1.7 percent of all households. But it accounts for 9.3 percent of the millionaire households in America. Thus, in terms of concentration, the Scottish ancestry group is more than five times (5.47) more likely to contain millionaire households than would be expected from its overall portion (1.7 percent) of American households.

The Scottish ancestry group ranks second in terms of the percentage of its clan that are in the millionaire league. Nearly twenty-one (20.8) in 100 of its households are millionaires. What explains the Scottish ancestry group's high ranking? It is true that many Scots were early immigrants to America. But this is not the major reason for their economic productivity. Remember that the English were among the earliest immigrants, yet their concentration numbers are far lower than those of the Scots. Also consider that the Scots did not enjoy the same solid economic status that the English enjoyed during the years the nation was in its infancy. Given these facts, one would think that the English ancestry group would account for a higher concentration of millionaire households than those in the Scottish group. But just the opposite is the case. Again, the Scottish ancestry group has a concentration level nearly three times that of the English group (5.47 versus 2.06). What then makes the Scottish ancestry group unique?

If an ancestry group has a high concentration of millionaires, what would we expect the income characteristics of that group to be? The expectation is that the group would have an equally high concentration of high-income producers. Income is highly correlated with net worth; more than two-thirds of the millionaires in America have annual household incomes of $100,000 or more. In fact, this correlation exists for all major ancestry groups but one: the Scottish. This group has a much higher number of high–net worth households than can be explained by the presence of high-income-producing households alone. High-income-producing Scottish-ancestry households account for less than 2 percent of all high-income households in America. But remember that the Scottish ancestry group accounts for 9.3 percent of the millionaire households in America today. More than 60 percent of Scottish-ancestry millionaires have annual household incomes of less than $100,000. No other ancestry group has such a high concentration of millionaires from such a small concentration of high-income-producing households.

If income does not come near in explaining the affluence of the Scottish ancestry group in America, what factors do shed light on this phenomenon? There are several fundamental factors.

First, Scottish Americans tend to be frugal. Given a household's income, there is a corresponding mathematical expectation of level of consumption. Members of this group do not fit such expectations. On average, they live well below the norm for people in various income categories. They often live in self-designed environments of relative scarcity. A household of Scottish ancestry with an annual income of $100,000 will often consume at a level typical for an American household with an annual income of $85,000. Being frugal allows them to save more and invest more than others in similar income groups. Thus the same $100,000 income–producing household of Scottish descent saves and invests at a level comparable to the typical American household that annually earns nearly $150,000.

In the chapters that follow, we reveal the highest prices typical millionaires reported paying for suits, shoes, watches, and motor vehicles. A significantly greater number of millionaires with Scottish ancestry reported paying less for each item than the norm for all millionaires in the sample. For example, more than two-thirds (67.3 percent) of Scottish millionaires paid less for their most expensive motor vehicle than the norm for all millionaires surveyed.

Because they accumulate wealth, the Scottish-ancestry affluent have wealth to pass on to their offspring. Our research reveals that Scottish offspring typically become economically and emotionally independent even as young adults. Thus, they tend not to drain their parents' wealth.

Members of the Scottish-ancestry group have been able to instill their values of thrift, discipline, economic achievement, and financial independence in successive generations. These values are also typical traits among most self-made millionaires.

SMALL POPULATIONS

Often small-population groups are underrepresented in studies of the affluent. Yet many contain high concentrations of wealthy households. What small groups in particular? We estimate that all of the fifteen small-population ancestry groups shown in Table 1-2 have at least twice the proportion of millionaires than the proportion for all U.S. households. Only about 3.5 percent of all U.S. households are in the million-dollar net worth league. All the groups listed in Table 1-2 are estimated to contain at least twice this proportion.

TABLE 1-2

THE TOP FIFTEEN ECONOMICALLY PRODUCTIVE SMALL-POPULATION ANCESTRY GROUPS[1]

Ancestry of Households	Proportion of Total U.S. Households	Ancestry High-Income Index[2]	Ancestry Dependency Index[3]	Ancestry Economic Productivity Index[4]	Ancestry Economic Productivity Rank
ISRAELI	0.0003	2.6351	0.3870	6.8095	1
LATVIAN	0.0004	2.4697	0.5325	4.6383	2
AUSTRALIAN	0.0001	2.1890	0.5329	4.1080	3
EGYPTIAN	0.0003	2.6546	0.6745	3.9357	4
ESTONIAN	0.0001	1.8600	0.4787	3.8855	5
TURKISH	0.0003	2.2814	0.6650	3.4305	6
ICELANDER	0.0001	1.8478	0.5600	3.2997	7
SYRIAN	0.0004	2.1659	0.6698	3.2335	8
IRANIAN	0.0009	2.0479	0.6378	3.2107	9
SLAVIC	0.0002	1.2292	0.4236	2.9018	10
LUXEMBOURGER	0.0002	1.1328	0.3992	2.8379	11
YUGOSLAVIAN	0.0009	1.3323	0.5455	2.4424	12
PALESTINIAN	0.0002	1.8989	0.7823	2.4274	13
SLOVENE	0.0004	1.0083	0.4246	2.3748	14
SERBIAN	0.0004	1.3184	0.5950	2.2157	15

[1]Small population ancestry groups are those with fewer than 100,000 households residing in the U.S., according to the 1990 Census of Ancestry of the Population of the United States.

[2]For example, households with Israeli ancestry have 2.6351 times greater the proportion of high-income ($100,000 and over) households than the proportion for all U.S. households.

[3]For example, households with Israeli ancestry have 0.3870 times the proportion of publicly assisted households than the proportion for all U.S. households.

[4]For example, the ancestry economic productivity index for households of Israeli ancestry (6.8095) is determined by taking their high-income index (2.6351) and dividing it by their dependency index (0.3870).

(In total, all fifteen account for less than 1 percent of all affluent households.) In fact, there is compelling evidence of an inverse relationship between the size of an ancestry group and the proportion of its members that are wealthy. In other words, larger ancestry groups contain smaller proportions of millionaires on average than smaller groups.

What about the number of years that an average member of an ancestry group has been in America? The longer the time here, the less likely it will produce a disproportionately large percentage of millionaires. Why is this the case? Because we are a consumption-based society. *In general, the longer the average member of an ancestry group has been in America, the more likely he or she will become fully socialized to our high-consumption lifestyle.* There is another reason. First-generation Americans tend to be self-employed. Self-employment is a major positive correlate of wealth.

This is not to suggest that self-employment and/or being first-generation American ensures membership among the ranks of millionaires. Most self-employed Americans will never accumulate even modest levels of wealth. The same is true for most first-generation Americans. But twenty-three million people in this country today were born elsewhere. That is a large gene pool. Note also that 12 percent of *INC.* magazine's top five hundred business entrepreneurs are first-generation American.

One might expect that the sons, daughters, grandsons, and granddaughters of these people would automatically become even more successful economically than they. Not really. We will discuss intergenerational transfers in more detail in Chapters 5 and 6, but allow us at this juncture to explain why the "next generation" is often less productive economically than the last.

VICTOR AND HIS CHILDREN

Take the case of Victor, a successful entrepreneur who is first-generation American. Entrepreneurs like him have typically been characterized by their thrift, low status, discipline, low consumption, risk, and very hard work. But after these genetic wonders become financial successes, then what? What do they teach their children? Do they encourage them to follow Dad's lead? Do their children also become roofing contractors, excavation contractors, scrap metal dealers, and so on? The chances are they don't. Fewer than one in five do.

No, Victor wants his children to have a better life. He encourages them to spend many years in college. Victor wants his children to become physicians, lawyers, accountants, executives, and so on. But in so encouraging them, Victor essentially discourages his children from becoming entrepreneurs. He unknowingly encourages them to postpone their entry into the labor market. And, of course, he encourages them to reject his lifestyle of thrift and a self-imposed environment of scarcity.

Victor wants his children to have a better life. But what exactly does Victor mean when he says that? He means that his children should be well educated and have a much higher occupational status than he did. Also, "better" means better artifacts: fine homes, new luxury automobiles, quality clothing, club membership. But Victor has neglected to include in this definition of better many of the elements that were the foundation stones of his success. He does not realize that being well educated has certain economic drawbacks.

Victor's well-educated adult children have learned that a high level of consumption is expected of people who spend many years in college and professional schools. Today his children are under accumulators of wealth. They are the opposite of their father, the blue-collar, successful business owner. His children have become Americanized. They are part of the high-consuming, employment-postponing generation.

How many generations does it take for an ancestry group that today contains thousands of Victors to become Americanized? Only a few. Most move into the "American normal" range within one or two generations. This is why America needs a constant flow of immigrants with the courage and tenacity of Victor. These immigrants and their immediate offspring are constantly needed to replace the Victors of America.

THE AUTHORS AND TODDY AND ALEX

Several years ago we were asked to conduct a study of the affluent in America. We were hired by Toddy, a corporate vice president of a subsidiary of a large corporation. Toddy's ancestors were English. His forefathers were in America before the Revolutionary War. More recently, they owned steel mills in Pennsylvania. Toddy, their direct descendant, attended an exclusive prep school in New England. Later he graduated from Princeton University. While in college, he played varsity football.

Toddy, like many people in this country, had always believed that wealthy people inherited their fortunes. Toddy also believed that most wealthy people had English roots. So what happened to Toddy's long-held opinions after he joined us out in the survey field, meeting America's millionaires? Most of the millionaire respondents Toddy met were first-generation affluent. And most were not of English origin. Most of them attended public schools; they drove American-made automobiles; they preferred club sandwiches to caviar. And, unlike Toddy, most were frugal.

Toddy's education was enhanced by another event. During the course of our assignment, an entrepreneur named Alex approached Toddy and the other senior officers of the corporation. Alex wanted to buy the firm that employed Toddy. Who was this Alex fellow, anyway? His father had immigrated to this country from Russia before Alex was born. His dad was a small business owner. Alex had graduated from a state university. "How could it be possible," Toddy asked, "that this fellow wants to, and has the resources to, buy the company?" Alex's dad answered the question quite succinctly:

Russians—they are the best horse traders.

Alex is a self-made multimillionaire. His is the prototypical American success story. Conversely, Toddy and others like him are an endangered species. Someday, they may even be extinct. This is especially true for those who spend a lot of time reminiscing about how their late ancestors founded steel mills, railroads, and pony express services long, long ago.

FRUGAL FRUGAL FRUGAL

THEY LIVE WELL BELOW THEIR MEANS.

he first time we interviewed a group of people worth at least $10 million (decamillionaires), the session turned out differently than we had planned. We were contracted to study the wealthy by a large international trust company. Our client wanted us to study the needs of high–net worth individuals.

To make sure our decamillionaire respondents felt comfortable during the interview, we rented a posh penthouse on Manhattan's fashionable East Side. We also hired two gourmet food designers. They put together a menu of four pâtés and three kinds of caviar. To accompany this, the designers suggested a case of high-quality 1970 Bordeaux plus a case of a "wonderful" 1973 cabernet sauvignon.

Armed with what we thought would be the ideal menu, we enthusiastically awaited the arrival of our decamillionaire respondents. The first to arrive was someone we nicknamed Mr. Bud. Sixty-nine and a first-generation millionaire, Mr. Bud owned several valuable pieces of commercial real estate in the New York metropolitan area. He also owned two businesses. You would never have figured from his outward appearance that he was worth well over $10 million. His dress was what you might call dull-normal—a well-worn suit and overcoat.

Nevertheless, we wanted to make Mr. Bud feel that we fully understood the food and drink expectations of America's decamillionaires. So after we introduced ourselves, one of us asked, "Mr. Bud, may I pour you a glass of 1970 Bordeaux?"

Mr. Bud looked at us with a puzzled expression on his face and then said:

I drink scotch and two kinds of beer—free and BUDWEISER!

We hid our shock as the true meaning of our decamillionaire's message dawned upon us. During the subsequent two-hour interview, the nine decamillionaire respondents shifted constantly in their chairs. Occasionally they glanced at the buffet. But not one touched the pâté or drank our vintage wines. We knew they were hungry, but all they ate were the gourmet crackers. We hate to waste food. How did we dispose of our food and drink? No, we did not have to throw it away. The trust officers in the next room consumed most of it. Of course, the authors helped! It seems that most of us were gourmets. However, none of us was a decamillionaire.

A FOUNDATION FOR BUILDING WEALTH

Today we are much wiser about the lifestyles of the affluent. When we interview millionaires these days, we offer a spread that is more congruent with their way of life. We provide them with coffee, soft drinks, beer, scotch (during evening sessions), and club sandwiches. Of course, we also pay them between $100 and $250 apiece. Occasionally, we offer additional incentives. Many respondents have picked a large and expensive teddy bear as one of their nonmonetary rewards; they tell us they have a grandchild who would be thrilled to receive a big bear.

It is unfortunate that some people judge others by their choice in foods, beverages, suits, watches, motor vehicles, and such. To them, superior people have excellent tastes in consumer goods. But it is easier to purchase products that denote superiority than to be actually superior in economic achievement. Allocating time and money in the pursuit of looking superior often has a predictable outcome: inferior economic achievement.

What are three words that profile the affluent?

FRUGAL FRUGAL FRUGAL

Webster's defines *frugal* as "behavior characterized by or reflecting economy in the use of resources." The opposite of frugal is wasteful. We define wasteful as a lifestyle marked by lavish spending and hyperconsumption.

Being frugal is the cornerstone of wealth-building. Yet far too often the big spenders are promoted and sensationalized by the popular press. We are constantly barraged with media hype about so-called millionaire athletes, for example. Yes, some of the members of this small population are millionaires. But if a highly skilled ball player makes $5 million a year, having $1 million in net worth is no big deal. According to our wealth equation, a $5 million earner who is thirty years of age should be worth $15 million or more. How many highly paid ball players have a level of wealth in this range? We believe only a tiny fraction. Why? Because most have a lavish lifestyle—and they can support such a lifestyle as long as they are earning a very high income. Technically, they may be millionaires (have a minimum net worth of $1 million or more), but they are typically low on the prodigious accumulator of wealth (PAW) scale.

How many households in America earn $5 million in one year? Fewer than five thousand of the nearly 100 million households. That's about one in twenty thousand. Most millionaires never earn one-tenth of $5 million in a year. Most never become millionaires until they are fifty years of age or older. Most are frugal. And few could have ever supported a high-consumption lifestyle and become millionaires in the same lifetime.

But the lavish lifestyle sells TV time and newspapers. All too often young people are indoctrinated with the belief that "those who have money spend lavishly" and "if you don't show it, you don't have it." Could you imagine the media hyping the frugal lifestyle of the typical American millionaire? What would the results be? Low TV ratings and lack of readership, because most people who build wealth in America are hard working, thrifty, and not at all glamorous. Wealth is rarely gained through the lottery, with a home run, or in quiz show fashion. But these are the rare jackpots that the press sensationalizes.

Many Americans, especially those in the under accumulator of wealth (UAW) category, know how to deal with increases in their realized income. They spend them! Their need for immediate gratification is great. To them, life is like a quiz show. Winners get quick cash and conspicuous gifts. Viewers of these quiz shows have lots of empathy for the contestants. Look at the top ratings such shows enjoy. People love to view their surrogate-other winning motor vehicles, boats, appliances, and money. Why don't quiz shows offer tuition scholarships as prizes? Because most people want immediate gratification. They don't want to trade a prize of, say, a camper van for eight years in night school, even though a college degree can translate into a value equivalent to more than a dozen vans.

THE LIFESTYLE OF THE TYPICAL AMERICAN MILLIONAIRE

Is a show about the typical American millionaire one the mass TV audience would enjoy? We doubt it. Why not? Let's take a look at why not.

The camera zooms in on the typical millionaire household of Mr. Johnny Lucas. Like most millionaires, Johnny, fifty-seven, has been married to the same woman for most of his adult life. He holds an undergraduate degree from a local college. He is the owner of a small janitorial contracting firm that has thrived in the last few years. All of his workers now wear nicely tailored uniforms, including hats that bear his company's logo.

To his neighbors, Johnny and his family appear to be nondescript, middle-class folks, but Johnny has a net worth of more than $2 million. In fact, in terms of wealth, Johnny's household ranks in the top 10 percent of all the households in his "nice neighborhood." Nationwide, his household is in the top 2 percent.

How will the TV audience respond to the description of Johnny's wealth and the images of Johnny on the screen? First, viewers will likely be confused, because Johnny does not look like the millionaire most people envision. Second, they may be uncomfortable. Johnny's traditional family values and his lifestyle of hard work, discipline, sacrifice, thrift, and sound investment habits might threaten the audience. What happens when you tell the average American adult that he needs to reduce his spending in order to build wealth for the future? He may perceive this as a threat to his way of life. It is likely that only Johnny and his cohorts would tune in to such a program. It would certainly bolster their views about life.

In spite of these concerns, let us assume that one of the major TV networks agrees to run at least a pilot program about the Johnnys of America. What will this program tell the viewing audience?

Here is Johnny Lucas, ladies and gentlemen. Mr. Lucas is a millionaire. I will ask Johnny some questions about his purchasing habits. These questions come from our TV audience.

CUSTOM-MADE, OR OFF THE RACK?

First, Johnny, Mr. J. G. from our audience wants to know: "What's the most you ever spent for a suit of clothing?"

Johnny closes his eyes for a moment. Obviously, he is deep in thought. The audience is silent. It is expecting him to say, "Somewhere between $1,000 and $6,000." But our research indicates that the audience's expectations are wrong. We predict that our prototypical millionaire would say:

The most I ever spent . . . the most I ever spent . . . including the suits I bought for myself and for my wife, June, and my sons, Buddy and Darryl, and my girls, Wyleen and

Ginger . . . the most I ever spent was $399. Boy, I remember that it's the most I ever spent. It was for a very special occasion—our twenty-fifth wedding anniversary party.

How will the audience respond to Johnny's statement? Probably with shock and disbelief. The audience's expectations are not congruent with the reality of most American millionaires.

According to our most recent survey, the typical American millionaire reported that he (she) never spent more than $399 for a suit of clothing for himself or for anyone else. Note the figures given in Table 2-1. Fifty percent or more of the millionaires surveyed paid $399 or less for the most expensive suit they ever purchased. Only about one in ten paid $1,000 or more; only about one in one hundred paid $2,800 or more. Conversely, about one in four million-

TABLE 2-1

PRICES PAID BY MILLIONAIRES FOR CLOTHING AND ACCESSORIES

SUIT OF CLOTHING			PAIR OF SHOES			WRISTWATCH		
Most Ever Spent	% That Paid This Amount or:		Most Ever Spent	% That Paid This Amount or:		Most Ever Spent	% That Paid This Amount or:	
	Less	More		Less	More		Less	More
$195	10	90	$73	10	90	$47	10	90
$285	25	75	$99	25	75	$100	25	75
$399	50	50	$140	50	50	$235	50	50
$599	75	25	$199	75	25	$1125	75	25
$999	90	10	$298	90	10	$3800	90	10
$1400	95	5	$334	95	5	$5300	95	5
$2800	99	1	$667	99	1	$15000	99	1

aires paid $285 or less, and one in ten paid $195 or less for his (her) most expensive suit.

These figures are for *all* millionaires in our survey. Keep in mind that almost 14 percent of those surveyed told us they inherited their wealth. What happens when we break out inheritors and self-made millionaires? Self-made millionaires spend significantly less for suits, as well as for most other high-status items, than do those who have inherited their wealth. The typical (50th percentile) self-made millionaire paid about $360 for a suit, while the typical inheritor of wealth reported paying more than $600.

How can the Johnnys of America get away with spending such modest amounts? Johnny does not need to wear expensive suits. He is not a successful attorney who must impress his clients. Nor does he ever have to impress a large audience of stockholders at an annual meeting, the financial press, or investment bankers. Johnny does not have to dress the part of a high-powered CEO who must constantly address a high-brow board of directors. Johnny does, however, need to impress his staff of janitors. How? By never giving them the impression that he is making so much money he can afford to have a tailor fit him for a suit priced in the low- to mid-four figures.

Most of the millionaires we have interviewed over the past twenty years have views similar to Johnny's. Then who purchases all those expensive suits? Our survey has revealed an interesting relationship. For every millionaire who owns a $1,000 suit, there are at least six owners who have annual incomes in the $50,000 to $200,000 range but who are not millionaires. Their shopping habits certainly have something to do with the fact that they are not wealthy. Who are these people? Typically, they do not own their own businesses. They are more likely to be corporate middle managers (especially those who are part of a working couple), attorneys, sales and marketing professionals, and physicians.

Why would anyone suggest that you spend more than the typical millionaire for a suit? In a recently published article, an owner of very expensive suits touted that they were an excellent investment (Lawrence Minard, "You're Looking Rather Prosperous, Sir," *Forbes*, April 8, 1996, pp. 132–133). Mr. Minard asks and answers the question of questions about investing in suits:

Can custom-made suits be worth $2,000? Mine are. Fourteen years and 14 pounds later, they still look good. . . . Believe it or not I made an excellent investment (Minard, p. 132).

Mr. Minard tells his readers how he was initially guided to the custom tailor shops of London's Savile Row by two senior-level executives whom he regarded as having "excellent taste" but were not "frivolous" in their buying habits:

They explained that to buy bespoke is to enter into a unique and personal relationship with your clothes (Minard, p. 132).

What is the meaning of *bespoke*? In middle-class American, it means custom-made. Johnny Lucas never bought a custom-made suit. Does he have a "unique and personal relationship" with his all-wool, top-of-the-line JC Penney suit? (Are you surprised to learn that some millionaires shop at Penney's? Perhaps even more surprising, about 30.4 percent of the respondents who are millionaires hold JC Penney credit cards.) Penney's private-brand Stafford Executive suits were recently given top scores for durability, cut, and fit by a leading consumer publication:

JC Penney . . . now subject[s] garments to tough tests for color matching, fabric shrinkage, and pilling. . . . When it comes to quality control Penney's is more demanding than any of the department stores (Teri Agins, "Why Cheap Clothes Are Getting More Respect," *The Wall Street Journal,* Oct. 16, 1995, pp. B1, B3).

Keep in mind that moths, cigar ashes, and other hazards do not care how much you paid for your wool suit. They do not understand the full meaning of *bespoke*. They are not interested in the fact that a suit with the same label was also worn by Dickens, de Gaulle, and Churchill. Nor do they care if your suits ever generate dividends or capital gains. But they can certainly ruin your investment portfolio of suits.

THEN CERTAINLY FOOTWEAR

Let us return to our proposed TV program. Mr. Lucas is still on stage. What type of shoes does Johnny Lucas purchase? The TV audience, if any are still tuned in, will again be surprised by his answer. Johnny, like most millionaires, does not buy high-priced footwear. About half the millionaires surveyed reported that they had never spent $140 or more for a pair of shoes. One in four had never spent more than $100. Only about one in ten had spent over $300. If not millionaires, then who is keeping the high-priced shoe manufacturers and dealers in business? Certainly some millionaires purchase expensive shoes. But for every millionaire in the "highest price paid" category of over $300, there are at least eight nonmillionaires.

But what does the popular press tell us? The press sensationalizes that very small proportion of Americans who purchase expensive shoes and related artifacts. Consider this news story about boxing promoter Don King, who spent two hours shopping for shoes in Atlanta. During that time, Mr. King purchased 110 pairs of shoes from one store, for which he paid $64,100, tax included. His purchase topped the previous sales record for the store, held by Magic Johnson, who spent $35,000 during one visit. Mr. King's record purchase translates into an average of $582.73 per pair. How much did Mr. King pay for his most expensive pair? It was reported that a pair of alligator loafers cost him $850 (Jeff Schultz, "King Foots $64,100 Bill at Shoe Store," *Atlanta Journal-Constitution*, June 4, 1995, p. 1).

Note that only 1 percent of the millionaires in our survey paid $667 or more for a pair of shoes. Mr. King's purchase of alligator shoes is rare even among millionaires. Nonetheless, the popular media enjoy touting abnormalities in buying behavior. As a consequence, our youth are told that buying expensive items is normal behavior for affluent people. They are led to believe that the wealthy have a high-consumption lifestyle. They learn that hyperspending is the main reward for becoming affluent in America.

Why does Johnny Lucas get ignored while Mr. King receives headlines? Because Johnny's consumption habits are mundane. His rewards are more intangible than product-related: financial independence; discipline; and being an excellent family provider, a fine husband, and a father of well-disciplined children.

THE LAST CHANCE FOR MR. LUCAS

Is there any life remaining for our proposed TV program about America's typical millionaire? Can Johnny Lucas still rally and bring back the audience he lost?

Johnny Lucas, the affluent business owner, is very punctual. He is never late for meetings and arrives at work each weekday at 6:30 A.M. How does he do this? It must be his wristwatch. Could it be that Johnny wears an expensive watch? By now you have probably guessed the answer. And once again, the audience is disappointed. Fully one-half of the millionaires surveyed never in their lives spent more than $235 for a wristwatch. About one in ten never paid more than $47, while about one in four spent $100 or less.

Certainly some millionaires purchase expensive watches. But they are in the minority. Even among millionaires, only 25 percent of those surveyed paid $1,125 or more. About one in ten paid $3,800 or more. About one in one hundred paid $15,000 or more.

Johnny would, we are sure, apologize to the TV audience for his mundane taste in clothing and jewelry. But we are sure that he would also define his position by reporting the following:

I live in a fine home . . . but have no mortgage. All my children's college accounts were more than fully funded before they even began attending college.

Unfortunately, Johnny's story, including his apology, will never get into syndication.

So Rare the Johnny Lucases

Why are so few people in America affluent? Even most households with six-figure annual incomes are not affluent. These people have a different orientation than does Johnny Lucas. They believe in spending tomorrow's cash today.

They are debt-prone and are on earn-and-consume tread-mills. To many of them, those who do not display abundant material possessions are not successful. To them, nondisplay-oriented people like Johnny Lucas are their inferiors.

Johnny Lucas is not likely to be held in high regard by many of his neighbors. On a social status scale, he is below average. But on what criteria? In his neighbors' eyes, Johnny has low occupational status. He is an owner of a small business. What happens when he occasionally comes home in one of his janitorial vans? The van stays in his driveway until he leaves the next morning. What are his neighbors to think? They do not know that Johnny is financially independent. They don't give him points for being married and never divorced, fully funding his children's college tuition, employing several dozen people, having integrity, being frugal, paying off his mortgage, and so forth. No, many of his neighbors would prefer that Johnny move out of the neighborhood. Why? Perhaps it's because he and his family don't look affluent, dress like the affluent, drive the vehicles of the affluent, or work in high-status positions.

PLAYING GREAT DEFENSE

The affluent tend to answer "yes" to three questions we include in our surveys:

1. Were your parents very frugal?
2. Are you frugal?
3. Is your spouse more frugal than you are?

This last question is highly significant. Not only are the most prodigious accumulators of wealth frugal, their spouses tend to be even more frugal. Consider the typical affluent household. Nearly 95 percent of millionaire households are composed of married couples. In 70 percent of these households, the male contributes at least 80 percent of the income. Most of these men play great offense in the game called income generation. Great offense in economic terms means that a household generates an income significantly higher than the norm, which in America is an annual realized income of approximately $33,000. Most of these households also play great *defense*; that is, they are frugal when it comes to spending for consumer goods and services. One frugal high-income producer within the married-couple category, however, does not automatically translate into a high level of net worth. Something else must be present. A self-made millionaire stated it best when he told us:

I can't get my wife to spend any money!

Most people will never become wealthy in one generation if they are married to people who are wasteful. A couple cannot accumulate wealth if one of its members is a hyperconsumer. This is especially true when one or both are trying to build a successful business. Few people can sustain profligate spending habits and simultaneously build wealth.

ODE TO HIS FRUGAL WIFE

How did the wife of a millionaire respond when her husband gave her $8 million worth of stock in the company he recently took public? According to her husband of thirty-one years, she said, "I appreciate this, I really do."

Then she smiled, never changing her position at the kitchen table, where she continued to cut out twenty-five- and fifty-cents-off food coupons from the week's supply of newspapers. Nothing is so important as to interrupt her Saturday-morning chores. "She just does today like she always has done, even when all we owned was a kitchen table. . . . It's how come we're well-off today. Made a lot of trade-offs . . . sacrifices early in our marriage."

Why aren't you wealthy, you ask? Well, let's examine your lifestyle. Is it one of great offense? Are you in the $70,000, $100,000, $200,000 income category? Congratulations, you play wonderful offense. But how is it that you keep losing the game called wealth accumulation?

Be honest with yourself. Could it be that you play terrible defense? Most high-income earners are in the same situation, but not most millionaires. Millionaires play both quality offense *and* quality defense. And quite often their great defense helps them outscore/outaccumulate those who outearn/have superior offenses. *The foundation stone of wealth accumulation is defense, and this defense should be anchored by budgeting and planning.* We have discovered that several occupational groups contain large numbers of budgeters and planners.

AFFLUENT AUCTIONEERS

Our latest survey of auctioneers found that more than 35 percent of them are millionaires. This percentage is slightly higher than the proportion of millionaire households living in America's finest urban and suburban neighborhoods.

Auctioneers have been on our list of highly productive types since we conducted our first study of occupations in

1983, when they ranked sixth among those with realized annual incomes of more than $100,000. But their income alone was not what caught our attention. Given the same level of income, who accumulates more wealth—an auctioneer residing in small-town America or someone who lives in a high-status urban or suburban neighborhood? As you can guess, it is the typical auctioneer.

Auctioneers are more frugal than their high-income-producing counterparts in prestige areas; they have lower overhead both for household and business expenditures. To some extent, these data are explained by the lower cost of living and doing business in small towns. Yet even when cost of living is taken into account, auctioneers are more prone to accumulate wealth. Consider the following:

◆ On average, millionaire auctioneers are about fifty years of age, six to eight years younger than their urban/suburban counterparts.

◆ The average millionaire auctioneer spends only 61 percent of the amount urban/suburban millionaires allocate for housing.

◆ Urban/suburban millionaires are more than three times more likely than millionaire auctioneers to own luxury foreign automobiles.

◆ Auctioneers hold a higher proportion of their wealth in appreciating assets than do other high-income producers, and they invest in categories in which they have expertise.

◆ Auctioneers have experience with bankruptcy. They are aware that consumer goods often generate few cents on the dollar. One auctioneer explained why she was so frugal:

When I was quite young, I watched a woman crying . . . sitting on a chair in her front yard. All the while, bidders were walking away with everything she once owned. I'll never forget that woman.

Let's ask the typical American self-made millionaire about her defense. We will refer to her as Mrs. Jane Rule. Mrs. Rule and her husband own a small business, an auctioneering/appraising company. They also invest in several of the categories of items they appraise. Mr. Rule is the visible manager of their business. He gets much of the credit for its success. After all, he speaks very well and very quickly. But it's actually Mrs. Rule who is the true force, the real leader, of this enterprise. It's her planning, designing, budgeting, bill collecting, and marketing that made this auctioneering company successful.

Why are Mr. and Mrs. Rule millionaires today? Because Mrs. Rule plays tremendous defense! She is responsible for budgeting and spending for both her household and their business. Is anyone in your household responsible for budgeting? All too often the answer is "not really." All too often people allow their income to define their budgets. When we tell our audiences about the budgeting and planning habits of the affluent, someone always asks a predictable question: Why would someone who is a millionaire need to budget? Our answer is always the same:

**They became millionaires by budgeting
and controlling expenses, and they
maintain their affluent status the same way.**

Sometimes we are forced to add analogies to make our point. We ask, for example:

Have you ever noticed those people whom you see jogging day after day? They are the ones who seem not to need to jog. But that's why they are fit. Those who are wealthy work at staying financially fit. But those who are not financially fit do little to change their status.

Most people want to be physically fit. And the majority know what is required to achieve this. But despite that knowledge, most people never become well conditioned physically. Why not? Because they don't have the discipline to just do it. They don't budget their time to just do it. It is like becoming wealthy in America. Oh, you want to all right, but you play lousy financial defense. You don't have the discipline to control your spending. You don't take the time to budget or plan. Note that under accumulators of wealth spend three times as much time exercising per month as they do planning their investment strategies.

Mrs. Rule is different. She's like most millionaires. She's disciplined. She takes time to plan and budget. This translates into wealth. Mrs. Rule's household income varies from year to year. (It is typical for auctioneers to have ups and downs in their cash flow. Often downturns in our nation's economy translate into increased demand for auctioneering services.) Over the past five years her annual income averaged around $90,000. But her net worth keeps increasing. Today Mrs. Rule has a net worth of more than $2 million. In our survey, she answered "yes" to four questions about planning and budgeting.

Do you wish to become affluent and stay affluent? Can you answer "yes" candidly and honestly to four simple questions?

QUESTION 1: DOES YOUR HOUSEHOLD OPERATE ON AN ANNUAL BUDGET?

Do you plan your consumption spending according to a variety of food, clothing, and shelter categories each year? Mrs. Rule does, and so do most millionaires. In fact, in our latest national survey of millionaires, we found that for every 100 millionaires who don't budget, there are about 120 who do.

We anticipate your question about those millionaires who don't budget. How did they become millionaires? How do they control spending? They create an artificial economic environment of scarcity for themselves and the other members of their household. More than half of the nonbudgeters invest first and spend the balance of their income. Many call this the "pay yourself first" strategy. These people invest a minimum of 15 percent of their annual realized income before they pay the sellers of their food, clothes, homes, credit, and the like.

What about those millionaires who don't budget *or* create an environment of relative scarcity? Some inherited all or most of their wealth. Another minority, accounting for fewer than 20 percent of millionaires, typically earn such high incomes that to some extent they can eat their income and still have a seven-figure net worth. In other words, their extraordinarily good offense compensates for a lack of defense. But so what if you earn $2 million a year and have a net worth of $1 million? Technically you're a millionaire. But spiritually you're an under accumulator of wealth. And it's likely that your millionaire status is temporary. These are the people you read about in the newspaper. The press loves to tout freaks of both nature and economics.

Will the popular press ever do a story on Mrs. Rule? It's unlikely. Who wants to read about Mrs. Rule's $140,000 home or her four-year-old "Detroit metal" sedan? Who wants to see her sitting at the kitchen table three nights in a row, putting together her family's annual budget? Is there anything exciting about computing and accounting for each dollar spent last year? Would you be thrilled to watch Mrs. Rule compute and allocate future dollars of income into dozens of consumption categories? How long could you stand to watch her carefully complete her annual allocations calendar? Well, it's not fun for Mrs. Rule, either. But in Mrs. Rule's mind there are worse things, such as never being able to retire and never being financially independent. It's much easier to budget if you visualize the long-term benefits of this task.

QUESTION 2: DO YOU KNOW HOW MUCH YOUR FAMILY SPENDS EACH YEAR FOR FOOD, CLOTHING, AND SHELTER?

Almost two-thirds of the millionaires surveyed (62.4 percent) answered "yes" to this question. So did Mrs. Rule. But only about 35 percent of high-income-producing nonmillionaires answered "yes" to this question. Many of these high-income/low–net worth types have no idea how much they spend each year for such items as food consumed at home, food consumed away from home, beverages, birthday and holiday gifts (for each category of recipient), each category of clothing for each household member at each store, baby-sitters, day-care fees, line of credit use, charitable contributions, financial advice, club dues, motor vehicles and related expenses, tuition, vacations, heating and lighting, and insurance.

Notice that we did not include mortgage payments in our list. Often high-income/low–net worth respondents boast about how much money they save on taxes via their mortgage deductions. Certainly most millionaires who have mortgages outstanding also take advantage of this provision. But most millionaires also account for their other categories of domestic expenditures. Ask typical high-income/low–net worth people about their goals. What will they tell you? A major goal they often name is to minimize their tax burden; they use the mortgage deduction as a way to accomplish this. Then why don't these same people compute their other domestic expenditures? Simply because they do not perceive any value in doing so. As they see it, most of their domestic spending is not deductible in computing one's taxable income.

But Mrs. Rule sees things differently. Her goal is to become financially independent—in her case, to have $5 million by the time she and her husband retire. She believes that budgeting and accounting for domestic consumption is directly related to achieving this goal. In her view, tabulating helps control consumption. It also reduces the probability of allocating too many dollars to product and service categories that are not really important. Mrs. Rule has always tabulated expenditures for her business. She realizes that the same system she used for business accounting can be used for domestic purposes. This is an advantage of being a self-employed business owner.

Mrs. Rule wants to be free of financial worry before her sixty-fifth birthday. Each time she tabulates, she tells herself she is reducing her fear of never being able to retire in comfort. Who has concern about their financial future? Not Mrs. Rule. Although she has an annual income of $90,000, she's worth more than twenty times that amount. And she is in control of her household's domestic spending.

Robert and Judy, on the other hand, are frightened. And they should be. This couple earns $200,000 annually, or more than twice what Mrs. Rule earns. Yet, like so many of today's high-income-producing couples, Robert and Judy have only a fraction of Mrs. Rule's wealth. They feel that consumption controls them, not the other way around. Even Mrs. Rule might find it daunting to have to account for $200,000 in expenditures each year. Robert and Judy have fourteen credit cards; the Rules have two (one for business use, the other for domestic spending).

Let's talk about credit cards for a moment. Ask a large sample of millionaires a simple question about their credit cards. The results will give you an excellent idea of who these millionaires really are.

> Mr./Mrs. Millionaire:
>
> Please indicate, by circling the appropriate number, the credit cards that you or any member of your house possesses. Circle all those that apply.

Now close your eyes and pretend you are a millionaire with a net worth of nearly $4 million. What credit cards would be congruent with your station in life? Perhaps at the top of your list would be American Express Platinum, Diners Club, or Carte Blanche. Perhaps you consider yourself a fashion-sensitive millionaire. You may list credit cards from Brooks Brothers, Neiman Marcus, Saks Fifth Avenue, Lord & Taylor, or even Eddie Bauer. You would be in the minority of millionaires if you did list these cards. The results from our national survey of millionaires reveal some interesting credit card preferences (see Table 2-2). Some highlights:

TABLE 2-2

CREDIT CARDS OF MILLIONAIRE HOUSEHOLD MEMBERS
(N=385)

CREDIT CARD	PERCENT POSSESSING
Visa	59.0
MasterCard	56.0
Sears	43.0
Penney's	30.4
American Express Gold	28.6
American Express Green	26.2
Lord & Taylor	25.0
Saks Fifth Avenue	25.0
Neiman Marcus	21.0
Brooks Brothers	10.0
Eddie Bauer	8.1
American Express Platinum	6.2
Diners Club	3.4
Carte Blanche	0.9

◆ Like most American households, most wealthy households have a MasterCard and a Visa card.

◆ The millionaire household is four times more likely to hold a Sears card (43 percent) than a Brooks Brothers card (10 percent).

◆ Both Sears and Penney's cards are significantly more popular among the wealthy than the cards of status retailers.

◆ Only 21 percent of the wealthy households in America hold the Neiman Marcus card; 25 percent, Saks Fifth Avenue; 25 percent, Lord & Taylor; and only 8.1 percent, the Eddie Bauer card.

◆ Only 6.2 percent of the millionaire respondents hold the American Express Platinum card; 3.4 percent hold Diners Club; and fewer than 1 percent own Carte Blanche.

QUESTION 3: DO YOU HAVE A CLEARLY DEFINED SET OF DAILY, WEEKLY, MONTHLY, ANNUAL, AND LIFETIME GOALS?

The source of this question came from a decamillionaire whom we interviewed a dozen years ago. He told us that he started a wholesale food business at the age of nineteen. He never finished formal high school but did eventually receive his high school equivalency diploma. We asked him to account for the fact that although he was a high school dropout, he had accumulated over $10 million. His response was as follows:

I have always been goal-oriented. I have a clearly defined set of daily goals, weekly goals, monthly goals, annual goals, and lifetime goals. I even have goals to go to the bathroom. I always tell our young executives that they must have goals.

Mrs. Rule also is goal-oriented. So are most other millionaires. For every 100 millionaires who answered "no" to this question, there are 180 who answered "yes." Who are the "noes"? Many of the high-income and inherited-wealth types discussed in the last section. Many senior citizens and retired millionaires who have already reached most of their goals also answered "no." You may wish to reflect for a moment on the comments made by an eighty-year-old multimillionaire:

Authors: The first question we always ask is about goals. What are your current goals?

Mr. Clark: It was $438 an ounce yesterday in London!

After Mr. Clark turned on his hearing aid, we repeated the question.

Mr. Clark: Oh, goals, not gold. . . . I see. My goals. I've accomplished what I've tried to do. . . . My long-range goal was, of course, to accumulate enough wealth so I can get out of business and enjoy life. I've been down the road. . . . I've got an international reputation. Mine is one of the greatest welding companies in the world. I never want to retire. But now my goal is my family and self-satisfaction about what I've accomplished.

Mr. Clark is typical of seniors who have accumulated significant wealth. By the way, only two millionaires of all those we interviewed ever told us that their goal was to "spend my last dollar the day that I die!"

Neither Mr. Clark nor Mrs. Rule has such a goal. Mrs. Rule plans to leave educational trusts for all her grandchildren. She also wants to enjoy life now and after she retires. She wants to be financially secure. Her financial goal is to accumulate $5 million. Mrs. Rule knows how much she needs to set aside each year to attain her goals.

But is she happy? That's a question very often asked of us regarding frugal millionaires. Yes, she is happy. She is financially secure. Mrs. Rule enjoys being part of a close-knit family. Her family is everything to her. Her life and her goals are simple. Mrs. Rule does not need a CPA to do her goal-planning for her, although she does seek his counsel in regard to both her domestic and business-related needs. But Robert and Judy, our high-income/low–net worth couple, are in dire need of a strong and intelligent guiding hand. They need a CPA who has considerable experience in changing his clients' orientations, one who will help them change their household environment from one of chaos and hyperconsumption to one of goal-oriented planning, budgeting, and controlling. Will they then be happy? We don't know, but we can tell you this:

> **Financially independent people are happier**
> **than those in their same income/age cohort**
> **who are not financially secure.**

Financially independent people seem to be better able to visualize the future benefits of defining their goals. Mrs. Rule, for instance, visualizes all her grandchildren graduating from college. She visualizes their success after college. She never sees herself being financially dependent on others, even if she is disabled in the future. Her goals are congruent with those of most millionaires in this regard.

QUESTION 4: DO YOU SPEND A LOT OF TIME PLANNING YOUR FINANCIAL FUTURE?

For every 100 millionaires who answer "no," there are 192 who answer "yes." Again, many who answer "no" are either high-income types with relatively low levels of accumulated wealth, those who inherited all or most of their wealth, or wealthy seniors/retirees.

People such as Mrs. Rule accurately label themselves as planners. In fact, the responses to this question are highly correlated to the actual hours the respondents allocate to planning their financial futures. On average, millionaires spend significantly more hours per month studying and planning their future investment decisions, as well as managing their current investments, than high-income nonmillionaires. The hours allocated to planning and managing finances are detailed in Chapter 3.

Millionaires like Mrs. Rule not only spend more time planning their finances than nonmillionaires, they also seem to get more out of their planning hours. Remember, Mrs. Rule is not only in the auctioneering business. Her job includes appraising the value of what her company auctions. Often Mrs. Rule invests in those same areas in which she has considerable expertise. In this regard she is like many millionaires. They astutely allocate their time so that they can plan their business and personal investing at the same time. We often find that highly productive auctioneers are also excellent investors. Take, for example, an auctioneer who specializes in auctioning commercial real estate. What area of investments does he know a great deal about? Commercial real estate. He is his own investment analyst. What if your auctioneering specialty is antique furniture and American firearms? Should you invest in high-tech securities? Probably not. But you would be wise to use your expertise to help you make your investments. If you're well versed in antiques, why not leverage your knowledge?

You don't have to be an auctioneer to benefit from your knowledge. One of our associates was formerly the head of strategic planning at a major corporation. Part of his job was to study a wide variety of trends across a wide variety of business categories. Years ago he discovered that the demand for

investment-grade baseball cards would likely explode someday. This was long before the market reflected this trend. He
invested heavily when the market was "asleep," in his words.
And he sold out all his holdings—including all his Mickey
Mantle rookie cards—at the top of the market. Another
acquaintance, a manager of a department store, always studied trade journals to learn how to make his store more productive. Later he leveraged his reading habits into investing in
growth stocks in the retailing area.

How much time do nonmillionaires allocate to planning
and managing? Not enough! As previously stated, much less
than millionaires. Although millionaires have much more
experience in making investment decisions, they allocate
significantly more hours than do nonmillionaires in an effort
to become even better investors. That is one of the main reasons that millionaires remain wealthy.

Business owners like Mrs. Rule certainly have more
freedom than people who are not self-employed. She can
and does leverage her business knowledge with her personal investing habits. She can pick her area of business and
the one she wants to study. Often employees don't have this
luxury. But even among those who do have significant
knowledge about excellent investment opportunities, many
do not leverage this knowledge. Consider the following
examples:

◆ A highly productive sales professional (we will call him
Mr. Willis) had Wal-Mart as a client for more than ten years.
All during this time, Wal-Mart was exploding in growth and
value. How many shares of Wal-Mart did Mr. Willis, the six-
figure-earning sales professional, ever purchase? Zero. Yes,
zero, even though he had considerable firsthand knowledge
of his client's success and an annual six-figure income. But

he did purchase a foreign luxury car every two years during this time.

◆ A high-income-producing marketing manager, Mr. Petersen, was employed in the high-tech field. But he never invested a dollar in Microsoft or any other growth company. Never, in spite of having considerable knowledge about many of the firms in the technology industry.

◆ The owner of a printing business enjoyed having one of the leading beverage companies in America as a customer. The customer bought millions of dollars' worth of printing from him annually. But how much money has the printer invested in his customer's equity offerings? Zero.

In all three cases, the person makes a higher income than does Mrs. Rule. Yet none is a millionaire. In fact, Mr. Petersen, the marketing manager, has zero invested in stocks. He never invests any of his income. But he lives in a $400,000 home that is surrounded by others in the high-tech field who have big hats and bigger mortgages, but no cattle. Too many high-income/low–net worth types live from paycheck to paycheck, fearing a sudden downturn in our economy.

OUR FRIEND THE UAW

What motivates Theodore "Teddy" J. Friend? Why does he work so hard? Why is he driven to earn so much money? Why does he spend so much? Teddy will tell you it's because he's competitive. But so are almost all top-producing sales professionals. His competitiveness is not the most important reason for his behavior.

When Teddy was growing up, his family was among the poorest in a blue-collar community. His family's small home was built from used lumber and similar discarded materials. Until Teddy was a freshman in high school, his father cut Teddy's hair, which did save money, although, according to Teddy, most people could tell that his "head was worked on by an amateur."

The public high school he attended attracted students from a wide variety of socioeconomic backgrounds. Many were from upscale homes. "Rich kids" were there in large enough numbers to fill the high school's parking lot with their nice cars. These cars always amazed Mr. Friend. Throughout high school his family owned one automobile. It was a well-used Ford that his dad had bought when it was ten years old.

During his high school years, Mr. Friend made a promise to himself that someday he would be a lot better off than his parents. "Better off" in his mind meant having a nice home in an upscale neighborhood, fine clothes for everyone in his family, classy cars, club memberships, and items purchased in the best stores. Mr. Friend realized that "better off" could be achieved by finding a high-paying position and working very hard.

Never did Mr. Friend equate "better off" with accumulating wealth. Again, being "better off" meant displaying one's high income via the conspicuous display of high-status artifacts. Teddy never gave much thought to the benefits of building an investment portfolio. To him, a high income was the way to overcome a feeling of social inferiority. A high income was the product of hard work. "Income in the form of capital gains" were foreign words to him.

Mr. Friend's father and mother were dysfunctional when it came to putting money away for a rainy day. Their financial plan was very simple: They spent when they had money. They stopped spending when they ran short of money. If they needed something, such as a washing machine or a new roof, they saved for it. But they also bought many items with installment loans. They never owned any stocks or bonds. Never did Teddy's parents set aside income for investment purposes. They did not understand or trust the stock market. The only real financial wealth the couple had was a small pension and the equity in their very modest home.

Today their son has a need to compensate for his "primitive blue-collar" background and his perceived educational deficiency. Mr. Friend never completed college. Even now he feels compelled to outperform all the college graduates against whom he competes. He will tell you that he enjoys dressing better, driving better, dwelling better, and, in general, living higher than all those "college kids" who operate within his territory.

Mr. Friend is the ultimate consumer. He has two boats, one jet ski, and six automobiles (two are leased; the others were purchased via credit). Interestingly, there are only three drivers in his household. He is a member of two country clubs and wears a watch that cost more than $5,000. He buys his clothes from the best stores. Mr. Friend also "owns" a vacation condo.

Last year Mr. Friend's income was approximately $221,000. Given his age, forty-eight, what is his expected net worth? According to our wealth equation, his net worth should be $1,060,800 (expected wealth = one-tenth age x total annual income). What is his real net worth? Less than one-fourth of the expected figure.

How is it possible that Mr. Friend has an actual net worth that is less than one-fourth of the expected value? The answer lies in how Mr. Friend thinks. Wealth accumulation is not what motivates him. Interestingly, Mr. Friend firmly believes that if he were really wealthy he would not be a top-income generator. He has often stated that people who come from wealthy backgrounds have little motivation to excel in the workplace.

Mr. Friend has found a method to sustain and even enhance his drive to perform at high levels. He has found that fear is a great motivator. So he buys more and more via credit. By increasing the amount he owes, he correspondingly increases the accountant's fear of default. In turn, this increasing level of debt-based fear encourages him to work harder and more aggressively. To him, a big home is a reminder of a big mortgage and the need to perform at a high level.

Mr. Friend is not a big spender across all categories of products and services. Ask him how much money he allocates for financial advice. In this category he is very price-sensitive. For example, his choice of an accountant was based almost exclusively on the accountant's fees, not on his quality. Mr. Friend has always believed that the quality of service that accountants deliver is about the same; only their fees are different. That's why he picked an accountant who has low fees. In sharp contrast, most wealthy people feel that you get what you pay for in the realm of financial advice.

Mr. Friend spends a considerable amount of time working. Still, he constantly worries that he will lose his so-called competitive edge. He is concerned that his need to outperform the rich kids, the college graduates, will wane someday. Mr. Friend constantly reminds himself about his humble background and lack of that all-important college degree. He constantly punishes himself psychologically. In his eyes he is inferior in pedigree to those very confident college graduates against whom he competes. He often wonders how they can be so content, given their less-than-exceptional performance in the workplace.

Mr. Friend never really enjoys his life. He owns a lot of upscale things, yet he works so hard and for so many hours during a typical day that he has no time to enjoy them. He has no time for his family, either. He leaves his house each day before dawn and rarely returns home in time for dinner.

Would you like to be Mr. Friend? His lifestyle is appealing to many people. But if these people really understood Mr. Friend's inner workings, they might evaluate him differently. Mr. Friend is possessed by possessions. He works for things. His motivation and his thoughts are focused on the symbols of economic success. He constantly needs to convince others of this success. Unhappily, he has never convinced himself. In essence, he works, he earns, and he sacrifices to impress others.

These factors underlie the thought processes of many under accumulators of wealth. More often than not, UAWs allow "significant others" to determine their financial lifestyle. Interestingly, these "significant others," or reference groups, turn out to be more imagined than real. Are you motivated by "significant others"? Perhaps you should consider a different approach to life. Perhaps you should reorient yourself.

Are all high-income people who came from humble beginnings destined to become UAWs? Will they all turn out to follow the ways of Mr. Friend? Absolutely not. There is a fundamental reason beyond Mr. Friend's perceived social and educational deficiencies that explains why he became a UAW: His parents taught him the ways of the UAW. In spite of their modest income, his parents were not frugal. They spent nearly all their income. They were professionals in expending resources. Any pending increase in income was immediately earmarked for consumption. Even anticipated income tax refunds were allocated for consumption—long before the checks were received. Their consumer behavior had an impact on their son. They constantly sent him a message:

One earns to spend.
When you need to spend more, you need to earn more.

LIFE AMONG FRIENDS

How did Mr. Friend's parents spend their money? He told us that throughout their marriage they ate a lot, smoked a lot, drank a lot, and shopped a lot. Their household was always overloaded with food. They stockpiled snack foods, prime meats, cold cuts, ice creams, and other desserts. Even breakfast was a feast. Bacon, sausage, home fries, eggs, English muffins, and Danish pastries were basics in the morning. Steaks and roasts were the preferred dinner offerings. The Friends never skipped a meal. Neighbors and relatives were frequent guests at the "Friends' Restaurant," as they referred to their home. Mr. Friend's parents, between them, smoked about three packs of cigarettes a day. During a normal week they consumed two cases of beer. On holidays, consumption of food, tobacco, and alcohol greatly increased.

Shopping and consuming were the Friends' main hobbies. More often than not, they shopped for fun, not necessity. On most Saturdays they would shop from the early morning until mid-afternoon. First they shopped for food. Then they spent countless hours shopping in discount stores. Mr. Friend pointed out that "most of the stuff they bought was junk."

His mother was an especially aggressive discount store shopper. She had a strong proclivity for purchasing large quantities of throw rugs, ashtrays, malted milk balls, caramel corn, towels of every color and style, casual shoes, wooden bowls, and cooking utensils. Many of these items were stockpiled, sometimes for years, before they were used. His father was also a recreational shopper. He spent hours each Saturday shopping for tools and hardware. In most cases, these items were rarely, if ever, used.

Clearly, Mr. Friend's parents were UAWs. He was well trained. But today he generates a much higher income than his parents ever earned. Why is he still a UAW? This income, in itself, is a result of parental guidance. His dad often told him to seek a job with high-income potential. To do so would enable Mr. Friend to buy the finer things in life. His father's message was clear: To purchase a fine home, luxury automobiles, and expensive clothing, one has to earn a large income. Mr. Friend found that several areas of the sales profession had excellent income-producing opportunities. He would have to earn big to spend big. No mention was ever made of the value of putting money aside for investing. Income was designed to be spent. Credit was used heavily for major purchases.

Mr. Friend and his parents have never appreciated the benefits of accumulating wealth via investing. Mr. Friend told us repeatedly that "it's hopeless." He just does not have any money to invest! How is it that someone with an income six times the average for American households has no money to invest? Mr. Friend spends more annually for his children's private school and college tuition than the average household earns in a year. He has an inventory of automobiles that is valued in excess of $130,000. He pays more than $12,000 each year for property taxes. His total annual mortgage payments are in excess of $30,000. Several of his suits cost $1,200 each.

But his insensitivity to the benefits of investing go beyond his need to consume. His parents had no understanding or appreciation of invested dollars. Nor does he. And his parents passed this lack of wisdom on to him.

Mr. Friend argues that his parents were people of modest means, people with no money to invest. Let's examine this perception. His parents smoked three packs of cigarettes each day. How many packs did they consume during their adult lifetimes? There are 365 days in a year. So they consumed approximately 1,095 packs per year. They smoked for approximately forty-six years. So in forty-six years, they smoked 50,370 packs of cigarettes. How much did the couple pay for these cigarettes? Approximately $33,190—more than the purchase price of their home! They never considered how much it cost to purchase cigarettes. They viewed such purchases as small expenses. But small expenses become big expenses over time. Small amounts invested periodically also become large investments over time.

What if the Friends had invested their cigarette money in the stock market (index fund) during their lifetimes? How much would it have been worth? Nearly $100,000. And what if they had used their cigarette money to purchase shares in a tobacco company? What if they had purchased, reinvested all dividends, and never sold shares in Philip Morris instead of smoking Philip Morris products for forty-six years? *At the end of forty-six years, the couple would have had a tobacco portfolio worth over $2 million*. But the couple, like their son, never imagined that "small change" could be transformed into significant wealth.

This change in behavior alone would have placed the Friends in the millionaire category. They would have been members of the PAW group, too, given their modest income. Perhaps they would have lived differently if someone had educated them about the mathematics of wealth appreciation. No one told them about this phenomenon. So it is not surprising that they failed to educate their son about the benefits of investing. But they did tell him not to smoke. His dad told him, "Don't ever put the first cigarette in your mouth. I'm hooked. There is nothing I can do to quit." His son followed this advice.

KICKING THE UAW HABIT

How long will Mr. Friend be able to fund his lifestyle? What if he were to stop working today? How long could he live off his current level of wealth? Only for about a year! No wonder he works so hard. Given his current circumstances, Mr. Friend will never be able to retire in comfort. In spite of being nearly fifty years of age, he has yet to figure this out for himself. But all is not hopeless. Mr. Friend can still become an accumulator of wealth.

We find that it is often useful for UAWs to be told the naked truth: *"Friend, you're worth less than one-half of the expected amount for those in your income/age group."* Such news can spur on UAWs who are competitive. How do they respond when told that their net worth places them in the bottom quartile for all people with similar income and age characteristics? Some are incredulous. Many want to change but are uncertain how to transform themselves. How can someone change when they have more than twenty years' experience as a UAW?

First, they must really want to change. Second, they will likely need some professional help. Ideally, they need to find a certified public accountant who provides financial planning. A professional of this type should have considerable experience and success with transforming UAWs. That is, they should have a strong track record in helping the Mr. Friends of the world become more PAW-like.

In extreme cases, a CPA/financial planner actually takes control of his client's purchasing behavior. He first audits the client's consumption habits over the past two years. He categorizes and tabulates each element. Then the accountant consults with the client. The client is put into a "cold turkey" cutback program, meaning that all elements of consumption are reduced by a minimum of 15 percent for the next year or two. Additional cutbacks follow. In some situations, the accountant/financial planner even keeps his client's checkbooks, writes all the checks, and pays all the bills. Cold turkey is not easy for most UAWs. But sometimes it's the only way to solve the problem.

THE ULTIMATE CONSUMPTION CATEGORY

The typical millionaire in our surveys has a total annual realized income of less than 7 percent of his wealth. This means that less than 7 percent of his wealth is subject to some form of income tax.* In our latest study of millionaires, the percentage was found to be 6.7 percent. Millionaires know that the more they spend, the more income they must realize. The more they realize, the more they must allocate for income taxes. So millionaires and those who will likely become affluent in the future adhere to an important rule:

---

*The value of private wealth in America is more than $22 trillion. Millionaires own approximately half of this amount, or $11 trillion. The total personal income for the same period is estimated to be about $2.6 trillion. Millionaires account for only about 30 percent of the total income, or $.78 trillion. This means that millionaires as a group realize the equivalent of only 7.1 percent of their total wealth each year ($.78 trillion income ÷ $11 trillion in wealth = 7.1 percent).

**To build wealth, minimize
your realized (taxable) income
and maximize your unrealized income
(wealth/capital appreciation without a cash flow).**

Income tax is the single largest annual expenditure for most households. It is tax on income, not on wealth and not on the appreciation of wealth if this appreciation is not realized; that is, if it does not generate a cash flow.

What is the message? Even many high-income-producing households are asset poor. One reason is that they maximize their realized incomes, often to support high-consumption lifestyles. Such people might wish to ask themselves a simple question: Could I live on the equivalent of 6.7 percent of my wealth? It takes much discipline to become affluent. We have interviewed many people worth $2 or $3 million who have total realized annual household incomes of less than $80,000.

How much does the typical American household realize in income each year? About $35,000 to $40,000, or nearly the equivalent of 90 percent of its net worth. The result is that the typical household in America pays the equivalent of more than 10 percent of its wealth in income taxes each year. How about the millionaires whom we surveyed? On average, their annual income tax bill is an amount equal to only a bit over 2 percent of their wealth. That is one of the reasons they remain financially independent.

CASE STUDY: SHARON AND BARBARA

Sharon is a high-income-producing health-care specialist. She recently asked us, "How is it that I make so much in terms of income but accumulate so little in terms of wealth?"

Last year Sharon's household had a realized total annual

income of approximately $220,000 (see Table 2-3), which places her household in the top 1 percent of all households in America. Sharon's household has a net worth of approximately $370,000. While Sharon's income is higher than 99 percent of the other households in America, her net worth is far below what it should be. Given her age, fifty-one, and her income, $220,000, Sharon should, according to the wealth equation (expected net worth = one-tenth age x income), be worth approximately $1,122,000.

Why is Sharon's level of accumulated wealth far below the norm? Because her realized, or taxable, income is too high. Last year she paid $69,440 in federal tax on her $220,000 income. This is the equivalent of 18.8 percent of her total wealth. Yogi Berra might say, "Sharon, you can't be wealthy. Your income is too high."

We believe that the average person in Sharon's income/age category pays the equivalent of only 6.2 percent of his wealth in annual federal tax, or $69,440 divided by $1,122,000. Thus, Sharon's tax equivalent, 18.8 percent of her wealth, is three times higher than the tax equivalent for the average person in her income/age category.

To view this another way, Sharon has an annual realized income that is equivalent to 59.5 percent of her total net worth of $370,000. How could anyone hope to become truly wealthy when the equivalent of nearly 60 percent of her wealth is subject to income tax each year? The average person in Sharon's income/age category realizes the equivalent of only 19.6 percent of his net worth in annual income. Thus, only about $1 in $5 of his net worth is subject to income tax.

What about people who have above-average levels of wealth? How much of their equivalent net worth is being taxed? Barbara is a typical member of the PAW category. Her realized annual income is approximately the same as

TABLE 2-3

CONTRASTS AMONG AMERICAN TAXPAYERS

HOUSEHOLD DESIGNATION	TOTAL ANNUAL PRETAX REALIZED INCOME FOR HOUSEHOLD	NET WORTH (ASSETS LESS LIABILITIES) FOR HOUSEHOLD	REALIZED INCOME AS A PERCENTAGE OF NET WORTH	FEDERAL INCOME TAX	TAX AS A PERCENTAGE OF INCOME	TAX AS A PERCENTAGE OF NET WORTH	CATEGORY OF WEALTH ACCUMULATION
Typical High-Income Household	$220,000	$1,122,000	19.6	$69,440	31.6	6.2	Average Accumulators of Wealth (AAWs)
Sharon's	$220,000	$370,000	59.5	$69,440	31.6	18.8	Under Accumulators of Wealth (UAWs)
Barbara's	$220,000	$3,550,000	6.2	$69,440	31.6	2.0	Prodigious Accumulators of Wealth (PAWs)
Ross Perot's	$230 million	$2.4 billion	9.6	$19.5 million	8.5	0.8	Prodigious Accumulators of Wealth (PAWs)
Typical American Household	$32,823 (Average)	$36,623 (Median)	89.6 (Average)	$4,248 (Average)	12.9 (Average)	11.6 (Average)	Under Accumulators of Wealth (UAWs)

Sharon's—$220,000. But Barbara's net worth is approximately $3,550,000. Therefore, the equivalent of only 6.2 percent of her wealth is subject to federal income tax. What percentage of Barbara's wealth is paid in federal income tax? Approximately 2 percent. In sharp contrast, Sharon paid the equivalent of 18.8 percent of her wealth in federal income tax, or more than nine times the percentage for Barbara.

The average American millionaire realizes significantly less than 10 percent of his net worth in annual income. In spite of having considerable wealth and substantial annual increases in wealth (in unrealized form), the typical American millionaire may personally be cash poor. More than 20 percent of Barbara's annual realized income is invested in financial assets that tend to appreciate in value without generating realized income. Sharon, on the other hand, invests less than 3 percent of her realized income. Most of her financial assets are in liquid form.

Sharon's economic situation is quite risky. She is the main breadwinner in her household, which has little investment income. If her employer eliminates her job, what then? There are not too many positions available today that pay $200,000 or more a year. Barbara, again in contrast to Sharon, has a business with more than sixteen hundred customers—that's sixteen hundred sources of income. This is much less risky than Sharon's position. Sharon could not survive for six months if she lost her source of income. But Barbara could easily survive for twenty or more years. Actually, she could retire at this point on the income from her financial assets alone.

Barbara, the prodigious accumulator of wealth, is just one of more than 3.5 million millionaires in America today. More than 90 percent have a net worth between $1 million and $10 million. How do these affluent people compare with the super-affluent? Indications are that the higher one's net worth, the better one is at minimizing one's realized income. The fact is that the super-affluent got to that position by being masters at minimizing their realized income.

Ross Perot is the perfect example of how the super-affluent stay affluent and even enhance their levels of wealth year after year. *Forbes* recently estimated that Mr. Perot's net worth was $2.4 billion (see Randall Lane, "What's Ross Perot Really Worth," *Forbes*, Oct. 19, 1992, p. 72). The Citizens for Tax Justice, a tax reform group headquartered in Washington, D.C., estimated that Perot's annual realized income in 1995 was approximately $230 million. Thus, he realized the equivalent of 9.6 percent of his wealth but paid only $19.5 million in tax, or 8.5 percent of his income (see "How Perot Caps His Rising Taxes at Only 8.5%," *Money*, Jan. 1994, p. 18). Compare this figure with the 31.6 percent of their income paid in tax by Barbara, Sharon, and many others in their income category (see Table 2-3).

How does Mr. Perot end up paying such a small percentage of his income in tax? According to a recent newspaper report:

Perot . . . minimizes his tax bill by investing heavily in tax-free municipals, tax-sheltered real estate, and stocks with unrealized gains (Tom Walker, "Perot's Tax Rate Is Lower Than Most, Magazine Says," *Atlanta Journal-Constitution*, Dec. 30, 1993, p. 1).

Of particular interest, Perot's tax rate as a percentage of his income—that is, 8.5 percent—is lower than that of the average American household. The average household in this country pays $4,248 in federal income tax each year, or the equivalent of 12.9 percent of their annual realized income of $32,823. Perot is super-affluent in terms of accumulated wealth, but he has less than the common man's marginal tax liability.

Even more interesting than the percentage of income paid in taxes is the percentage of wealth paid in taxes. The typical American household has a total net worth, including equity in the home, of $36,623. They pay the equivalent of 11.6 percent of their net worth in income tax. What about Mr. Perot, the billionaire? In one year, it is estimated, he paid the equivalent of only 0.8 percent of his wealth in tax. In terms of income tax paid as a percentage of wealth, the typical household paid 14½ times more.

Most millionaires measure their success by their net worth, not by their realized income. For the purposes of wealth building, income doesn't matter that much. Once you're in a high-income bracket, say $100,000 or $200,000 or more, it matters less how much more you make than what you do with what you already have.

WORKING FOR THE TAX MAN

Assume for a few moments that you are Mr. Bob Stern, a scholar who works for the IRS. One morning your manager, Mr. John Young, calls you into his office. He gives you an assignment: to enhance his understanding of the relationship between income and wealth.

Mr. Young: Bob, I keep reading reports about the growth of the millionaire population.

Mr. Stern: Yes. I have a pile of articles and clippings on the same topic in my desk.

Mr. Young: Well, here is the problem. The number of wealthy people keeps rapidly increasing. But our income tax revenue for a lot of these people is not keeping pace.

Mr. Stern: I read somewhere that the wealthiest 3.5 percent of the households in this country account for more than half of the personal wealth. But these same folks account for less than 30 percent of the income.

Mr. Young: I wish Congress would wake up. What this country needs is a tax on wealth. Even in biblical times the rich had to pay 10 percent of their wealth each year in taxes. Now that's what I call the ultimate tax reform.

Mr. Stern: I know what you mean. But sooner or later we will get 'em. Remember, it's inevitable—death and taxes.

Mr. Young: The estate tax area is not your specialty, Bob. You are a little naive on this issue. You are thinking that we will eventually take a big bite out of all the millionaires in this country by taxing their estates.

Mr. Stern: The Grim Reaper is on our side.

Mr. Young: Not so fast, Bob. Just think of all the millionaires in this country. Most of them own some kind of a business, and a whole bunch own stocks. What do these folks do with their money? They sit on it, or they plow it back into their business. They hold on to all those stocks that keep appreciating.

Mr. Stern: But what about the Grim Reaper?

Mr. Young: Look at it this way, Bob. We have often looked at estate returns in the $1-million-and-above level. Last year there were only about 25,000. But, Bob, at the same time there were 3.5 million millionaires alive and kicking. That means that 0.7 percent were picked up by the Reaper. This number should be twice as high. But you know what a lot of millionaires do? Before the Reaper shows up, they transform themselves. It's like magic.

Mr. Stern: How do they do it? They can't just vanish. Do they move offshore before the Reaper shows up?

Mr. Young: Offshore is not a significant factor. But I would not be surprised if we found that half of the millionaires transform themselves into nonmillionaires BR.

Mr. Stern: What do you mean by BR?

Mr. Young: It's an insider term. BR means "Before the Reaper," or prior to death, as opposed to AR, or "After the Reaper." Look at this case study. Here's a woman, Lucy L., who had $7 million just a year before she died. She lived on her pension money. Never in her life sold a share of stock out of her portfolio. Her wealth doubled in just the six years between her seventieth and seventy-sixth birthdays. But what did we get out of it? In terms of income tax, nearly zip. She essentially had no realized income from her portfolio. I hate unrealized income.

Mr. Stern: You're right. It is a clever enemy. But the Reaper —he got her, right? Death and taxes.

Mr. Young: Wrong, Bob. She died last year. And do you know what her net worth was at the time the Reaper finally showed up? Less than $200,000. No estate taxes. Another former millionaire moves on without leaving a taxable estate. Some days I wish I were in another line of work. The enemy is winning.

Mr. Stern: But where did all her money go?

Mr. Young: She gave it to her church, two colleges, and a dozen or more charitable organizations. She also gave $10,000 to every one of her children, grandchildren, and nieces and nephews. She's real country—loaded with relatives, like a lot of mountain people.

Mr. Stern: And what did we finally end up with?

Mr. Young: You're not listening, Bob. We, the government, got zippo! Can you believe it? Her own government. There's just no justice in America. We need a wealth tax.

Mr. Stern: Well, she sounds like a pretty nice person to give so much money to a church, colleges, and charities.

Mr. Young: Bob, shame on you. She and her ilk are the enemy. America needs their wealth to keep our government operating. We need her money to pay off the federal debt. We need to fund all our social programs.

Mr. Stern: Perhaps she feels that her church, the colleges, and the charities also have needs.

Mr. Young: Bob, you are so naive. This woman is an amateur. What type of experience does she have doling out her wealth? We are her government. We're experts in redistributing wealth. We should decide where and how wealth is distributed. We are the pros. We have to start taxing wealth before all the millionaires transform themselves into nonmillionaires.

Mr. Stern: What about all those famous people we read about in the newspaper? The ones who have very high incomes?

Mr. Young: God bless them, Bob. They are our best customers. I love people who are big earners. Realized income is our salvation. I want you to study these types. But I also want you to find out how these other types can exist without realizing a lot of income. Some of them must live like monks. What's wrong with these people? Why don't they sell a few million dollars' worth of stock and buy a mansion?

Mr. Stern: Is that why you have all those pictures of America's highest-paid celebrities on the walls of your den at home?

Mr. Young: You bet. I love those people. They've got a real bad case of the "spends." And to spend they have to have realized income. Look at it this way. When a ball player buys a $2 million boat, we become his partner. He will need to realize $4 million to pay $2 million for his boat. We are his partner.

Mr. Stern: Ball players? Are they good role models for our youth?

Mr. Young: Absolutely. They are high-income spenders. They tell our youth to earn and spend. It's realized income that our youth need to learn about. These spender types are true patriots. That's why I keep *Webster's* definition of patriot on my wall. Why don't you read it to me, Bob?

Mr. Stern: Patriot: one who loves his country and zealously supports its authority and interests.

Mr. Young: Yes, Bob—zealously supports its authority and interests. You know, Bob, the real patriots out there are people who earn big incomes—$100,000, $200,000, and $1 million or more a year—and spend it all. Congress should mint a new medal for this type of patriotism, Bob. It would be called the Congressional Medal of Taxation and Consumption. And as long as these patriots keep training their kids to be medal winners, we are in good shape. Bob, do you think we should start sending out holiday greeting cards to all those companies that promote luxury cars, yachts, million-dollar homes, and expensive clothes and accessories? These people are really patriots in their own way. They encourage spending. They are keeping us in business. Well, Bob, it's getting late. You have your assignment. I want to know more about the medal winners. But I also want you to study the ways of those who don't spend their money.

What evidence is there that the government knows the formula for becoming financially independent in America? Just read some of the articles its employees have written recently. Many well-trained economists and other scholars who work for our government frequently conduct studies about the rich (or, as they refer to them, the "top wealth holders"). We are particularly interested in the articles published in the Internal Revenue Service's *Statistics of Income*, a quarterly report. It's a research scholar's paradise, providing mountains of statistics on income. But income is not the government's only focus. It also studies top wealth holders. We are envious. We have to do our own surveys of the affluent. That's our main source for understanding the "How to Get Rich" formula.

C. Eugene Steuerle is assistant director of the Office of Tax Analysis in the U.S. Department of the Treasury. He is also a scholar and talented researcher. He asks the same question we do: What is "the relationship between realized income and wealth"? (*SOI Bulletin*, Department of the Treasury, Internal Revenue Service, vol. 2, no. 4, Spring 1985) What does he find? That people accumulate significant wealth by minimizing their realized/taxable income and maximizing their unrealized/nontaxable income.

In the study that Mr. Steuerle conducted, he compared the income tax returns that top wealth holders filed while they were alive with the estate returns their executors filed after the subjects passed away. He studied a national sample of estate tax returns. Then he matched each of these with their respective income tax returns from previous years. Why all this contrasting? Mr. Steuerle wanted to study the correlation between realized income as documented in income tax returns and the actual net worth of each subject in the sample. Of special interest was the relationship between realized income generated from investments and their actual market value.

Why would a scholar who works for our treasury department spend so much time conducting a study like this? We consider the staff of the IRS a clever bunch. They study their target market. And they lust for its wealth. They want to know how many affluent people generate so few dollars of realized income. Since owners of closely held businesses are especially adept at this strategy, Mr. Steuerle selected for study those estates in which the value of the closely held business(es) exceeded 65 percent of the estates.

Here are some of the findings of Mr. Steuerle's study:

♦ The income realized from the assets of closely held businesses was only 1.15 percent of the appraised value of the assets. Note that even this small percentage is likely to be biased in the upward direction, since there are estate tax advantages for heirs and executors who provide conservative appraisals.

♦ The total income realized from all assets and all salary, wages, and income combined was only 3.66 percent of the value of all assets.

What do these results tell you about the affluent? They suggest that a business owner who is worth, say, $2 million on average has an annual realized income of only $73,200, or 3.66 percent of $2 million. Could you live on $73,200 today and still invest a minimum of 15 percent each year? No, it's not easy. But it's not easy being financially dependent, either.

FINANCIAL INDEPENDENCE

We once asked a high-income/low–net worth corporate manager (we will refer to him as Mr. Rodney) a simple question:

Why is it that you never participated in your corporation's tax-advantaged stock purchase plan?

This manager's employer offered him a matching stock purchase plan. Each year the manager could purchase the equivalent of 6 percent of his income in shares of the corporation, which would reduce his realized taxable income. Also, the corporation would match his purchase of company stock up to a certain percentage of his income.

Mr. Rodney reported that, unfortunately, he could not afford to participate. It seemed that all his income went toward his $4,200 monthly mortgage payment, two leased vehicles, tuition bills, club dues, a vacation home that needed to be fixed up, and taxes.

Ironically, Mr. Rodney wants "eventually to become financially independent." But like most UAWs, Mr. Rodney is not realistic in this regard. He has sold his financial independence. What if he had taken full advantage of the tax-advantaged benefit from the time he was first employed? Today he would be a millionaire. Instead, he is on the perpetual earn-and-consume treadmill.

We have interviewed countless high-income/low–net worth people. Sometimes it can be depressing, especially when the respondents are seniors. How would you like to be a sixty-seven-year-old cardiologist who has:

No pension plan . . . never had a pension plan

in spite of earning millions during his lifetime? His total net worth is less than $300,000. No wonder he started asking us questions such as:

Will I ever be able to retire?

Even more revealing are the interviews we hold with the widows of UAWs. In many cases, the widow has been a housewife throughout her long marriage. Often her mate, a high-income/low–net worth type, was underinsured or had no life insurance at all.

My husband always said not to worry about money. . . . "I'll always be here," he said. Can you help me? What should I do?

This is not a fun situation. How can well-educated, high-income people be so naive about money? Because being a well-educated, high-income earner does not automatically translate into financial independence. It takes planning and sacrificing.

What if your goal is to become financially independent? Your plan should be to sacrifice high consumption today for financial independence tomorrow. Every dollar you earn to spend is first discounted by the tax man. Earning $100,000 may be required to purchase a $68,000 boat, for example. Millionaires tend to think this way. That's why only a minority own boats. Do you plan to live on a boat after you retire? Or would you prefer to live on a $3 million pension plan? Can you do both?

HIGH-STATUS NEIGHBORHOODS

If you read the last section about the IRS's study of the affluent carefully, a question may have come to your mind. Are the results of the surveys we conducted different than those generated from income tax and estate tax returns? You will recall that, on average, the millionaires in our latest survey had a total realized income that was about 6.7 percent of their total net worth. The results from the income tax and estate tax data, however, indicated that top wealth holders realized only 3.66 percent of their wealth. How can this difference be explained? And what does it mean?

We employed a different sampling method than that used by the IRS in its study of income tax and estate tax returns. Our survey was based on sampling households that resided in high-status neighborhoods, whereas the IRS sampled from all income tax and estate tax returns. Since about half of the millionaires in America today do not live in so-called high-status neighborhoods, we also surveyed affluent farmers, auctioneers, and other wealthy people who live in nonstatus neighborhoods. Why do millionaires from high-status areas realize significantly more of their wealth (6.7 percent) than those top wealth holders selected from a national sample of all affluent decedents (3.66 percent)? Because the millionaires from high-status neighborhoods have to realize more income to live in these areas. What are the implications of our findings? *It's easier to accumulate wealth if you don't live in a high-status neighborhood.* But even those millionaires who do live in high-status areas realize only 6.7 percent of their wealth each year. Think of their non-affluent neighbors who, on average, must constantly realize more than 40 percent of their wealth just for the joy of living in a high-status gulch.

Perhaps you aren't as wealthy as you should be because you traded much of your current and future income just for the privilege of living in a home in a high-status neighborhood. So even if you're earning $100,000 a year, you're not becoming wealthy. What you probably don't know is that your neighbor in the $300,000 house next to yours bought his house only *after* he became wealthy. You bought yours in *anticipation* of becoming wealthy. That day may never come.

Each year you are forced to maximize realized income just to make ends meet. You can't afford to invest any money. Essentially, you're at a stalemate. Your high domestic overhead requires full commitment of all your income. You will never become financially independent without purchasing investments that appreciate without income realization. So what's it going to be? Will you choose a lifetime of high taxes and high-status living, or will you change your address? Allow us to help you in your decision making. Here is another one of our rules.

If you're not yet wealthy but want to be someday, never purchase a home that requires a mortgage that is more than twice your household's total annual realized income.

Living in less costly areas can enable you to spend less and to invest more of your income. You will pay less for your home and correspondingly less for your property taxes. Your neighbors will be less likely to drive expensive motor vehicles. You will find it easier to keep up, even ahead, of the Joneses and still accumulate wealth.

It's your choice. Perhaps you will make a better one than a young stock broker, Bob, we recently advised. We gave him the same advice about the ideal ratio of home price to income. This thirty-seven-year-old broker had a total realized income of $84,000. He wanted our advice about buying a $310,000 home. He planned to make a down payment of $60,000. He also planned to become wealthy. Carrying a $250,000 mortgage, we felt, would be an impediment to his goal.

We suggested that he buy something less expensive, such as a $200,000 home with a $140,000 mortgage. This would be within the parameters of the rule. Bob rejected this advice. He did not want to live in a neighborhood full of "truckers and construction workers." After all, he is a financial consultant and a college graduate.

But what Bob does not realize is that many construction workers and their spouses have combined incomes of more than $84,000. Of course, his mortgage broker told him he was qualified for a $250,000 mortgage. But that's like asking a fox to estimate the number of chickens in your coop.

TIME, ENERGY, AND MONEY

**THEY ALLOCATE THEIR TIME, ENERGY, AND MONEY
EFFICIENTLY, IN WAYS CONDUCIVE TO BUILDING WEALTH.**

Efficiency is one of the most important components of wealth accumulation. Simply: People who become wealthy allocate their time, energy, and money in ways consistent with enhancing their net worth. Although both prodigious accumulators and under accumulators of wealth state similar goals about achieving wealth, these groups have completely different orientations when it comes to how much time they actually spend on wealth-building activities.

**PAWs allocate nearly twice the number
of hours per month to planning their
financial investments as UAWs do.**

There is a strong positive correlation between investment planning and wealth accumulation. UAWs spend less time than PAWs consulting with professional investment advisors; searching for quality accountants, attorneys, and investment counselors; and attending investment-planning seminars. PAWs, on average, spend less time worrying about their economic well-being. We have determined that under accumulators are much more concerned than prodigious accumulators with the prospects of:

◆ not being wealthy enough to retire in comfort.

◆ never accumulating significant wealth.

Are their concerns realistic? Yes. Yet UAWs spend more time worrying about these issues than taking proactive steps to change their tendencies to overconsume and underinvest.

What type of person recently indicated that he was afraid and worried about the following two issues?

1. Experiencing a significant reduction in his standard of living.
2. Not having an income high enough to satisfy his family's purchasing habits.

Who is this person? Perhaps he is a mail carrier with two children in college. Or perhaps he is a single, low-income parent who has to raise three children. Do you envision a middle-aged corporate manager who recently found out that his position would be eliminated? Certainly these are logical guesses. People in these categories would very likely express fear about having to reduce their standard of living and not having the income to satisfy their family's buying habits. But none of these people is the one we are about to profile.

The respondent who actually expressed these fears and worries is a surgeon in his fifties whom we shall call Dr. South (see Table 3-1). He is married and has four children. Why should he be worried about his standard of living and his income? Could it be that he's down on his luck, perhaps

TABLE 3-1

CONCERNS, FEARS, AND WORRIES: DR. NORTH VS. DR. SOUTH

	PAW Dr. North	UAW Dr. South
Type of Wealth Accumulator:		
I. YOUR ECONOMIC WELL-BEING		
Not being wealthy enough to retire in comfort	Low	Moderate
Not having an income high enough to satisfy your family's purchasing habits	Low	Moderate
Having to retire	Low	Low
Having your job/occupational position eliminated	None	None
Experiencing a significant reduction in your standard of living	Low	High
Never accumulating significant wealth	Low	Moderate
Having your own business fail	Moderate	Low
Not being able to protect your family financially in case of premature death	High	Low
II. YOUR CHILDREN		
Having to support your adult children financially	Low	Moderate
Having adult children who spend more than they earn	Low	Moderate
Having children who are underachievers	Moderate	Low
Finding that your adult children have moved back home	Low	Moderate
Finding out that your son/daughter married an unfit spouse	Moderate	Moderate
Having adult children who think that your wealth is their income	Low	Moderate
III. YOUR PHYSICAL WELL-BEING		
Having cancer and/or heart disease	Moderate	Low
Having visual or hearing problems	Moderate	None
Being mugged, raped, robbed, or burglarized	Low	Moderate
Contracting AIDS	None	Low
IV. YOUR GOVERNMENT		
Increased government spending/federal deficit	Low	High
Increased government regulation of business/industry	Low	High
Paying increasingly high federal income taxes	Low	High
A high rate of inflation	None	Moderate
Having your family pay high taxes on your estate	Low	Low
V. YOUR DOMESTIC TRANQUILITY		
Having your children feud over your wealth	Low	Moderate
Having your family fight over your estate	Low	Moderate
Being accused of financially favoring one adult child over the other(s)	Low	Moderate
VI. YOUR FINANCIAL ADVISOR		
Being swindled by a financial advisor	Low	Moderate
Not receiving high-quality investment advice	None	Moderate
VII. YOUR PARENTS, CHILDREN, AND GRANDCHILDREN		
Having your children exposed to drugs	None	Low
Having your parent(s)/in-law(s) move into your home	Moderate	Low
Having too little time to devote to your children/grandchildren	Low	Low

unable to continue to practice medicine because of a disability? No. Actually he is a fine physician who earned more than $700,000 during the year prior to our interview with him! But in spite of his high income, his net worth in real terms is declining. He has reasons to be afraid and worried.

Dr. North is very similar to Dr. South in age, income, and family composition. But Dr. North is a PAW. His profile is also detailed later in this chapter. Dr. North has far fewer worries than Dr. South. He is not afraid of being forced to reduce his standard of living. Unlike Dr. South, he is not concerned that his income will not be high enough to satisfy his family's purchasing habits. This is especially interesting given that both Dr. South and Dr. North have similar incomes. The case studies that follow will introduce you to these physicians and their families. You will learn a lot about how each man makes use of his time, energy, and money. But before we profile these two physicians in detail, we will discuss the income and wealth-accumulating habits of physicians in general.

DOCTORS, PAWS, AND UAWS

On average, physicians earn more than four times the income of the average American household: $140,000 versus $33,000. But Dr. South and Dr. North are hardly average physicians. They are gifted and highly trained specialists. In fact, the average annual income for someone in their specialty is more than $300,000. But again, they are extraordinary even among their cohorts. Last year they each earned more than $700,000.

In spite of his income, Dr. South has a relatively small level of accumulated wealth. He spends a lot, invests little. Our research has found that physicians in general do not tend to be wealth accumulators. In fact, among all major high-income-producing occupations, physicians have a significantly low propensity to accumulate substantial wealth. For every one doctor in the PAW group, there are two in the UAW category.

Why are doctors lagging behind on the wealth scale? There are several reasons. Foremost among them is the correlation between wealth and education. This relationship may surprise some people. For all high-income earners (those earning at least $100,000 annually), the relationship between education and wealth accumulation is *negative*. High-income PAWs are significantly *less* likely than UAWs to hold graduate degrees, law degrees, or medical degrees. Millionaires typically indicate on our survey "business owner" with "some college," "four-year college graduate," or "no college."

Warning: Parents should not suggest that their children drop out of college and start a business. Most businesses fail within a few years of their conception. Only a small minority of business owners ever earns a six-figure income. But those who do tend to accumulate more wealth than others in the same income cohort.

The "some college," "four-year college graduate," and "no college" types who have high incomes often had a head start on many well-educated workers. Doctors and other well-educated professionals get a very late start in the earnings race. It is difficult to accumulate wealth when one is in school. The longer one stays in school, the longer one postpones producing an income and building wealth.

Most experts on wealth agree that the earlier one starts investing one's income, the greater the opportunity to accumulate wealth. Mr. Denzi, for example, is a business owner with two years of technical school training in data processing.

He started working and building wealth at the age of twenty-two. Today, thirty years later, he has benefited greatly from the meteoric increase in the value of his pension plan.

In sharp contrast, consider the situation of Dr. Dokes, who graduated from high school the same year as Mr. Denzi. Dr. Dokes opened his private medical practice more than a dozen years after his classmate, Mr. Denzi, started a business. During that twelve-year period, Dr. Dokes spent his time studying and spending his savings, his parents' money, and money he borrowed for tuition and living expenses. During the same time, Mr. Denzi, who designated himself as "not college material," focused his resources on building his business and becoming financially independent.

Who is in the UAW category today? Is it the "not-college-material" business owner, Mr. Denzi, or the valedictorian of his high school class, Dr. Dokes? The answer is obvious. Mr. Denzi is a prototypical PAW, while Dr. Dokes is a UAW. Interestingly, both earned approximately the same income last year (nearly $160,000). But Mr. Denzi has five to six times the wealth of his high school classmate. And he has no debt.

Mr. Denzi can teach us all something about accumulating wealth. *Begin earning and investing early in your adult life.* That will enable you to outpace the wealth accumulation levels of even the so-called gifted kids from your high school class. Remember, wealth is blind. It cares not if its patrons are well educated. So the authors have an excuse. How else does one explain why two experts on wealth are not wealthy? In part, because they spent a combined total of nearly twenty years pursuing higher education!

Another reason very well-educated people tend to lag behind on the wealth scale has to do with the status ascribed to them by society. Doctors, as well as others with advanced degrees, are expected to play their parts. Mr. Denzi is a small business owner. In spite of being wealthy, he is not expected by society to live in an exclusive neighborhood. He would not be out of place living in a modest home or driving a nondescript sedan. His domestic overhead is significantly lower than Dr. Dokes's.

Many people tell us that you can judge a book by its cover, meaning that high-grade doctors, lawyers, accountants, and so on are expected to live in expensive homes. They also are expected to dress and drive in a style congruent with their ability to perform their professional duties. How do you judge the professionals you patronize? Too many people judge them by display factors. Extra points are given to those who wear expensive clothes, drive luxury automobiles, and live in exclusive neighborhoods. They assume a professional is likely to be mediocre, even incompetent, if he lives in a modest home and drives a three-year-old Ford Crown Victoria. Very, very few people judge the quality of the professionals they use by net worth criteria. Many professionals have told us that they must look successful to convince their customers/clients that they are.

Of course, there are exceptions. But people who spend many years in college, professional school, or graduate school are more likely to have higher levels of household overhead than less educated people. As a rule, doctors have exceptionally high levels of domestic overhead. The concern in many of these households is with consuming, not investing.

Physicians often find that there are disadvantages to living in affluent neighborhoods. People who live in expensive areas are often bombarded with solicitations from "cold-calling" investment experts. Many of these callers assume that people in upscale areas have money to invest. In reality, many people who live in luxury have little money left over after funding their high-consumption lifestyles.

Some naive cold callers purchase prospect lists that fit two criteria. First, prospects must be physicians. Second, they must live in exclusive neighborhoods. It's no wonder physicians are the favorite targets of some of America's most aggressive sellers of investment ideas. Too often doctors who receive such solicitations assume that the callers are "just as professional as physicians." Many physicians have told us that they have had bad experiences with investing via cold callers. In fact, many have been burned so badly that they never again invested in the stock market. This is unfortunate given the overall growth in the real value of the equity market. And, in rejecting the stock market, they figured that left them with more money for spending. This attitude is not as rare as one might think:

> A plastic surgeon added that he had three boats and five cars but hadn't gotten around to assembling a pension plan. Financial investments? Didn't have those, either. Speaking of his colleagues, the surgeon said, "I don't know even one guy who hasn't been beaten to death in the financial markets. As a result, they don't have anything. At least I'm going to enjoy spending my money."
>
> Later on, this doctor summed up his financial philosophy: "Money," he said, with a wave of his hand, "is the most easily renewable resource" (Thomas J. Stanley, "Why You're Not As Wealthy As You Should Be," Medical Economics, July 1992).

What other factors explain why so many doctors are members of the UAW group? Our research shows that they are generally unselfish. On average, they contribute a higher percentage of their incomes to noble causes than do other high-income producers. Also, doctors are among the least likely to receive inheritances from their parents. Their less-educated brothers and sisters are significantly more likely to inherit money. In some cases, physicians are asked by their elderly parents to "help out [their] less fortunate brothers and sisters after [the parents] are no longer able to help pay their bills." These findings are detailed in Chapter 6.

Doctors often allocate large amounts of their time to serving patients. They rarely work fewer than ten hours a day, thus expending most of their time, energy, and intellect on patients. In so doing, they tend to neglect their economic well-being. Some doctors figure that working hard translates into a large income and that, therefore, there is no need to design a household budget. Some ask why they should waste time planning a domestic budget and investments when there is so much income to be made. Many high-income-producing UAWs feel this way.

PAWs tend to have just the opposite feelings. To them, money is a resource that should never be squandered. They know that planning, budgeting, and being frugal are essential parts of building wealth, even for very high-income producers. Even high-income producers must live below their means if they intend to become financially independent. And if you're not financially independent, you will spend an increasing amount of your time and energy worrying about your socioeconomic future.

PLANNING AND CONTROLLING

Planning and controlling consumption are key factors underlying wealth accumulation. Thus, one should expect that PAWs like Dr. North take the time to plan their budgets. They do. Conversely, Dr. South has no control over his family's consumption, other than his household's income limit. We asked Drs. South and North about their respective planning and controlling systems.

Question: Does your household operate on a fairly well-thought-out annual budget?

Dr. South: *No.*

Dr. North: *Yes . . . absolutely!*

Operating a household without a budget is akin to operating a business without a plan, without goals, and without direction. The Norths have a budget that calls for them to invest at least one-third of their pretax household income each year. In fact, during the year that we interviewed Dr. North, he and his wife invested nearly 40 percent of their annual pretax income. How were they able to do this? In short, they consume at the same level as the average family that earns about one-third as much as they do.

What about the Souths? They consume at the same level as the average household that earns nearly two times *more* than they do. In fact, their hyperuse of credit is more in line with that of households that earn several million dollars each year. The Souths essentially spend all of or more than their income each year. This income is their only restraint.

We asked both doctors another set of questions:

1. Do you know how much your family spends each year for food, clothing, and shelter?

2. Do you spend a lot of time planning your financial future?

3. Are you frugal?

You probably predicted the outcome. Dr. South responded with three noes, while Dr. North responded in true PAW fashion, with three yeses. Consider the frugal orientation of Dr. North. He stated emphatically, for instance, that he never bought a suit that was not offered at a discount or a special price. This is not to suggest that Dr. North is poorly dressed. Nor does he wear cheap suits. Rather, he purchases quality clothing, but not at full price and never on impulse. This behavior was part of his socialization process as a youth:

When I was going to school, my wife taught. We had a small income. . . . Even then we always had a rule . . . to save— even then we saved. You can't invest without something. . . . The first thing is to save.

Even when I was eleven years old, I saved my first $50 from working in a grocery store. It's just like today . . . only today the number of zeros change. . . . More zeros, but it's the same rule, same discipline.

You must take advantage of investment opportunities. . . . You have to have something to take advantage of excellent opportunities. . . . It's part of my background.

Dr. South reported having just the opposite orientation. How much did he and his family spend on clothing during the year prior to our interview? About $30,000 (see Table 3-2). Thus, the Souths spend nearly as much on clothing

TABLE 3-2
CONSUMPTION HABITS: THE NORTHS VS. THE SOUTHS

CONSUMPTION CATEGORY	ANNUAL AMOUNTS SPENT	
	NORTHS	SOUTHS
Type of Wealth Accumulator:	PAW	UAW
Clothing	$8,700	$30,000
Motor Vehicles	$12,000	$72,200
Mortgage Payments	$14,600	$107,000
Club Dues/Fees/Expenses	$8,000	$47,900

each year as the average American household earns in total—that is, $33,000.

THE HOME TEAM

Most high-income households consist of traditional married couples with children. Both the South and North households are traditional. We determined long ago that the habits of both husband and wife account for variations in accumulating wealth. Your spouse's orientation toward thrift, consumption, and investing is a significant factor in understanding your household's position on the wealth scale.

Who is the tightwad in your household? In the case of Dr. North's family, both he and his wife fit the profile. Both live well below their means. Both contribute to planning their well-thought-out annual budget. Neither objects to buying used motor vehicles. Both can tell you how much their family spends each year for a variety of products and services. Neither objected to sending their children to public elementary and high schools. Both place a high priority on being financially independent. Yet these goals never translated into shortchanging their three children. The parents funded their children's college educations as well as their graduate school and law school tuition and fees. They also provided them with funds to purchase homes and for related expenditures. The Norths paid for these expenditures out of investments that they set aside for their children. Conversely, the Souths are not investors. Almost all such allocations in the South household come from current earned income.

What if your household generates even a moderately high income and both you and your spouse are frugal? You have the foundation for becoming and maintaining PAW status. On the other hand, it is very difficult for a married couple to accumulate wealth if one is a spendthrift. A household divided in its financial orientation is unlikely to accumulate significant wealth.

Even worse are cases in which both the wife and her husband are spendthrifts. This is the domestic situation the Souths find themselves in today. Interestingly, Dr. South reported to us that he is the "tightwad" in his household. Is he? True, he takes aim at the shopping and consumption habits of his spouse. But spending all or even most of their annual income takes a team effort. Both are hyperconsumers. Both contribute to their lower-than-expected position on the wealth scale.

Let's evaluate Dr. South's wealth-building performance. He is responsible for his household's income. And there is no argument that he is extraordinary in this regard. His performance places him in the 99.5 percentile of all income earners in America. But he is also responsible, in part, for making other decisions for his household. He buys the motor vehicles and financial advice. He also makes investment decisions. But neither he nor his wife does any budgeting for the family.

Mrs. South is responsible for buying the family's clothing. In one year she spent about $30,000 on clothes for herself and her family. She also contributed significantly to the decision to spend more than $40,000 for country club fees and related expenses. Both decided to spend $107,000 per year in mortgage payments. Most UAWs will tell you that their big mortgage helps reduce their taxable income. Of course, if the Souths keep saving money this way, they may never be able to retire.

Often people who purchase expensive homes and automobiles are criticized for their extravagant lifestyle. But at least homes, in most cases, hold their value, if only in a nominal sense. Even automobiles hold some value for a few years after they are purchased. Large allocations for homes and automobiles can have a dampening effect on wealth building, but again, at least you can trade up, out, or down with such items. There are worse culprits.

How much is the Souths' $30,000 clothing purchase that they made last year worth today? How much will the $7,000 vacation they recently took be worth tomorrow? How much value is there remaining from the more than $40,000 they spent last year for country club–related expenses? Add to these gourmet restaurant patronage, maid services, tutors, lawn care/landscaping services, decorating consultants, insurance, and more.

The Souths' consumption habits are related to the fact that they have no centralized control over their expenditures. Much of their consumption is a function of independent action in this household drama. This is not the case in the North household. Dr. North and his wife both play active roles in budgeting and spending. They plan together and consult with each other regarding expenditures. We will detail their system. But first let us examine the Souths' situation.

Mrs. South is responsible for purchasing a wide variety of products and services for her household. She did not consult with anyone before spending $30,000 for clothing last year. She does her thing, and her husband does his. She has her set of credit cards, and he has his.

Mrs. South is a particularly ardent patron of upscale department stores. These include Neiman Marcus, Saks Fifth Avenue, and Lord & Taylor. She carries credit cards for each of these stores. In addition, she and her husband hold a MasterCard (gold) and a Visa (preferred) card. Dr. South also has the American Express platinum card.

What's the problem? Often Dr. and Mrs. South have little or no idea what their counterpart is buying or how much each is spending. This is especially true for soft goods and intangibles, such as clothes, gifts, and entertaining. Both are susceptible to solicitations from everyone from store clerks to financial advisors, from automobile sales personnel to credit officers at banks. If you were one of these people, who would you call? Who would you keep abreast of new product and service offerings? Who would you advise about a special showing of the latest fashions and motor vehicles?

Why does Mrs. South spend so much money? In classic UAW fashion, her husband has encouraged her to do so. He was the product of a high-income-producing, indulgent set of parents. He, in turn, has given his wife almost a blank check when it comes to shopping. And, of course, the Souths associate with other hyperconsumers. But there is something she and her husband don't know. They are unique. They are not typical consumers. No one ever told them that most people in their income bracket, including the Norths, never spend money like the Souths do. Unfortunately, the Souths never learned about the prodigious accumulators of wealth.

The Norths are very different from the Souths in their

spending behavior. Both Dr. and Mrs. North come from backgrounds of frugality and thrift. Throughout their marriage they have communicated with each other about resource allocations. Their budgeting system is basic to their controlled-consumption lifestyle. Unlike the Souths, the Norths own no credit cards for upscale department stores. That's right. The North family, whose net worth is more than eighteen times that of the Souths ($7,500,000 versus $400,000), holds no cards from Neiman Marcus or from Saks Fifth Avenue or from Lord & Taylor. They are only "special-occasion" shoppers at such stores. Almost all of their household purchases are placed on one "central" credit card, a Visa (preferred) card. Both their purchases are listed on one single statement each month. Each month they determine how much remains to be allocated for each consumption category, and at the end of each year they refer to these statements to compute their total expenditures for each category. Using this statement facilitates budgeting and making appropriations for the following year. Most important, their planning, budgeting, and consuming are coordinated events. Unlike the Souths, the Norths have one joint checking account to help facilitate the budgeting of items not paid for with their credit card.

What if you want to budget but don't like the process? We recently interviewed a CPA who offers a household budgeting and consumption planning service. Mr. Arthur Gifford has several hundred high-income-producing clients. Most are either self-employed professionals or business owners. Some are PAWs. Some are UAWs.

We asked Mr. Gifford who uses his budgeting and consumption planning system. His response was predictable in light of the case studies of the Souths and Norths:

Only those clients with considerable wealth want to know exactly how much their family spends on each and every category.

Mr. Gifford is correct. But aren't PAWs usually price sensitive when it comes to purchasing services? Not always. *They are much less price sensitive when buying services that will help them control their family's consumption behavior.*

Do you know exactly how much your family spent last year for each and every category of product and service? Without such knowledge, it's difficult to control your spending. If you can't control your spending, you're unlikely to accumulate prodigious amounts of wealth. A good start is to keep an accurate record of each and every expenditure that your family makes each month. Or ask your accountant to help you set up a system for tabulating and categorizing these expenditures. Then work with her to develop a budget. The goal is to enable you to set aside for investing purposes at least 15 percent of your pretax income each year. By the way, this "15 percent method" is Mr. Gifford's simple strategy for becoming affluent.

CAR-SHOPPING METHODS

The Souths outpace the Norths in several consumption categories. During the year prior to our interview, they allocated six times more money for motor vehicles than the Norths ($72,200 versus $12,000). Dr. South also purchased a $65,000 Porsche during the year of our interview. Dr. South is, in fact, a true connoisseur of fine motor vehicles. He spends little time preparing a budget for his household and even less time planning his financial future. But he has a very different orientation when it comes to purchasing automobiles.

There is an inverse relationship between the time spent purchasing luxury items such as cars and clothes and the time spent planning one's financial future.

High-income-producing UAWs like Dr. South spend a great deal of their incomes on expensive automobiles and clothing. But it takes more than money to acquire and maintain large inventories of luxury goods. Such purchases have to be planned. It takes time to shop, and it takes time to care for large quantities of expensive high-status artifacts. Time, energy, and money are finite resources, even among high-income generators. Our research indicates that even these top earners cannot have their cake and eat it, too. Dr. North and PAWs in general, on the other hand, allocate their spare time to activities that they hope will enhance their wealth (see Table 3-6 later in chapter). Such activities include studying and planning their investment strategies and managing current investments. We will study this issue in greater detail later in this chapter.

Conversely, UAWs such as Dr. South work hard to maintain and enhance their high standard of living. Often these high-income-producing UAWs, Dr. South included, outspend their six-figure incomes. So how do they balance their need to maintain their high standard of living with a finite income? Many aggressively shop for bargains.

THE SOUTH METHOD

Examine the activities that Dr. South undertakes prior to purchasing an automobile. You might get the impression that he is a tightwad. Most UAWs like Dr. South bolster their hyperconsumption behavior by telling would-be critics that everything they buy is purchased near cost, at cost, below cost, and so on. It is true that Dr. South is an aggressive bargain shopper. But he just paid more than $65,000 for an exotic sports car. Is this really a bargain? Dr. South made this purchase at "near dealer's cost." But what were the costs of this so-called deal in time and effort? Most high-income generators, whether they are PAWs or UAWs, work more than forty hours a week. Typically, the amount of time remaining each week is allocated in ways that are congruent with their goals.

All too often high-income-producing UAWs spend countless hours studying the market—but not the stock market. They can tell you the names of the top auto dealers, but not the top investment advisors. They can tell you how to shop and spend. But they can't tell you how to invest. They know the styles, prices, and availability at various car dealers. But they know little or nothing about the various values of equity market offerings.

As an example, contrast Dr. South's most recent automobile-shopping activities with that of typical millionaires. On average, the American millionaire employs four to five simple bargain-shopping techniques when buying a motor vehicle. Dr. South does it differently. He uses at least nine bargaining/shopping tactics and strategies when negotiating with dealers.

Consider the level of car-purchasing knowledge Dr. South has recently acquired that will never pay capital gains or real dividends or enhance the productivity of his business. He now has knowledge about every Porsche dealer within a four hundred–mile radius of his home. Dr. South also can tell you immediately the dealer's cost on nearly every

Porsche model, the cost of options and accessories, and the performance characteristics of most models. It takes much time and effort to acquire such information.

Dr. South has an interesting style when purchasing automobiles. He first decides on the make and model of the vehicle he wants and the corresponding accessories. Then he goes all-out into information seeking and negotiating. It is not unusual for him to shop around for months "for the very best deal." In the process he usually discovers the dealer's cost on the vehicle. This is done prior to entering into serious negotiations with a dealer. Then he telephones all the dealers (his long list) and invites them to compete for his business. He has no problem buying a Porsche from a low-price-oriented, out-of-town dealer. Those dealers who designate themselves as price-oriented are then placed on Dr. South's short list. The others are dropped from consideration.

Dealers on his short list are contacted once again. During this stage of the process, Dr. South quizzes the dealers about their willingness to sell at below cost. While doing so, he reminds them of the low prices quoted by other dealers. He also asks about program/off-lease vehicles. But his heart is always set on a brand new model.

At the end of the month, Dr. South recontacts all the low-price-oriented dealers. Dr. South does this because he feels that dealers have "sales quotas and bank notes due" at that time. He invites all these dealers to give their "final lowest bid" for his business. For his most recent purchase, during the last day of the month and after a flurry of phone calls, he finally accepted a bid from an out-of-town dealer.

Dr. South is penny-wise, pound-foolish when purchasing motor vehicles. But he has convinced himself that he is a prudent buyer. After all, he spends much time and energy trying to buy cars at or near dealer cost. But perhaps dealer cost was too high a price to pay. It is difficult to accumulate wealth if you spend much of your time, energy, and money for a so-called dealer cost price on an extremely expensive motor vehicle.

Consider this fact: Most millionaires we have interviewed never in their lifetimes spent near $65,000 for an automobile. In fact, as we will report in Chapter 4, more than half the millionaires we interviewed never paid more than $30,000 for a motor vehicle. Remember, though, Dr. South is not a millionaire. Certainly in terms of net worth, millionaires are better able to afford a $65,000 automobile. But they ignore such opportunities. As so often is said, "That's why they're millionaires!"

Certainly the consumption of very expensive automobiles has a dampening effect on the probability that one will ever accumulate significant wealth. During the year we interviewed him, Dr. South spent more than $70,000 for his most recent motor vehicle purchase, related sales tax, and insurance. Yet for the same period, how much did he place in his pension plan? About $5,700! In other words, only about $1 in every $125 of his income was set aside for retirement. The amount of time Dr. South took to find the best deal on his car was also counterproductive. We estimated that it took him more than sixty hours to study, negotiate, and purchase his Porsche. How much time and effort does it take someone to place money in a pension plan? A small fraction of this time and energy. It is easy for Dr. South to say he wants to accumulate wealth, but his actions speak much louder than his words. Perhaps that explains why he has lost a considerable amount of wealth through imprudent investing. Investing when one has little or no intellectual basis for one's decisions often translates into major losses.

THE NORTH METHOD

Dr. North is not a connoisseur of motor vehicles, although he is price-sensitive when making purchasing decisions. We asked Dr. North about his most recent automobile purchase. Remember that Dr. South's most recent purchase was the current year's model. Note that fewer than 25 percent of America's millionaires are driving the current year's model. And, of course, Dr. South is not a millionaire.

Dr. North proudly informed us that he purchased his most recent automobile six years ago. We anticipate your question: Do you mean he has not purchased a new automobile in six years? Not only has Dr. North not purchased a *new* automobile in six years, but the one he purchased six years ago was a three-year-old Mercedes-Benz 300 that he bought for $35,000.

Dr. North loves the car: great price, excellent fuel economy—"It's a diesel." And, of course, diesel Mercedes often can last for hundreds of thousands of miles before they need an overhaul. It also has classic styling.

How much time and energy did Dr. North expend in purchasing his Mercedes? Let's examine his decision-making process. First, he decided that he needed to replace his "old car." After all, it was twenty years old. He knew that many European luxury automobiles depreciate rapidly during the first three years following their initial purchase. So he figured that he might be able to save a considerable amount if he purchased a three-year-old Mercedes-Benz.

He confirmed this speculation by determining the original retail price of the model he was interested in purchasing. A quick trip to a local dealer was all that was required to gain this knowledge. Dr. North then decided that his best choice would be a three-year-old model. He telephoned a few dealers and advised them of his interest. He also examined several advertisements in the classified section of the paper. Finally he decided on a low-mileage model offered by a local dealer. As he explained:

Automobiles? I have always placed a premium on quality. But I never lease, never finance. I drive a Mercedes-Benz. Since I started my practice, I have only had two cars. The first, a Mercedes, I purchased new just after I opened my practice. . . . Kept it twenty years. Then I bought my second car . . . a three-year-old Mercedes. I went to a dealer. . . . He wanted to sell me a new one. But it was $20,000 more than the used one on the lot.

Then I just asked myself a simple question: Is the "pride of new car ownership"—and that's all it is, pride—worth $20,000? The cars are the same. The answer is no. The "pride of new car ownership" is not worth $20,000.

The North method took only a few hours. Contrast this with Dr. South's automobile-purchasing crusade—a process that took him at least sixty hours. And, of course, Dr. North likes to keep his cars for a long time. So his allocation of purchasing time is spread over several years. On average, he devotes less than an hour a year to purchasing motor vehicles. But Dr. South likes to buy a new car every year. Thus, his sixty-hour project is typically allocated to only one year.

FEARS AND WORRIES

What do you spend time worrying about? Are your concerns congruent with wealth accumulation? Or do you spend time thinking about issues that are impediments to becoming affluent? How do PAWs and UAWs differ in regard to their fears and concerns? In simple terms, UAWs worry more than PAWs. PAWs and UAWs also worry about different issues. Overall, PAWs have significantly fewer concerns and fears than their counterparts.

What if you spend much of your time thinking about a lot of issues that concern you? You will spend less time taking action to solve these problems. And what if your fears provide a foundation for increased spending? You may be a member of the UAW group.

Fears and concerns can be both a cause for becoming a UAW as well as a result. Will a person who constantly worries about earning more money to enhance his lifestyle become wealthy? Probably not. Dr. South is not wealthy, in part because he concerns himself with such issues. Dr. North is wealthy today because he placed much less priority on standard-of-living issues than did Dr. South.

Dr. South told us that nineteen issues were of high or moderate concern to him (see Table 3-1). Dr. North was concerned with only about seven issues. Thus, it's only logical to conclude that the Dr. Norths of this country have more time and energy to devote to wealth-enhancing activities. Let's examine how these doctors' fears and worries—or lack of them—have affected their lives.

THE CHILDREN OF UAWS AND PAWS

The Souths have four children. Two are adults. Dr. South has serious, well-founded concerns about their future. UAWs tend to produce children who eventually become UAWs themselves. What is expected of children who are exposed to a household environment predicated upon very high consumption, few—if any—economic constraints, little planning or budgeting, no discipline, and pandering to every product-related desire? Like their UAW parents, as adults, these children are often addicted to an undisciplined, high-consumption lifestyle. Further, these children typically will never earn the incomes necessary to support the lifestyle to which they have grown accustomed.

Certainly Dr. South's parents' indulgent lifestyle contributed to his becoming a UAW. And he learned so well. His lifestyle is even more consumption-oriented than that of his mother and father. His upper-middle-class lifestyle was never interrupted even when he was in graduate school and medical school. His parents paid for his home and all other expenses. They provided him with substantial gifts of cash each year. In essence, he never really had to change his consumption habits or standard of living after leaving home. Fortunately for him, he has the income to support his addiction to consumption. But what about his children? They have lived in a high-consumption environment that would be extremely difficult to replicate on their own. The curtain is coming down on the third generation. Dr. South indicated in our interviews with us that he believed his children would never generate even a fraction of the income he currently earns.

In comparison, Dr. North's adult children are demonstrating more independence and discipline, in part because they have been exposed to a much more frugal, well-planned, and disciplined lifestyle. As we noted, the Norths consume at a level that is more congruent with a household earning less than one-third of their income. This living below their means is precisely why PAWs throughout the income spectrum tend to produce children who are economically disciplined and self-sufficient adults. PAWs tend to produce children who become PAWs.

Dr. South, as indicated, has accumulated considerably less wealth than Dr. North. He is significantly less able than Dr. North to support the economic outpatient care of his adult children. But ironically it is Dr. South who is burdened by having economically dependent adult children.

We questioned both Dr. South and Dr. North about their fears and worries concerning their children. As you may have already predicted, Dr. South is much more concerned about this issue. He specifically expressed fears of

1. having adult children who think his wealth is their income.
2. having to support his adult children financially.

Imagine how disconcerting it is for someone like Dr. South to face the prospect of supporting his extended family. Chapters 5 and 6 will explore the implications of "economic outpatient care" in great detail. However, there is an important point to note at this time: *Having adult children who are UAWs greatly reduces the probability that their parents will ever become wealthy!*

Dr. South wonders where his children got the idea that their parents would provide them with substantial economic outpatient care. He worries that he will not have the resources to provide his children with all the subsidies his parents gave him. There is yet another fear Dr. South must face. He is becoming more and more worried that his children will not get along with each other. Much of this concern is rooted in their need for economic support from their parents. Dr. North does not worry about such issues.

We asked both doctors about these types of concerns. Dr. South worried that

3. his family/children will fight over his estate.
4. he will be accused of financially favoring one adult child over another.

Are Dr. South's fears justified? Ask yourself this question: What is the greatest fear of the thirty-year-old sons and daughters of the Dr. Souths of America? That the economic outpatient care they receive from their parents will stop. Many "thirty-something" UAWs cannot maintain anywhere near the lifestyle they had while living with Dad and Mom. In fact, many are unable to purchase even a modest home without financial subsidies from their parents. It is not unusual for these "rich kids" to receive substantial cash and other financial gifts until they are in their late forties or even early fifties. Often these adult UAWs compete with each other for their parents' wealth. What would you do if your economic subsidy was being threatened by the presence of your equally dependent brothers and sisters?

Dr. South is not only worried about *his* problems; he is also worried about his children's problems. Consider for a moment the legacy he is leaving them. What are the ramifications of being an economically dependent adult? How much insecurity and fear will they have to deal with in the future? How will they be able to have harmonious, loving relationships with each other? These are among the issues Dr. South spends more and more time contemplating.

Dr. North is much less concerned with such problems. His adult children are accustomed to living in a much more frugal and disciplined environment. They are less likely to have a perceived need for major doses of economic outpatient care.

TABLE 3-3
INCOME AND WEALTH CONTRASTS

Households	Total Annual Realized Income	Total Income Tax	Tax As % of Realized Income	Total Net Worth	Tax As % of Net Worth
THE NORTHS	$730,000	$277,000	38	$7,500,000	4
THE SOUTHS	$715,000	$300,000	42	$400,000	75

TAXES, GOVERNMENT, AND GOVERNMENT

Many high-income earners in America—both PAWs and UAWs—are greatly concerned about the actions of the federal government. These actions are external forces—those over which an individual has no control. Dr. South indicated that he feared four external forces that are government-related. Interestingly, these issues are not of major concern to Dr. North. Let's look at these four concerns:

1: Paying increasingly high federal income taxes

Both physicians think that the federal government is likely to require high-income producers to pay more in taxes. But tax increases are more the concern of Dr. South than of Dr. North. Why is Dr. South concerned about this issue? Because he needs to maximize his realized income to support his hyperconsumption lifestyle. If the government requires Dr. South to pay a higher share of his income, his lifestyle will be threatened.

What about Dr. North? He told us that he had a low level of concern over the prospects of the federal government increasing the share of his realized income that he must pay in taxes. Last year Dr. North paid approximately $277,000 in income taxes (see Table 3-3). This may seem like a big bite. But look at it through the eyes of Dr. North. He looks at income tax more as a portion of his total wealth than a portion of his realized income.

What if the government doubled the tax rate on high incomes? This is very unlikely, but just as an example, Dr. North would then have to pay the equivalent of 8 percent of his wealth each year. By comparison, Dr. South would be at a "wealth rate" of 150 percent! Is it any wonder Dr. North is much less concerned about paying increasingly higher federal income taxes than Dr. South is?

2: Increased government spending and the federal deficit

Dr. South is very concerned about this issue. He believes that increased spending on the part of the government will translate into higher taxes on his income. Dr. North is not overly concerned for the reasons stated above.

3: A high rate of inflation

Dr. South is also concerned that such government action as increased spending and an increase in the deficit will precipitate a significant increase in the inflation rate. Dr. South has a moderate level of concern about this issue because he, like many UAWs, keeps trading up to more and more expensive homes, cars, clothes, and so on. On the other hand, Dr. North feels that inflation will significantly increase the value of at least part of his investment portfolio!

4: Increased government regulation of business and industry

Most physicians feel that this type of government action is targeted at them. They interpret increases in government regulation as preceding the advent of socialized medicine.

Both physicians feel that this would have a dampening effect on the fees they generate for their professional services. Dr. South indicated that this issue is of significant concern to him, while Dr. North viewed such action as only a minor concern.

Why do these two respondents perceive things so differently?

The actions of the government are often a threat to high-income earners who use most of their incomes to support their lifestyles. This is especially true when there is political gain for those in power in targeting the "wealthy." Actually, the people the politicians are targeting are high-income earners. Most politicians don't understand the difference between having a high income and having high levels of wealth. They have a more difficult time targeting people with high levels of net worth.

Most millionaires who are PAWs are self-employed. Being self-employed gives one much more control over one's economic future than does working for others. Conversely, employees today, even high-income-producing executives, have less control over their livelihoods than ever before. Downsizing, for example, is taking its toll, even among the most productive employees. More often than not, even high-income-producing employees are not likely to be millionaires.

UAWs who are employees (not self-employed) are particularly vulnerable to external forces that threaten their ability to earn a living. We found that only 19 percent of PAWs versus 36 percent of high-income-producing nonmillionaires (UAWs) were concerned about having their jobs eliminated (see Table 3-4). But in spite of the "handwriting" that is often "on the wall," even most high-income-earning employees are consumption-oriented.

TABLE 3-4
CONCERNS, FEARS, AND WORRIES: PAWS VS. UAWS

% with High or Moderate Concern, Fear, and/or Worry:	PAW[1] N=155	UAW[2] N=205	Significant Difference[3]
I. YOUR ECONOMIC WELL-BEING			
Not being wealthy enough to retire in comfort	43	60	Yes
Not having an income high enough to satisfy your family's purchasing habits	31	37	No
Having to retire	20	18	No
Having your job/occupational position eliminated	19	36	Yes
Experiencing a significant reduction in your standard of living	44	44	No
Never accumulating significant wealth	32	42	Yes
Having your own business fail	38	32	No
Not being able to protect your family financially in case of premature death	22	32	Yes
II. YOUR CHILDREN			
Having to support your adult children financially	23	17	No
Having adult children who spend more than they earn	39	25	Yes
Having children who are underachievers	34	30	No
Finding that your adult children have moved back home	13	11	No
Finding out that your son/daughter married an unfit spouse	36	34	No
Having adult children who think that your wealth is their income	20	18	No
III. YOUR PHYSICAL WELL-BEING			
Having cancer and/or heart disease	61	58	No
Having visual or hearing problems	47	40	No
Being mugged, raped, robbed, or burglarized	38	45	No
Contracting AIDS	13	11	No
IV. YOUR GOVERNMENT			
Increased government spending/federal deficit	88	78	Yes
Increased government regulation of business/industry	82	76	No
Paying increasingly high federal income taxes	80	79	No
A high rate of inflation	64	52	No
Having your family pay high taxes on your estate	65	41	Yes
V. YOUR DOMESTIC TRANQUILITY			
Having your children feud over your wealth	10	11	No
Having your family fight over your estate	17	11	No
Being accused of financially favoring one adult child over the other(s)	7	8	No
VI. YOUR FINANCIAL ADVISOR			
Being swindled by a financial advisor	26	29	No
Not receiving high-quality investment advice	40	33	No
VII. YOUR PARENTS, CHILDREN, AND GRANDCHILDREN			
Having your children exposed to drugs	47	59	Yes
Having your parent(s)/in-law(s) move into your home	12	19	Yes
Having too little time to devote to your children/grandchildren	44	56	Yes

[1]The 155 PAWs in this sample had an average realized annual income of $151,656 and average net worth of $2.35 million. Their average age was 52.

[2]UAWs in this sample had an average realized annual income of $167,348 and a net worth of $448,618. Their average age was 48.

[3]Probability at less than 0.05 level

FINANCIAL GOALS: WORDS VERSUS DEEDS

Many high-income-producing PAWs and UAWs share similarly stated goals concerning wealth accumulation. For example, more than three-fourths of both groups indicated they had the following goals:

◆ To become wealthy by the time they retire

◆ To increase their wealth

◆ To become wealthy through capital appreciation

◆ To build their capital while conserving the value of their assets

But having a set of stated goals does not necessarily mean that one is committed to achieving them. Most of us want to be wealthy, but most of us do not spend the time, energy, and money required to enhance our chances of realizing this goal.

TIME ALLOCATION

Most PAWs agree with the following statements, while most UAWs disagree:

◆ I spend a lot of time planning my financial future.

◆ Usually, I have sufficient time to handle my investments properly.

◆ When it comes to the allocation of my time, I place the management of my own assets before my other activities.

Conversely, UAWs tend to agree with the following statements:

◆ I can't devote enough time to my investment decisions.

◆ I'm just too busy to spend much time with my own financial affairs.

TABLE 3-5

**INVESTMENT PLANNING AND DEMOGRAPHIC CONTRASTS:
MIDDLE-INCOME PAWS VS. UAWS**

| Planning for Investment Decisions | Wealth Accumulator: | |
| (Average Number of Hours Allocated) | PAW | UAW |
	N=205	N=215
Per Month	8.4	4.6
Per Year	100.8	55.2
Demographic Characteristics		
Age (Average Years)	54.4	56.0
Annual Realized Household Income (Average/$000's)	51.5	48.9
Net Worth (Average/$000's)	629.4	105.7
Net Worth of $1 Million or More (%)	59.6	0.0
Expected Net Worth[1] (Average/$000's)	280.2	273.8
Realized Income As a Percent of Net Worth	8.2	46.3
Percent Self-Employed	59.1	24.7

[1]Expected net worth was computed via the wealth equation: expected net worth = 1/10 age x annual realized household income.

PAWS and UAWS also differ in the amount of time they actually allocate to planning their investments.

Planning is typically found to be a strong habit among people who have a demonstrated propensity to accumulate wealth. *Planning and wealth accumulation are significant correlates even among investors with modest incomes.* In our survey of 854 middle-income respondents (see Table 3-5), for example, a strong positive correlation was found between investment planning and wealth accumulation.

One of the more interesting findings in our studies of the affluent relates to why many people spend so little time planning their investments. Many people who do little or no investment planning often feel the way these respondents did:

It's hopeless. . . .

I never have the time needed to make it pay off.

We never have made so much. . . . But the more we earn, the less we seem to accumulate.

Our careers take up all our time.

I don't have twenty hours a week to fool with investing my money.

But PAWs do not spend anywhere near twenty hours a week in this way. If you study Table 3-5, you will notice that, on average, even prodigious accumulators of wealth do not need to devote a large proportion of their time to planning their investment strategies.

We found that these middle-income PAWs spend an average of only 8.4 hours per month planning their investments. This translates to about 100.8 hours per year. Given that there are 8,760 hours in a year, PAWs allocate approximately 1.2 percent of their time planning their investments.

UAWs, on average, spend 4.6 hours per month planning their investments, or about 55.2 hours per year. In other words, PAWs spend an average of 83 percent more hours (100.8 versus 55.2) planning per month than do UAWs. UAWs allocate only 1 in 160 hours of their total available time to planning their investments. PAWs allocate 1 in 87 hours.

Will UAWs automatically become PAWs simply by doubling the number of hours they devote to planning their investments? Not likely. Planning is only one of many key ingredients in building wealth. Most PAWs have a regimented planning schedule. Each week, each month, each year, they plan their investments. They also start planning at a much earlier age than do UAWs.

UAWs, on the other hand, are much like some overweight people who occasionally starve themselves to reach their ideal weight. But more often than not, they regain all the weight they lost and more. UAWs may start the new year with a plan that outlines a variety of investment goals. These goals may be the product of a couple of days of aggressive planning that specifies the number of dollars allocated to investments. Also included in the plan may be a significant "cold-turkey" reduction in the consumption of goods and services. More often than not, this "shock planning" and corresponding radical change in lifestyle are so severe that they do not work. The typical UAW, in this case, quickly becomes disenchanted with his new model for wealth building. Soon he "falls off the wagon," once again breaking his promise of planning, investing more, and consuming less.

Many UAWs think that a professionally prepared plan

will make them PAWs overnight, but even the best financial plans are ineffective if you don't follow them. All too often UAWs think that others "can lose weight" for them.

The UAWs in such cases would greatly benefit from understanding how PAWs operate. PAWs do a little planning each and every month. Again, only about eight hours a month. UAWs might do more planning if they knew that it would not require them to "quit their day jobs"! PAWs build wealth slowly. They do not live a spartan existence, but they do have a regimen when it comes to balancing working, planning, investing, and consuming.

YOUR TIME IS YOUR OWN

The work factor is an important part of understanding the differences between PAWs and UAWs. Note in our study of middle-income respondents the percentage (59.1 versus 24.7) of PAWs versus UAWs who are self-employed (see Table 3-5). In this study, self-employment correlated significantly with planning investments. Overall, the self-employed spend more time planning their investment strategies than those who work for others. The self-employed, even those with middle incomes, typically integrate investment planning into their work lives. Most employees, in sharp contrast, have a set of job-related tasks that are independent of planning their investment strategies. Why is this so?

Those who succeed among the ranks of the self-employed never take their economic position for granted. Most middle-aged people who are self-employed have seen good as well as bad economic times. They tend to offset the inevitable changes in their revenue by planning and investing. They must build and manage their pension plans by themselves. They have to rely on themselves for their current and future financial situations. More often than not, only the well-disciplined self-employed survive economically over the long run.

But, you may ask, don't these people work long and hard? Yes, most successful people who are self-employed work ten to fourteen hours per day. In fact, this is why many employees shy away from even considering "going out on their own." They want something less demanding. They want to be employees. But most workers, even those with middle-level incomes, also work long and hard. As for employees who earn annual incomes in the upper five or lower six digits, much of their time and energy is allocated to their jobs. They usually don't have the benefit of writing their own job descriptions. And their occupational tasks typically don't include setting aside a few hours per week to plan their investments. In contrast, the self-employed, especially in the high-income category, have a different set of occupational goals; one of them is to become financially independent. Conversely, employees are too often fully dependent on their employers. Thus they tend to be less self-reliant when it comes to planning their investments in a way that will facilitate accumulating wealth.

There is another issue to consider in the planning equation: UAWs spend less time planning their investments than do PAWs, in part because of the nature of their investments. UAWs consider cash/near cash and equivalents, such as savings accounts, money market funds, and short-term treasury bills, to be investments. UAWs are nearly twice as likely as PAWs to hold at least 20 percent of their total wealth in cash/near cash. Most of these cash categories are federally insured. Most are easily accessed when consumption needs arise. And, of course, it takes less time to plan cash-related investments than it does to allocate wealth the way PAWs tend to do.

PAWs are more likely to invest in categories that usually appreciate in value but do not produce realized income. They tend to have a greater percentage of their wealth invested in privately held/closely held businesses, commercial real estate, publicly traded equities, and their pension plans/annuities and other tax-deferred categories. These types of investments require planning. They are also the foundation for wealth. UAWs hold a larger percentage of their wealth in motor vehicles and other assets that tend to depreciate.

ACTIVE OR INACTIVE TRADER?

Nearly all (95 percent) of the millionaires we surveyed own stocks; most have 20 percent or more of their wealth in publicly traded stocks. Yet you would be wrong to assume that these millionaires actively trade their stocks. Most don't follow the ups and downs of the market day by day. Most don't call their stock brokers each morning to ask how the London market did. Most don't trade stocks in response to daily headlines in the financial media.

Do you define active investors as people who, on average, keep an investment for days? Of the millionaires we interviewed, fewer than 1 percent of those who own stock are in this league. How about weeks? Another 1 percent. Let's move up to those who, on average, hold on for months but less than a year. Fewer than 7 percent are "monthly" investors. Overall, only about 9 percent of the millionaires we have interviewed hold their investments for less than one year. In other words, fewer than one in ten millionaires are "active investors." One in five (20 percent) hold, on average, for a year or two; one in four (25 percent) hold for between two and four years. About 13 percent are in the four-to-six-year category. More than three in ten (32 percent) hold their investments for more than six years. In fact, *42 percent of the millionaires we interviewed for our latest survey had made no trades whatsoever in their stock portfolios in the year prior to the interview.*

The so-called active investor is one of the more difficult types of millionaires to find for interview purposes. He may be an ideal target market for stock brokers. He certainly spends considerable amounts for brokerage fees related to his trading. But he represents a very small minority of the millionaire population. In fact, we have encountered more nonmillionaire active traders than millionaires who actively trade. How can this be possible? Because it is very expensive to buy and sell, buy and sell, buy and sell one's equity holdings each day or week or month.

Often, active investors spend more time trading than studying and planning their investments. Conversely, millionaires spend more time studying far fewer offerings. Thus, they can focus their time and energy—the resources needed to master their understanding of a much smaller variety of offerings in the market.

We have always been interested in studying the wealth

TABLE 3-6

HOURS ALLOCATED:
DR. NORTH VS. DR. SOUTH CONTRASTED WITH
SAMPLES OF PAWS AND UAWS

HOURS SPENT IN AN AVERAGE MONTH FOR:	Dr. North	(PAW) N=155	Dr. South	(UAW) N=205
Studying/planning future investment decisions	10.0	(10.0)	3.0	(5.5)
Managing current investments	20.0	(8.1)	1.0	(4.2)
Exercising	30.0	(16.3)	10.0	(16.7)

accumulation habits of stock brokers. Compared with the members of other industries, stock brokers earn high incomes. They have access to large amounts of research data. Also, they pay less than other people when they trade securities because they earn their own commissions. Are all these high-income-producing investment advisors wealthy? Not by a long shot.

We have asked many stock brokers about this issue. Perhaps one individual stock broker stated it best when he told us:

I'd be rich if I would just keep . . . [my stocks, but I] can't help but make trades in my own portfolio. I'm looking at the screen every day.

Keep in mind that this broker's net annual income is in excess of $200,000. But because he's a very active investor, he rarely allows the investment seeds he sows to grow. Any short-term realized gains he enjoys are taxed immediately. He is not the type of broker a millionaire prefers to patronize. Then what type do they prefer? Far less active investors. They prefer to deal with those who believe in buying based on considerable studying and then holding.

Let's return to our case studies, Drs. North and South, to see financial planning in action.

COMPARING TIMES

Dr. North allocates about ten hours in a typical month, or 120 hours a year, to studying and planning his future investment decisions (see Table 3-6). In contrast, Dr. South allocates three hours a month, or fewer than forty hours a year.

Who spends more time managing his current investments? Again, the answer is predictable. Dr. North, on average, allocates about twenty hours a month, or 240 hours in a typical year, for this purpose, while his counterpart reported spending only one hour per month managing his current investments. Certainly, this is a contributing factor to Dr. South's low net worth.

Dr. North is a focused investor. He has two favorite investment categories, agricultural land and stocks from the medical industry:

First, a fellow I attended medical school with . . . He saved the life of a patient who believed in investing in grade A agriculture/orchards. My colleague invested and told me about it. He told me that these people were very honest. I met them and agreed. I have been investing ever since . . . still investing regularly today.

I have made most in the stock market from the medical industry. . . . Drug companies and medical instrument companies . . . I know this area. I do research on the medical . . . drug field. . . . That's what Warren Buffett does . . . invests in companies that he knows and understands. But you must have seed money [savings to invest] in areas you have knowledge. I have over $2 million in my profit-sharing plan.

Dr. South is responsible for making the major investment decisions in his family. It was his decision to have accounts at four different full-service brokerage firms. But surprisingly, Dr. South has less than $200,000 in securities. Then why does he have four different financial advisors? Because he believes, incorrectly, that he does not need to spend time making his own investment decisions. He admitted to us that he would be "really" affluent if he did not take advice from these so-called experts. But even bad advice does not come cheap. We estimated that Dr. South spent over $35,000 in a single year for advice and trades related to his poorly performing $200,000 portfolio. What about Dr. North? During the same period he spent zero dollars for transaction fees and zero dollars for financial advice. He is his own financial advisor. He rarely sells stocks. Also, there are no transaction fees for his direct investing in farmland and its products.

Dr. South, in traditional UAW fashion, has been burned by financial advisors. Too often people in his position respond to cold calls from brokers who are touting the stock of the week. Too often Dr. South is late entering the up market and exits it too early. In sharp contrast, most of the PAWs we have interviewed make their own investment decisions. They take the time and energy to study investment opportunities. They consult with financial advisors, but ultimately their investment decisions are their own.

Dr. South has a history of trading rapidly among his brokers' "flavors of the month." He spends many dollars for these trades. If these "flavors" appreciate in value, they precipitate capital gains taxes. On the other hand, when stocks in a pension plan are traded, they are not subject to capital gains taxes. Unfortunately, Dr. South is not a big fan of pension plans. We estimated that he had less than $40,000 in his plan at the time of our interview with him!

WHO ARE YOUR SUPPLIERS?

How did you hire your household's financial advisor? Did you list the position in the help-wanted section of your local newspaper? Did you evaluate the stacks of resumes your advertisement generated? Or did you ask your accountant, attorney, or minister to help you find a quality advisor?

Many people tell us that such methods are just too much work.

This is unfortunate. The more intellect, time, and energy you spend in hiring a financial advisor, the more likely you will be to find a suitable one. Perhaps you're not convinced about the need to exert yourself in this task. Look at it another way.

How much time and effort did it take you to find your most recent employment position? What are the chances that you could call General Motors, IBM, or Microsoft and obtain a job today by phone? What theme would you use?

Hi, I'm a red-hot potential employee. I can greatly enhance the productivity of any department in which I'm placed. I'm smart, efficient, positive, personable, well groomed, resourceful, and have empathy for the needs of others. When do you want me to start?

Your chances of being hired by placing a telephone call, especially a cold call, are near zero. Then why do so many people hire their financial advisor after he or she made a cold call to them? Because they are not experienced in hiring employees.

Why aren't you as wealthy as you should be? It may be because of the way you operate your household. Would a business, especially a very productive one, ever hire a key employee without doing a serious background check and an in-depth interview? No! Yet most people, even those with high incomes, hire financial advisors after obtaining little or no background information about these "employment candidates."

Some high-income people have responded to our views on this topic by stating: "But I'm not hiring an employee— I'm just doing some investing with the fellow who called on me." Our response to such statements is simple: Operate your household like a productive business. The best businesses hire the best people. They also patronize the best suppliers. Utilizing the best human resources and top suppliers are two major reasons the most productive organizations succeed while others fail. You should view all financial advisors who solicit you as a client merely as applicants. View them as prospective employees or suppliers for your household. Then ask yourself some simple questions: What criteria would a productive personnel manager use in evaluating each of these applicants? Would a skilled purchasing agent and/or a chief financial officer of an organization buy investment information and products from this potential supplier? What criteria, what key pieces of background information, would be used to evaluate potential suppliers?

Before a well-run business would ever hire a financial advisor or a supplier of investment intellect, it would insist on many vital pieces of hard copy, including the following:

◆ Several references

◆ An official college transcript

◆ A credit check

◆ A series of personal interviews

◆ Completion of a detailed employment application

◆ Documents attesting to the ability of the applicant to perform the duties and tasks required

Your ability to hire high-grade financial advisors is directly related to your propensity to accumulate wealth.

This, in turn, relates to one of the fundamental reasons business owners outpace all other occupational categories in accumulating wealth. Most high-income business owners have more experience in evaluating potential suppliers, employee applicants, and human resources in general than do individuals in other occupational groups. Being in business requires the constant evaluation of such resources.

THE MARTIN METHOD

Several years ago we had the pleasure of interviewing Mr. Martin, a very astute investor and a self-made millionaire. Mr. Martin participated in a focus group interview we conducted with eight multimillionaires. To be included in the group, respondents had to have a net worth of $5 million or more. Building a net worth of $5 million or more in one generation is quite an accomplishment. But Mr. Martin is rare even within this category, since he never had an earned annual income (from employment) of more than $75,000! How did Mr. Martin become so wealthy? He is one of the best investors we have ever interviewed. Mr. Martin made his fortune via the stock market. We found him to be extremely bright and well informed about various investments. He is also an excellent judge of investment advisors.

As you may expect, Mr. Martin subscribes to a wide variety of investment-related publications. Several of these sell their mailing lists to brokers. Thousands of financial advisors have access to Mr. Martin's address and telephone number. Mr. Martin estimates that each week at least three or four brokers attempt to solicit his investment dollars via cold calls. How does Mr. Martin deal with these callers? He instructs his secretary to follow the "Martin Method," which

is used to debrief all callers. What is the "Martin Method"?
Here is what he told us during the interview:

*I am a businessman who goes out and tests people. Brokers
call me a lot. They say, "I have a great deal of experience in
Wall Street's best offerings. . . . I have a fantastic track
record of making money for my clients."*

*I always say: "Do you have some good investment ideas for
me—really good?" He says, "Absolutely, especially if
you're willing to make trades in your portfolio. I only handle accounts with a minimum of $200,000."*

*Then I tell him, "So you're really good. Well, I'll tell you
what. Send me a copy of your personal income tax returns
from the last few years and a list of what you have had in
your own portfolio for the past three years. If you made
more money than I did from investments, I'll invest with you.
Here's my address."*

*When they say, "We can't show that to you," I tell them,
"You are likely to be full of baloney." This is my strategy for
checking people out. It works. I check them all out this way.
I mean it very honestly.*

Perhaps you're asking yourself how Mr. Martin finds time
to evaluate all those stacks of credentials he receives from
cold callers. During the many years Mr. Martin has been an
active investor, he has received countless telephone solicitations. How many of these solicitors "applied for the job" as
financial advisor to the Martin household by submitting their
credentials? Zero! Not one of the dozens of cold callers sub-
mitted his income and wealth appreciation data to Mr. Martin.

According to Mr. Martin, "If these guys were really good, they would not spend all their time calling me." Well, fair enough, Mr. Martin. But not everyone in America has your investment intellect, income, and net worth. Many people would be better off financially if they used the services of a financial advisor, even one who cold called them, for the simple reason that most financial advisors are significantly more knowledgeable about investing than the average high-income UAW.

How one comes into contact with one's financial advisor is a correlate of wealth appreciation. How did Mr. Martin come into contact with his? Like the majority of PAWs, he used interpersonal communication. Early in his career he asked his accountant for a referral to a quality financial advisor. The accountant provided the names of several such advisors. Mr. Martin also asked for referrals from those of the accountant's clients whose investments always seemed to do well. Mr. Martin has patronized several financial advisors since first being introduced via his accountant. He also relies on others for investment advice, including his attorney and CPA.

Mr. Martin always felt his financial advisors were credible sources of investment wisdom because all were endorsed by his CPA and/or his CPA's most successful investors. Also, Mr. Martin reasoned quite correctly that these financial advisors would treat him as a special client. And, indeed, they went out of their way to provide him with good advice and timely forecasts. Why? To do otherwise would jeopardize their relationships with their referral network. What would Mr. Martin do if his advisors provided him with poor service and low-quality advice? He would complain to the CPA who endorsed these people. The CPA would not enjoy losing Mr. Martin as a client and would likely cast these advisors out of his referral network. No financial advisor would enjoy being fired in this way. Even better-grade advisors seem to turn up their level of service for members of important referral networks.

What is to be learned from this case scenario? Choose a financial advisor who is endorsed by an enlightened accountant and/or his clients with investment portfolios that in the long run outpace the market. If you don't have an accountant, hire one.

Another correlate of wealth accumulation is employment of a CPA, not just to do taxes but also to provide various kinds of investment advice. To find a high-quality accountant, ask friends or associates who fit the PAW profile. You may wish to call the accounting department at your state's university. Speak with several accounting faculty. Ask them for the names of their former students who have established track records in helping clients make enlightened financial decisions. Another method is to call the local offices of national accounting firms, which are often very selective in their hiring. Even large firms have many smaller accounting/financial planning clients. We selected our CPAs based on two criteria. First, the CPAs were recommended by professors of accounting. Second, the CPAs were initially hired out of college by major accounting firms and later started their own successful accounting firms. We find that many of the very best CPAs and financial planners follow this career path.

Some CPAs are better than others at helping clients accumulate wealth. Interview several. Choose the one who has the highest concentration of PAWs as clients. You may have to explain the concept to them.

YOU AREN'T WHAT YOU DRIVE

THEY BELIEVE THAT FINANCIAL INDEPENDENCE
IS MORE IMPORTANT THAN DISPLAYING
HIGH SOCIAL STATUS.

Mr. W. W. Allan is a self-made multimillionaire. He and his wife have lived in the same three-bedroom house in the same middle-class neighborhood for nearly forty years. Mr. Allan owns and manages two manufacturing businesses in the Midwest. During his entire married life, he has owned only full-sized General Motors sedans. He will tell you that he never burdened himself with status vehicles or products of any kind. Mr. Allan's businesses, as well as his household, are highly efficient operations. The productivity of his businesses, coupled with his household's moderate consumption habits, produced many surplus dollars. These, in turn, were reinvested in his businesses, commercial real estate, and the common stocks of a variety of high-quality American corporations. Mr. Allan is what we call a super-PAW. His net worth exceeds the expected value for people in his income/age category by more than tenfold!

During the course of his career, Mr. Allan has helped many other entrepreneurs. He has acted as a mentor to dozens of business owners and has saved many businesses from going under by giving financial assistance to struggling entrepreneurs. But he never extended credit to people who exhibited the big-hat-no-cattle philosophy. In his mind, such people would never be able to repay their debts. These types, according to Mr. Allan, "spend, spend, spend, in anticipation of having money before they even earn it."

Mr. Allan, as well as those people whom he has backed financially, have never felt that their purpose in life was to look wealthy. According to Mr. Allan, "That's why I'm financially independent":

If your goal is to become financially secure, you'll likely attain it. . . . But if your motive is to make money to spend money on the good life, . . . you're never gonna make it.

Many people who never achieve financial independence have a much different set of beliefs. When we ask them about their motives, they speak in terms of work and career. But ask them why they work so hard, why they selected the careers they did, and their answers are much different from Mr. Allan's. They are UAWs, and UAWs, especially high-income producers, work to spend, not to achieve or become financially independent. UAWs view life as a series of trade-ups from one level of luxury to the next.

So who enjoys working? Who really gets satisfaction from their careers, PAWs or UAWs? *In most of the cases we have examined, PAWs love working, while a large proportion of UAWs work because they need to support their conspicuous consumption habit.* Such people and their motives offend Mr. Allan. He stated numerous times:

Money should never change one's values. . . . Making money is only a report card. It's a way to tell how you're doing.

NO ROLLS-ROYCE, PLEASE

Mr. Allan is extremely perceptive in his understanding of under accumulators of wealth. In essence, he feels that products change people. If you acquire one status product, you will likely have to purchase others to fill up the socially conspicuous puzzle. Before long, your entire lifestyle will have changed. Mr. Allan clearly understands the complementary nature of status products and a high-consumption lifestyle. He will have none of these artifacts. They are a threat, as he sees it, to his rather simple yet highly efficient lifestyle:

Building wealth is not something that will change your lifestyle. Even at this stage of life, I don't want to change the way I live.

Mr. Allan's values and priorities were recently tested. Several of those people whom Mr. Allan helped stay in business decided to purchase a special birthday gift for him. What a nice gesture, they thought. But status gifts, whether from friends or rich parents, are not always congruent with the recipient's values and lifestyle. And often such gifts place tremendous pressure on the recipients to spend more and more of their income to "fill in the picture."

Some wealthy parents buy their adult children homes in affluent neighborhoods. Great idea? Perhaps they should realize that "affluent neighborhoods" are high-consumption neighborhoods. From property taxes to the pressure to decorate, from the perceived need to send their children to expensive private schools to the $40,000 four-wheel-drive luxury Suburban, the children are now on the earn-to-spend treadmill. Thanks, Mom and Dad!

As Mr. Allan, the super-PAW, told us:

Something interesting recently happened. I discovered I was to be given a surprise present [from several close business associates]. A Rolls-Royce for a present! It was ordered for me . . . special color, special interior. . . . [They] ordered it about four months before [I found out about it]. . . . Still had about five months [before delivery].

How do you go . . . and tell somebody who [wants to] give you a Rolls-Royce that you don't want it?

Why did Mr. Allan refuse to accept such a marvelous gift?

There's nothing the Rolls-Royce represents that's important in my life. Nor would I want to have to change my life to go along with [owning] the Rolls. I can't throw fish in the back seat of the Rolls, like I do right now when I go fishing. I'm gonna have to get you all to the lake. . . . I'm out fishing here every weekend. We have some of the best freshwater fishing in the country. Right out here . . . where I keep my fishing boat.

Mr. Allan's type of fishing includes throwing bloody fish in the back seat of his four-year-old, full-sized, American-made, nonluxury vehicle. But such behavior is incongruent with driving a Rolls-Royce down to the lake. It would be out of place. Mr. Allan would not feel comfortable with such a vehicle. Thus, he contended, he had to change his behavior by ceasing to fish or refuse the gift.

Let's consider Mr. Allan's dilemma further. His office is located in his manufacturing plant, which is in an old industrial area. An automobile like the one being offered might well be out of place in such an environment. And, of course, Mr. Allan does not want to operate two vehicles. That would be inefficient. Mr. Allan also feels that a luxury car would alienate many of his workers. They might get the feeling that their boss was exploiting them. How else could he afford such an expensive vehicle? There are other considerations as well:

With a Rolls, I can't go to some of the crummy restaurants I enjoy going to. . . . Can't drive up in a Rolls-Royce. So, no, thank you. And so I had to call and say, "I really got to tell you something. That I don't want it." It's totally unimportant. . . . There are some things that are more fun to do . . . more interesting to do [than owning a Rolls].

Mr. Allan recognizes that many status artifacts can be a burden, if not an impediment, to becoming financially independent. Life has its own burdens. Why add excess baggage?

BUYING CARS, MILLIONAIRE STYLE

How do millionaires go about acquiring motor vehicles?* About 81 percent purchase their vehicles. The balance lease. Only 23.5 percent of millionaires own new cars (see Table 4-1). Most have not purchased a car in the last two years. In fact, 25.2 percent have not purchased a motor vehicle in four or more years.

How much do millionaires pay for these vehicles? The typical millionaire (those in the 50th percentile) paid $24,800 for his most recent acquisition (see Table 4-2). Note that 30 percent spent $19,500 or less.

*We use the term motor vehicles to include sports utility vehicles, pickups, and so on, as well as cars.

Also note that the average American buyer of a new motor vehicle paid more than $21,000 for his most recent acquisition. This is not much less than the $24,800 paid by millionaires! Moreover, not all of these millionaires purchased new vehicles. How many indicated that their most recent vehicle was used? Nearly 37 percent. In addition, many millionaires indicated that they traded down recently—that is, purchased lower-priced vehicles than they had before.

What is the most that these millionaires ever paid for their motor vehicles? Fifty percent of the millionaires we surveyed never spent more than $29,000 in their entire lives for a motor vehicle. About one in five, or 20 percent, never spent more than $19,950. Eighty percent paid $41,300 or less to acquire their most expensive motor vehicle.

What if we separate out from our sample those millionaires who told us they had inherited their wealth—nearly 14 percent of the millionaires in our sample? The typical wealth inheritor spent in excess of $36,000 for his most expensive motor vehicle. In sharp contrast, the typical *self-made* mil-

TABLE 4-1
MOTOR VEHICLES OF MILLIONAIRES: MODEL-YEAR

LATEST MODEL-YEAR OF VEHICLE OWNED[1]	PERCENT OF MILLIONAIRES
Current Year	23.5
Last Year's/One Year Old	22.8
Two Years Old	16.1
Three Years Old	12.4
Four Years Old	6.3
Five Years Old	6.6
Six Years Old or Older	12.3

[1]Those purchasing motor vehicles accounted for 81 percent of this sample of millionaires; those leasing accounted for 19 percent.

TABLE 4-2

MOTOR VEHICLES OF MILLIONAIRES: PURCHASE PRICE

Amount Spent for Latest Model Purchased	Percent Who Paid This Amount or:		Most Amount Ever Spent for a Motor Vehicle	Percent Who Paid This Amount or:	
	Less	More		Less	More
$13,500	10	90	$17,900	10	90
$17,500	20	80	$19,950	20	80
$19,500	30	70	$23,900	30	70
$22,300	40	60	$26,800	40	60
$24,800	50	50	$29,000	50	50
$27,500	60	40	$31,900	60	40
$29,200	70	30	$35,500	70	30
$34,200	80	20	$41,300	80	20
$44,900	90	10	$54,850	90	10
$57,500	95	5	$69,600	95	5

lionaire paid much less—approximately $27,000, or almost $9,000 less than millionaires who inherited their wealth. Thus, the typical American buyer of a new motor vehicle today spends about 78 percent of what the typical self-made millionaire does for his most expensive motor vehicle.

You can look at all of this another way. The typical millionaire in our survey (one in the 50th percentile) spent about $29,000 for his most expensive motor vehicle. This equates to less than 1 percent of his net worth. The average buyer of a motor vehicle in America has a net worth that is less than 2 percent of that of these millionaires. Do they buy motor vehicles that cost 2 percent of what millionaires pay? If they did, they would spend, on average, about $580 (2 percent of $29,000). Instead, typical motor vehicle buyers spend the equivalent of at least 30 percent of their net worth for such purchases. Note also that, on average, American consumers buy new motor vehicles at a price that is 72 percent of the most that a typical millionaire ever spent on a motor vehicle. Does this give you some idea of why so few Americans are millionaires?

Those millionaires who lease vehicles are a minority—fewer than 20 percent. What was the "price" of their most recent acquisition/lease? We estimate that 50 percent leased vehicles that were priced at $31,680 or less. About 80 percent leased vehicles valued at or under $44,500. People often ask us, "Should I lease?" Our answer is always the same:

More than 80 percent of millionaires purchase their vehicles. If and when more than 50 percent begin leasing, we will change our recommendation.

MAKES OF MOTOR VEHICLES

What types of motor vehicles do millionaires drive? U.S. car manufacturers may be pleased to note that their makes account for 57.7 percent of the vehicles millionaires are driving; Japanese makes account for 23.5 percent, while European manufacturers hold 18.8 percent. What makes of cars are most popular with millionaires? The following are listed in rank order according to their respective market shares:

1. Ford (9.4 percent). The most popular models include the F-150 pickup and the Explorer sports utility vehicle. (American sports utility vehicles in general are becoming increasingly popular with the affluent.) About three in ten millionaire Ford drivers own F-150 pickups. About one in four drive Ford Explorers. Note that the F-150 pickup is the number-one vehicle sold in America. Thus, drivers of pickups have something in common with many million-aires.

2. Cadillac (8.8 percent). More than 60 percent of Cadillac owners drive the De Ville/Fleetwood Brougham.

3. Lincoln (7.8 percent). About half have Lincoln Town Cars.

4. A three-way tie: Jeep, Lexus, Mercedes (6.4 percent each). Almost all millionaires who own Jeeps choose the Grand Cherokee sports utility model. In fact, this model ranks first among all models owned by millionaires. Nearly two-thirds of Lexus drivers choose the LS 400 model. The favorite model of Mercedes-Benz is the S Class.

5. Oldsmobile (5.9 percent). The overall favorite model is the Olds 98.

6. Chevrolet (5.6 percent). Ten different models are represented. The most popular include the Suburban and the Blazer sports utility vehicles.

7. Toyota (5.1 percent). The Camry model accounts for more than half of this segment.

8. Buick (4.3 percent). The Le Sabre and Park Avenue models were found to be most popular.

9. A two-way tie: Nissan and Volvo (2.9 percent each). The most popular Nissan is the Pathfinder sports utility vehicle; for Volvo, it is the 200 Series.

10. A two-way tie: Chrysler, Jaguar (2.7 percent each).

Other popular makes include Dodge, BMW, Mazda, Saab, Infiniti, Mercury, Acura, Honda, GMC, Volkswagen, Land Rover, Subaru, Pontiac, Audi, Isuzu, Plymouth, and Mitsubishi. The top three manufacturers are General Motors Corporation, with approximately 26.7 percent of the millionaire population; Ford Motor Company, with 19.1 percent; and Chrysler, with about 11.8 percent. As you can see, most millionaires are driving so-called Detroit metal. Most Americans who own motor vehicles also drive Detroit metal. How then can you tell if your neighbor who is driving a Ford, a Cadillac, or a Jeep is a millionaire or not? You can't. It's not easy to judge the wealth characteristics of people by the motor vehicles they drive.

An increasing number of affluent people are purchasing vehicles produced by American manufacturers, especially Buicks, Cadillacs, Chevrolets, Chryslers, Fords, Lincolns, and Oldsmobiles. This trend is related to the growing popularity of sports utility vehicles produced by Chrysler, Ford, and General Motors. What is it about Detroit metal that appeals to the wealthy? We can answer that question by reflecting on something that took place more than fifteen years ago.

After interviewing a group of ten millionaires, we walked into the parking lot of the research facility. We were very surprised to see that almost all of the millionaires we had just interviewed were driving full-sized Detroit metal, including Buicks, Fords, and Oldsmobiles. We looked at each other; one said: "These people are not into status; they buy automobiles by the pound!"

It's true. Many American millionaires have a propensity to purchase full-sized automobiles that have a low cost per pound. The average per pound price for all new motor vehicles is $6.86. The full-sized Buick four-door sedan currently sells for less than $6.00 a pound; the Chevrolet Caprice, about $5.27 per pound; the Ford Crown Victoria, about $5.50; the Lincoln Town Car, less than $10.00 a pound; and the Cadillac Fleetwood, $8.26 a pound. The Ford Explorer sells for about $5.98 a pound. The most popular model among millionaires is the Jeep Grand Cherokee, which sells for $7.09 per pound.

How do these costs per pound compare with those of full-sized foreign cars? The BMW 740 sedan costs more than $15.00 per pound; the Mercedes-Benz 500 SL is priced at more than $22.00 per pound; and the Lexus LS400 is now selling for more than $14.00 per pound. What about the Ferrari F40? It's $175.00 per pound! (The estimated price per pound for most currently offered motor vehicles is provided in Appendix 2 of this book.)

Many affluent respondents take joy in driving vehicles that do not denote so-called high status. They are more interested in objective measures of value. Some millionaires do spend considerable dollars for top-of-the-line luxury automobiles. But they are in the minority. For instance, approximately 70,000 Mercedes were sold in this country last year. This translates into about one-half of 1 percent of the more than fourteen million motor vehicles sold. At the same time, there were nearly 3.5 million millionaire households. What does this tell us? It suggests that the members of most wealthy households don't drive luxury imports. The fact is that two out of three purchasers or leasers of foreign luxury motor vehicles in this country are not millionaires.

Domestic brands have long been in favor with older millionaires. We believe this attitude is becoming more common even among younger millionaires. Why? Because the real growth in the millionaire market continues to come from the entrepreneurial segment. Entrepreneurs, as a rule, are more price-sensitive than others when it comes to acquiring motor vehicles. Successful entrepreneurs judge each expenditure in terms of productivity. They often ask themselves the impact heavy spending for motor vehicles will have upon their business's bottom line and ultimately their wealth. More often than not, they determine that investments for such items as advertising and new equipment are much more productive than very expensive motor vehicles.

PURCHASE BEHAVIOR

What thought and behavioral processes do millionaires go through before buying a car? We have done extensive research on the various types of vehicle buyers that exist among the ranks of millionaires. It seems that rich people differ significantly even among themselves. Studying these various findings reveals valuable information about the attitudes and behaviors necessary to accumulate wealth.

There are four distinct buyer types within the millionaire population. Underlying these four types are two fundamental factors. First is dealer loyalty. Some buyers have a proclivity to patronize the same dealer over and over again. In other words, when "dealer loyalists" want to acquire a motor vehicle, they are inclined to work with the dealer who sold them their last vehicle (and the vehicle before that). About 45.7 percent of the affluent are dealer loyalists (see Table 4-3).

All the other millionaires are shoppers. They account for 54.3 percent of the population. These people have no desire to patronize the same dealer. They are very aggressive, price-oriented buyers. Often they take months to make their price-related vehicle purchase.

The second factor underlying buyer types is vehicle choice—new or used. Among the affluent, 63.4 percent prefer and buy new cars. The balance, 36.6 percent, have a very strong proclivity to purchase used vehicles only. Putting these two factors together produces four types of millionaire car buyers (see Table 4-3):

◆ Type 1: New Vehicle–Prone Dealer Loyalists (28.6 percent)

◆ Type 2: New Vehicle–Prone Dealer Shoppers (34.8 percent)

◆ Type 3: Used Vehicle–Prone Dealer Loyalists (17.1 percent)

◆ Type 4: Used Vehicle–Prone Shoppers (19.5 percent).

NEW VEHICLE–PRONE DEALER LOYALISTS (28.6 PERCENT)

People with this orientation buy new vehicles only and have at least conditional loyalty to a dealer or set of dealers. Most affluent people have strong make/brand preferences concerning motor vehicles. So when they decide to buy a particular make of vehicle, loyalists already have a dealer in mind. They see certain benefits in buying new vehicles from the same dealer(s). But this doesn't mean they walk into their favorite dealership, lie down, and roll over. On the contrary, price—even for them—is an important consideration. Perhaps you think these dealer loyalists are lazy. Could they be members of the so-called idle rich? No, this is not the reason they patronize the same dealer again and again. Perhaps

TABLE 4-3

MOTOR VEHICLE ACQUISITION ORIENTATIONS OF MILLIONAIRES

ORIENTATION TOWARD DEALERS:

	Loyalists	Shoppers	TOTALS
VEHICLE TYPE ORIENTATION:	1	2	
	% of All Millionaires Who Are:	% of All Millionaires Who Are:	% of All Millionaires Who Are:
New Vehicle-Prone	New Vehicle-Prone Dealer Loyalists = 28.6	New Vehicle-Prone Dealer Shoppers = 34.8	New Vehicle-Prone = 63.4
	% of All Loyalists = 62.5	% of All Shoppers = 64.1	
	% of All New Vehicle-Prone = 45.1	% of All New Vehicle-Prone = 54.9	
	3	4	
Used Vehicle-Prone	% of All Millionaires Who Are: Used Vehicle-Prone Dealer Loyalists = 17.1	% of All Millionaires Who Are: Used Vehicle-Prone Shoppers = 19.5	% of All Millionaires Who Are: Used Vehicle-Prone = 36.6
	% of All Loyalists = 37.5	% of All Shoppers = 35.9	
	% of All Used Vehicle-Prone = 46.8	% of All Used Vehicle-Prone = 53.2	
TOTALS	% of All Millionaires Who Are: Dealer Loyalists = 45.7	% of All Millionaires Who Are: Dealer Shoppers = 54.3	

you might speculate that these buyers just like their dealer. Well, affection is not the answer either.

Quite simply, new vehicle–prone dealer loyalists prefer to minimize their effort in choosing both a dealer and their type of vehicle (i.e., new versus used). New vehicle–prone loyalists put a tremendous amount of time and effort into generating their high incomes. They believe there is significantly more money to be gained from working than from going from dealer to dealer or looking for a "real buy" on a used vehicle. This group patronizes particular dealers because they also feel that these sellers give them the best packages overall. Some of the components of "these packages" go far beyond the price and physical dimensions of a motor vehicle.

Why do these millionaires purchase new vehicles instead of used ones? Why are they less sensitive to the price variations of vehicles than are buyers of used cars? First, purchasers of new vehicles like new vehicles, although this is not the only reason they buy them. In their minds, buying new instead of used is much simpler; it requires less time and effort. To them, new vehicles are more reliable and more readily available in the models and colors and with the accessories they demand. In essence, they feel they must pay more to get more.

Yet price is somewhat important even for this group. Before they visit their favorite dealer, nearly half (46 percent) determine the dealer's cost of a particular model. About one in three contacts at least two competing dealers to get "some feel for the impending deal." Some study consumer magazines and other periodicals and price guides that reveal dealer cost figures. Location is another factor in understanding the behavior of this group. Many will contact dealers who are located outside their trade area, but most of these contacts are made merely to test local offers. Only about one in ten patronizes out-of-town dealers repeatedly.

There is another factor that explains the orientation of new vehicle–prone dealer loyalists:

More than one in five patronize dealers who are their clients or customers.

Networking is alive and well among the affluent in America. Many wealthy self-employed business owners believe strongly in reciprocity. Think for a moment. If you were a paving contractor, for example, where would you go to buy your vehicles? Would you buy from a stranger with a firm handshake, or from the automobile dealer who just gave you a contract to pave his parking lot? The answer should be obvious.

Many loyalists who are self-employed professionals, such as physicians, attorneys, CPAs, financial planners, and architects, also believe in this kind of reciprocity. The more enlightened ones tend to patronize those vehicle dealers who patronize them. It is not at all unusual for the owner of a dealership to have more than one hundred different suppliers who provide his business with products and services. Accordingly, there is some expectation on his part that these suppliers will return the favor. Many affluent dealer loyalists receive customer referrals from car dealers whom they patronize. In turn, 25.5 percent of the loyalists indicate that they refer their associates and friends to selected dealers. The dealers reciprocate by giving these buyers significant price discounts on their purchases.

Many millionaires are dealer loyal for another reason. About 20 percent patronize dealerships that are owned by a relative or close personal friend. Many also prefer to deal directly with the owner of the dealership they patronize; 37 percent deal exclusively with the owners. Why? Because they believe this will assure them of getting an excellent overall package.

NEW VEHICLE-PRONE DEALER SHOPPERS (34.8 PERCENT)

The affluent with this orientation believe that the price discounts they get through aggressive shopping and negotiating with multiple dealers are more than worth the time and energy exerted. On average, they have spent about 9 percent less than new vehicle–prone dealer loyalists for the most expensive motor vehicle they ever purchased. On their most recent purchase, they paid about 14 percent less than loyalists.

Loyalists tend to purchase somewhat more expensive cars, which accounts for about half the variation in the average prices paid by members of the two groups. In contrast, new vehicle–prone dealer shoppers are more sensitive to the price variations of competing dealers. Shoppers are typically experienced negotiators; many enjoy shopping and haggling. In contrast with dealer loyalists, dealer shoppers are significantly less likely to patronize dealerships owned by relatives or close personal friends, to refer others to dealers who reciprocate by giving them significant price discounts, to purchase exclusively from the owners of dealerships, or to buy from dealers who do business with them. On the other hand, they are much more likely to take weeks—even months—"to shop around for the very best deal," demand a "dealer-cost" or "below-cost" price, or "purchase a new model that is heavily discounted and resell it within a year or two at nearly the same or higher price."

BIDDING FOR YOUR BUSINESS

If you dread the thought of shopping in person for your next motor vehicle, consider an alternative method. Mr. Mark R. Stuart is a friend of ours who has purchased many motor vehicles by visiting competing dealers. But he had never purchased a sports utility vehicle until this year. Although he lacked experience with buying this kind of vehicle, he thought of a way to avoid spending countless hours visiting competing dealers. Below is the fax that Mr. Stuart sent to the sales managers of six local area Ford dealers.

Three sales managers responded immediately by faxing their very competitive bids to Mr. Stuart, who accepted one of these. It seems that his past experience as a procurement officer for the U.S. Army was useful in civilian life. Do you have a fax machine and a need for a new sports utility vehicle?

TO:_____
Sales Manager of new cars

FROM: Mark R. Stuart
      Fax: (404)XXX-XXXX

RE: Request for Quotation

If you are interested in earning my business, please reply to me by fax at (404)XXX-XXXX. This is a cash purchase (no trade), subject to sales tax in _____ County. If you do not have this vehicle in stock or on order, I am in no rush and can wait for delivery. Specifications are as follows:

    Current Model Year Ford Explorer Limited 4X4
    Ivory Pearlescent, Saddle Leather
    Options: Sun roof
    CD player
    Front license plate bracket

Your quotation should detail the price by line item, including tax, tag, title and any other fees. I look forward to receiving your reply by fax. Please do not call me. If you have any questions, please include them in your fax reply. I will call you if I have any questions. Thanks.

USED VEHICLE–PRONE DEALER LOYALISTS (17.1 PERCENT)

Why do millionaires such as those in this group with annual incomes in excess of $300,000 and a net worth of nearly $4 million have to buy used vehicles? They don't.

Overall, these millionaires get more satisfaction from acquiring used instead of new. In purchasing cars that are two or three years old, they feel that the original owner has paid while the vehicle was depreciating in value. They often plan to resell their used acquisition in two or three years and recoup much of their initial payout. Many also feel that aggressive bargain shopping for new vehicles is a waste of time and energy. They believe that new cars are overpriced at the manufacturer's or wholesale level; in their minds, one can't even hope to buy a new vehicle for much less than the dealer paid for it. For many, the real discounts on motor vehicles can be found in the used-vehicle market.

Used vehicle–prone dealer loyalists have the highest percentage of entrepreneurs among their ranks. Entrepreneurs are extremely price-sensitive when acquiring motor vehicles. Their preference to invest much of their income in assets that appreciate, however, must be balanced with the need of many successful entrepreneurs to drive quality motor vehicles. For this group, the acquisition of quality late-model used vehicles is the solution. Their favorite makes/models include used Jeep Cherokees, Cadillac De Villes, Ford F-150 pickups and Explorers, Lincoln Town Cars, Chevrolet Caprices and Suburbans, and Infiniti Q45s.

The members of this group spend less money on such acquisitions than do the members of either of the new vehicle–prone groups. The percentage of their incomes allocated for motor vehicle purchases is also the lowest of all the groups. On average, they spent only 7.6 percent of their income on their most recent acquisition, and only 9.9 percent for their most expensive purchase. As a percentage of their net worth, these purchases represent only 0.68 and 0.89 percent of their net worth respectively.

How do the members of this group make purchase and dealer patronage decisions? First, most determine the dealer cost on a new model of their preferred vehicle. Then they determine the vehicle's projected depreciation. This information is used to bolster their decision to purchase a used version of their chosen model. Information about the current retail and wholesale value of used vehicles is available at many libraries and book stores. Often, enlightened CPAs provide this information to their clients.

Used vehicle–prone dealer loyalists then examine the offerings of several dealers. This is done to judge the willingness of local area dealers to "earn the business" of the members of this group. Some check the prices of vehicles offered by individuals as listed in the classifieds. Often, they telephone those listing their vehicles and ask private-party sellers if they would be willing to lower their asking price. In most cases, the callers are just conducting price-sensitivity research. The used vehicle–prone dealer loyalist uses the information he gathered as a bargaining chip in negotiating with his chosen dealer(s). In most cases, the chosen dealer will meet or beat the prices offered by the so-called competition.

Millionaires in this buyer group patronize the same dealer(s) repeatedly. Buyers feel that repeat patronage can earn them price and even service concessions, but this is not the only reason for their loyalty. Like many new vehicle–prone dealer loyalists, 36 percent of used vehicle–prone dealer loyalists told us that they buy used cars from dealers who do business with them. Many also patronize dealers who go out of their way to refer customers to them. Remember that this group contains a high concentration of entrepreneurs, self-employed professionals, and very successful sales and marketing types. Obviously, they believe in reciprocity. About one in four acquires his vehicle from relatives or close friends who are in the automotive industry. One in three used vehicle–prone dealer loyalists makes his purchase by negotiating exclusively with the owner of the dealership. One in five deals exclusively with the top sales professional at a chosen dealership. Such buyers feel that top sales professionals have great leverage in persuading sales managers to agree to sell at low prices.

USED VEHICLE–PRONE SHOPPERS (19.5 PERCENT)

Those in this group are the most price-sensitive and the most aggressive bargain hunters of all those we have profiled. They spend less on average than do the members of any of the other groups. They paid an average of $22,500 for their most recent acquisition, under $30,000 for their most expensive. Their latest purchase represents less than 0.7 percent of their wealth; their most expensive acquisition, less than 0.9 percent. This group contains the smallest proportion who have clients, friends, or relatives in the automotive industry. Given that they don't have a friend in the automobile business, how do they go about finding a good deal? First and foremost, they don't buy new vehicles. Also, you will note that the title of this group—used vehicle–prone *shoppers*—does not contain the word *dealer*.

These people buy their used vehicles from all types of seller. Most often they buy from private parties, but they often shop at dealerships, leasing companies, financial institutions, consignment companies, auction companies, and agents.

Used vehicle–prone shoppers are extremely patient people. They are the most likely of all millionaire car buyers to take months to find the best overall deal. They never seem to be in a hurry to buy. In some ways, they are always looking for a deal. They are in a semi-searching/buying state all the time.

In one instance, a member of this group casually looked around for a deal on a late-model Chevrolet for more than seven months. But unlike Dr. South from Chapter 3, this bargain shopper never spent a great deal of time making this acquisition. It seems that on his long commute to work, he routinely passed by three dealers. If he noticed a vehicle that caught his eye, he would contact the dealer by phone. At the same time he would telephone sellers who had their vehicles listed in the classifieds. He eventually made a purchase from a private party at a price substantially lower than at any dealer he had contacted. He told the seller:

I am not in a hurry. Give me a call in a month or so and I'll make you an offer. But right now you're asking nearly as much as all the dealers I have been in contact with in the past few weeks.

He tells the same thing to all the people he contacts.

He also has a favorite time of the year to negotiate. He claims he is most successful in cutting deals from the last two weeks of December into February. During the winter season, he says, sellers don't find a lot of shoppers out and about. Christmas-related expenses and activities and the cold weather distract and discourage most potential buyers from shopping during this period. They do not discourage many used vehicle–prone shoppers. It is not at all unusual for buyers in this group to have four or more sellers competing simultaneously for their business during these months!

The members of this group typically acquire low-mileage vehicles that are two to four years old. Their favorite makes include Fords, Mercedes, Cadillacs, Lexuses, Chevrolets, Nissans, and Acuras.

WHAT BUYING HABITS REVEAL

One can learn a great deal about affluent people by analyzing their vehicle-buying habits. For instance, note that most millionaires are dealer shoppers as opposed to dealer loyalists. Not by a large margin (54.3 versus 45.7 percent), you may logically counter. But this margin is a bit misleading. Net out the percentage of dealer loyalists who are so inclined because they have strong reciprocal relationships with their favorite dealer. Factor out also those loyalists who patronize dealerships owned by relatives and close personal friends. Then ask about the percentages of loyalists versus shoppers. If you do, you will find that there are at least two shoppers for every loyalist among the ranks of American millionaires.

What about vehicle purchasers in general? Most vehicle buyers are not wealthy. Thus, one might logically expect them to spend more time and energy shopping for the best deal. Our research shows the opposite. Those who are not wealthy are less likely to shop, haggle, and negotiate than those who are millionaires. Car-buying behavior does indeed help explain why some people are wealthy while most are not and never will be.

More aggressive bargain shoppers for motor vehicles also tend to bargain hunt for other consumer products. These people also tend to plan their expenditures. Given these findings, what buyer type of the four profiled above would you expect to be the most frugal in general?

Have you guessed that it is the used vehicle–prone shoppers? Used vehicle–prone shoppers are the most aggressive and most price-sensitive when it comes to acquiring motor vehicles. They shop using a wide variety of sources. And, on average, they pay significantly less for their vehicles than do members of the other groups.

Of all the types studied, used vehicle–prone shoppers are the most illuminating for those interested in studying the path to affluence. Why? Because of all the groups studied, its members have the highest ratio of net worth dollars for each dollar of income: For every one dollar used vehicle–prone shoppers realize in income, they have $17.2 of net worth. They have the lowest average income of all the groups, yet, on average, they have been able to accumulate more than $3 million. How did they do it? Their wealth development strategy is worth detailing.

MILLIONAIRES WHO ARE USED VEHICLE–PRONE SHOPPERS

What factors explain variations in wealth accumulation? Income is a factor. People with higher incomes are expected to have higher levels of wealth. But note again that members of this group of used-vehicle buyers have a significantly

TABLE 4-4

ECONOMIC LIFESTYLES OF MOTOR VEHICLE ACQUISITION TYPES

Economic and Financial Lifestyle Correlate	New Vehicle-Prone Dealer Loyalists (28.6%)	New Vehicle-Prone Dealer Shoppers (34.8%)	Used Vehicle-Prone Dealer Loyalists (17.1%)	Used Vehicle-Prone Shoppers (19.5%)
Consumption Inoculation "Most people who live in up-scale neighborhoods have little real wealth."	59[1] Low (4)	106 High (2)	111 Low (3)	136[2] High (1)
Self-Designated Thrift Orientation "I have always been frugal."	82 Low (4)	108 High (2)	89 Low (3)	121 High (1)
Legacy of Thrift Orientation "My parents are [were] very frugal."	91 Low (4)	99 Average (3)	105 Average (4)	111 High (1)
Household Budgeting Orientation "Our household operates on a fairly well-thought-out annual budget."	95 Average (3)	101 Average (2)	85 Low (4)	118 High (1)
Fastidious Record-Keeping Orientation "I know how much our family spends each year for food, clothes, and shelter."	101 Average (2)	94 Average (4)	96 Average (3)	112 High (1)
Bargain-Oriented Clothes Shopper "I never bought a suit that was not on sale (discounted)."	69 Low (4)	89 Low (3)	123 High (2)	145 High (1)
Discount Store Patronage Orientation "I often buy my suits at factory outlets."	62 Low (4)	106 Average (3)	111 High (2)	136 High (1)

[1]For example, new vehicle-prone dealer loyalists have a significantly lower score (59) on the consumption inoculation scale when compared to the composite score for all millionaires (100). They rank last/fourth on this consumption inoculation scale.

[2]For example, used vehicle-prone shoppers have a significantly higher score (136) on the consumption inoculation scale when compared to the composite score for all millionaires (100). They rank first on this consumption inoculation scale.

lower income than the average for the other groups of millionaires. About two-thirds have incomes in the high-five- or low-six-figure range.

Occupation is another factor. We have noted many times that entrepreneurs account for a disproportionately large share of the millionaires in America. Conversely, most of the other high-income-producing occupations contain disproportionately smaller portions of high–net worth types. These include physicians, corporate middle managers, executives, dentists, accountants, attorneys, engineers, architects, high-income-producing civil servants, and professors. But there are exceptions. For example, each of these nonentrepreneurial occupations is represented in the used vehicle–prone shopper group we are profiling.

Used vehicle–prone shoppers are unique even among their millionaire cohorts. Note that, on average, they have the highest score values on all seven measures of frugality (see Table 4-4).

Behind their frugal behavior is a strong set of beliefs. First, they believe in the benefits of being financially independent. Second, they believe that being frugal is the key to achieving independence. They inoculate themselves from heavy spending by constantly reminding themselves that many people who have high-status artifacts, such as expensive clothing, jewelry, cars, and pools, have little wealth. They often tell the same thing to their children. In one case we studied, a youngster had once asked his dad why their family didn't have a swimming pool. His dad answered with the "big-hat-no-cattle" response that many frugal people articulate. He told his son that they *could* have a pool installed, but that a new pool would mean the family would not be able to send the son to Cornell.

Today the son, Carl, is a Cornell graduate. No, his folks

never had a swimming pool installed. What will happen when Carl's children ask about their father's proclivity to frugality? Will he be able to defend his purchasing orientation and his frugal nature in general? The answer to this question is reflected in the results given in Table 4-4. Used vehicle–prone shoppers are significantly more likely to report the following:

◆ My parents are [were] very frugal.

Once a member of the used vehicle–prone shopper group told us about his frugal habits. He explained that his parents were farmers:

My family in Nebraska understood the value of a dollar. Dad used to say seeds are a lot like dollars. You can eat the seeds or sow them. But when you would see what seeds turned into . . . ten-foot-high corn . . . you don't want to waste them. Consume them or plant them. I always get a kick out of watching things grow.

This man derived considerable enjoyment in his nondescript, four-door, three-year-old American-made sedan. He believed that his vehicle never revealed to the public that he was very affluent. Nor, according to him, would it ever encourage thieves to follow him home to burglarize his property. He often referred to his car as "the last one that would ever be stolen out of the airport parking lot!"

FRUGALITY TRANSLATES INTO WEALTH

Being frugal is a major reason members of the used vehicle–prone group are wealthy. Being frugal provides them with a dollar base to invest. In fact, they invest a significantly larger portion of their annual income than do any of the other types of vehicle buyers. This also applies to their contributions to pension/annuity programs. As you may have already predicted, the used vehicle–prone shopper group also contains the highest percentage of prodigious accumulators of wealth. This group is significantly more likely to agree with this statement:

◆ Our household operates on a fairly well-thought-out annual budget.

To budget properly, one must keep records of disbursements. Here again, the used vehicle–prone shopper is more fastidious than any of the other types. More of them agree that:

◆ I know how much our family spends each year for food, clothing, and shelter.

Used vehicle–prone shoppers are also bargain-oriented when it comes to buying clothing. Their score of 145 was the highest overall (see Table 4-4). A significantly higher percentage agreed with this statement:

◆ I never bought a suit that was not on sale (discounted).

Used vehicle–prone shoppers are significantly more likely to be discount-store patrons than other types of vehicle buyers. This is evident from their positive response to the following statement:

◆ I often buy my suits at factory outlets.

In addition, they are significantly more frequent shoppers at Sears than any of the other types of millionaire vehicle buyers. This group, on average, spends considerably less for a variety of items. As discussed in Chapter 2, we asked all our millionaire respondents to tell us the most they ever paid for (1) a wristwatch, (2) a suit of clothing, and (3) a pair of shoes. Once again, the used vehicle–prone shopper demonstrated his frugality. Members of this group spent only 59 percent as much as the other millionaires in our survey for a wristwatch, 83 percent for a suit, and 88 percent for a pair of shoes.

The majority of people do not have the ability to increase their incomes significantly. Yet income is a positive correlate of wealth. What, then, is our message? If you cannot increase your compensation significantly, become wealthy some other way. Do it defensively. This is how most of the used vehicle–prone shoppers did it. They successfully inoculated themselves from contracting the high-consumption lifestyle that many of their neighbors adopted. *More than 70 percent of their neighbors earn as much or more than they earn. But fewer than 50 percent of their neighbors have a net worth of $1 million or more.*

Most of these millionaires' high-income, low–net worth neighbors make the wrong assumption. They assume that by focusing their energy on generating high incomes, they will automatically become affluent. They play excellent offense in this regard. Most are positioned in the top 3 or 4 percent or higher of the income distribution for all U.S. households. Most look the part of millionaires. Yet they are not wealthy. They play lousy defense. We have stated many times the belief of countless millionaires who have told us:

It's much easier in America to earn a lot than it is to accumulate wealth.

Why is this the case? Because we are a consumption-oriented society. And the high-income-producing non-millionaire neighbors of used vehicle–prone shoppers are among the most consumption-oriented people in America.

CASE STUDIES

MR. J. S., CPA: NEW VEHICLE–PRONE DEALER LOYALIST

Mr. J. S. is one of three senior partners in a small but highly productive CPA firm. He is also a millionaire. Mr. J. S. enjoys buying new vehicles and is completely turned off by the idea of buying used cars. To him, owning a used vehicle is like wearing someone else's old clothes. Mr. J. S. is a dealer loyalist in part because "[his] time is more valuable than shopping for a so-called big discount." In addition, Mr. J. S. buys from a dealer with whom he does business.

Again, networking and reciprocity are major factors underlying the motor vehicle purchasing habits of many new vehicle–prone dealer loyalists. How did Mr. J. S. acquire the motor vehicle dealer as his accounting client? By referring more than a dozen of his clients to the owner of the dealership before ever selling the dealer any of his accounting services. Previously, the owner had dealt with another accounting firm for years before realizing that this accounting firm had never referred one of its clients to him.

Now the dealer and Mr. J. S. have a strong reciprocal bond. One of the great advantages of being a self-employed business owner is the ability to leverage your organization's patronage habits. In the case of Mr. J. S., he also leverages his influence over several of his clients. He is the dealer opinion leader for many of his clients. Mr. J. S. makes it clear to each client he refers that the dealer is also a client. The dealer, in turn, is likely to give favorable service and price concessions to these clients. Over the past ten years, Mr. J. S. has essentially sold more than three dozen motor vehicles for his client, the car dealer. At the same time, the dealer has expended many thousands of dollars for accounting services from Mr. J. S.

MR. T. F., STOCK BROKER: USED VEHICLE-PRONE DEALER LOYALIST

Mr. T. F. is a stock broker and a millionaire who enjoys purchasing late-model, used, luxury automobiles. After purchasing several models from the same dealer, Mr. T. F. had an idea: He would make a personal sales call to the owner of the dealership. Mr. T. F. first reminded the owner that he had purchased three cars from him in the past five years and had referred several of his clients to the dealer. Mr. T. F. then asked the dealer if he would reciprocate by giving him some of his investment business. The dealer's response was very frank. He told Mr. T. F. that he sold vehicles to dozens of stock brokers and that he could not do business with all of them.

Mr. T. F. understood the dealer's position. So he made a counterproposal. He asked if the dealer would be so kind as to give him the names of his top five suppliers:

Assume that you were asked to nominate the suppliers of the year in this state. Who would be on the top of your list? Who put the new roof on this place? Can I mention that you suggested I call him?

The dealer did refer several of his key suppliers to Mr. T. F. Mr. T. F. still buys his vehicles from this dealer and makes referrals on his behalf. In turn, the dealer refers business to Mr. T. F.

AUTHOR TOM STANLEY SELLS A CAR

Just before Christmas, I placed a classified ad in the local newspaper to sell my family's Acura Legend. Prior to doing so, I called our dealer. He advised me about the upper-limit price I could anticipate receiving for the car, and that was the price that we advertised. I have always meticulously maintained our motor vehicles. Our Legend had nearly every conceivable option, including the so-called Gold Package. The car was always garaged. Our Acura dealer did all the prescribed maintenance and tune-up procedures. We even used Mobil One synthetic oil! The car had a good set of Michelin MXV4 tires with a few thousand miles on them. And, perhaps most important, we had purchased the car new. My classified ad outlined many of these characteristics.

Allow me to profile some of the characters who took the time to stop by and look over our car.

Shopper One: a senior marketing officer, female

She arrived driving an Infiniti Q45. When I saw the car, I asked her why she was interested in a Legend, since her Q45 appeared to be nearly new. She told me that the Q45 was her husband's and that they had purchased it used nearly a year ago. In fact, she had just finished looking over "previously owned" Legends and Infinitis at several dealers. She made it very clear that her household had a used-vehicle orientation. It was not particularly loyal to any make of automobile, but she and her husband did prefer a narrow set of vehicles.

These included Acura Legends, Infiniti Q45s, and the Lexus 400 series.

The day she visited me, she had taken the afternoon off from work. She had a map of the Atlanta area and had marked the location of selected dealers and the addresses of private sellers. In this way, she made it very clear to me that she was well aware of many "compelling" opportunities.

It was obvious to me that this woman was very skilled in evaluating used cars. She immediately pointed to a small ding on the driver's door. She examined the interior, the engine compartment, and the car's sheet metal. Then she asked me why I had to sell the Legend. I responded by saying that "my teenage children have an aversion to four-door sedans. To them, a Legend is well suited for middle-aged, unexciting people like their parents! They would much prefer even a well-used 4 x 4 sports utility vehicle or a sporty two-door number."

She paused and reflected on my comments. Now that I think about it, I suspect she would have preferred another answer. She would have wanted me to say that I was selling the vehicle because of financial obligations. This would have put her in a much stronger bargaining position. Nonetheless, she attempted to negotiate a lower price. She asked, "What's the lowest you are willing to take for the car?" I responded by telling her, "If I don't sell it in thirty days, I will consider lowering the price." I then pointed to the portfolio in the front seat, which contained all the maintenance records, original window sticker, and so on. She turned around, got back in her husband's previously owned Q45, and left. I never heard from her again. I am convinced that she found exactly what she was looking for—that is, a real deal on a late-model, used vehicle from someone who was in a hurry to sell.

Shopper Two: a vice president at a regional financial institution, male

You may find it particularly interesting to learn this fellow's specific job title. He was vice president of the motor vehicle leasing department. I guess you could say he had an excellent understanding of the true value of motor vehicles. He also understood the relative advantages of buying versus leasing. It seems that this expert on leasing new vehicles spends his time searching for deals on used ones.

Shopper Two was also looking for a real deal. He was interested in several makes of quality Japanese cars, but, like Shopper One, had no great loyalty to any specific make. He spent a considerable amount of time going over the maintenance and other records for the Acura. Then he asked the same question Shopper One did: "Without you hitting me on the head, what is the least you would take for the Acura?" I gave him the same answer I'd given Shopper One. He also left. I am still waiting for his call.

Shopper Three: a wealthy former business owner, male

Shopper Three was the most interesting of the people with whom I came into contact. When he called me, he mentioned that he was intending to drive his wife to a local shopping center. He asked about our location, which he found ideal relative to the shopping center. He and his wife arrived shortly after our phone conversation in a 5 series BMW. The car looked like it had just come out of a showroom. So I asked him about his need to purchase the Acura. He informed me that the BMW was his wife's car. He then scrutinized the Acura from top to bottom.

While he was doing so, I had an interesting conversation with his wife. She informed me that her husband had recently sold his share in a successful software operation. They were millionaires. Her husband still acted as a consultant to the organization, but now he had more time to do other things. She also told me that her husband had never purchased a new car in the thirty years that they had been married. Apparently, he is in a semi-constant search for real deals on automobiles. He is particularly prone to purchasing quality used Japanese and German vehicles. But he is absolutely never in a hurry to make such purchases. Like many people in the used vehicle–prone shopper group, he gets immense pleasure from finding good deals from private sellers with too much car, too little capital.

I suspect that is why he spent time debriefing me. He asked me what I did for a living. He asked me how well my business was operating. Perhaps he had thought I was an out-of-work corporate executive. Why else would I be at home in the middle of the afternoon in my khaki pants and flannel shirt? I told him I was an author, working on book number four. Then he inquired about how well my other books were selling. "Great," I answered. He then frowned and asked the question of questions: "Would you be interested in knocking $1,500 off the asking price?" Again I responded, "Perhaps in thirty days if I don't sell it before then." I am still waiting to hear from him, too! He did seem impressed with the way I maintained automobiles, so just before he left, he asked if I intended to sell any of my other cars. He pointed to my high-performance Z28 Camaro. I had to turn him down on that offer, too.

Shopper Four: a schoolteacher, female

Isn't it interesting that a disproportionately high number of used-car shoppers come from the ranks of teachers and professors? Shopper Four called me late one Friday evening.

(When do weekend telephone rates go into effect?) She had a battery of questions to ask me. After this intense debriefing, she informed me that she lived several hundred miles from Atlanta in "cotton" country. She said she was in the process of calling many of the people who had listed Acura Legends in the Atlanta classifieds.

She promised to get back in touch with me the following Wednesday. She kept her promise and asked if I could fax her evidence that there were no outstanding liens on the vehicle. She also asked if it would be possible to have a more detailed list of the car's accessories. I faxed her the title and a copy of the original window sticker, with prices and options. She then advised me that she planned to come to Atlanta that Friday and look at several vehicles that were for sale.

She and her husband, a successful cotton farmer, arrived at our house on Friday. They were driving a late-model Nissan Maxima. The automobile appeared to be in excellent condition. Shopper Four drove her husband and me around the community for about twenty minutes, test-driving the Acura. During that time I had a chance to debrief them. Why did they drive all the way from cotton country? Why were they interested in buying a used vehicle? Aren't farmers supposed to be frugal?

It seems that this couple shops for a late-model, quality, used Japanese vehicle every two or three years. They find the prices and availability significantly better in the big city. (They are nearly 150 miles from the nearest Acura dealer.) They buy cars like mine and resell them in two or three years in their rural community for close to what they paid for them.

Shopper Four and her husband convinced me that they were frugal. They arrived with a certified check in an amount that was $1,000 less than my asking price. The farmer, upon returning from the test drive, asked his wife, "Aren't you going to try to negotiate with this guy?" She, in turn, said, "This fellow doesn't need to sell this car. And it's in great condition." Her husband agreed. Thereupon, she handed me the certified check and ten $100 bills. After all the papers were signed and the deal was complete, she told me that my car sold for at least $3,000 more at the dealer nearest her farm. I responded that her colleagues would likely be impressed with this car when she drove up to school on Monday. Her husband commented that the other teachers would really be impressed if they knew how little she had paid for it.

One comment he made was of particular interest to me: "My wife works with a woman who drives a new, comparably equipped Mercedes-Benz. She leased it for sixty months, $600 per month. Do you know how much cotton you have to grow to make those payments?"

A PROFESSOR OF THRIFT HAS UAWs FOR NEIGHBORS

How did Dr. Bill, an engineering professor who never had a total household income of more than $80,000, become a millionaire? He inherited nothing. He never won the lottery or hired an investment advisor who turned a few thousand of his dollars into a fortune. His success in accumulating wealth is based on living well below his means. This professor is a classic example of a used vehicle–prone shopper. But like most of those in this buyer group, he never neglected his family. He provided funds for his children's college tuitions in full and more. He and his family live in a fine home in an upper-middle-class neighborhood. In fact, about

80 percent of his group live in homes valued at $300,000 to $500,000.

Dr. Bill's goal always was to become financially independent, but he never wanted to become an entrepreneur. Often, entrepreneurs become wealthy by taking substantial risks and by leveraging the labor and talent of dozens, even hundreds, of others. Dr. Bill was never cut out to be anything but a professor. He is not alone. *Most people in this country are not the entrepreneurial type. But this does not mean that they can't become millionaires.*

People often confuse our message about the relationship between being wealthy and being an entrepreneur. We're not telling people to give up doing their own thing in medicine, law, accounting, and other occupations and join the ranks of the entrepreneurs in this country. Don't even consider such a change unless you really want to and are fully capable of succeeding. If you can generate a reasonably good income—say, twice the norm for households in America, or $65,000 to $70,000—then you may become wealthy one day if you follow the defensive strategy developed by millionaires who are used vehicle–prone shoppers.

Most of Dr. Bill's nonmillionaire neighbors have no household budget. They do no consumption planning. As a result, they have no restrictions on their domestic expenditures except one—the upper limits of their income. Yet these are the very types who are prone to whisper criticisms about frugal neighbors such as Dr. Bill.

Mr. Norman is an executive who lives in a $400,000 home in Dr. Bill's neighborhood. His household income last year was in excess of $150,000. But he has next to zero invested in anything other than home equity, motor vehicles, and a corporate pension plan. Mr. Norman's household has a net worth of under $200,000. Mr. Norman and his wife are each fifty years old. So are their neighbors, the used vehicle–prone shopper, Dr. Bill, and his wife. Bill earns only about half of what the Normans earn. But Bill's household has a net worth that is nine times greater than the Normans. Can this be possible?

It's more than possible. It is probable and predictable. *Great offense and poor defense translate into under accumulation of wealth.* But the Normans are not alone. There are many more under accumulators in their neighborhood than there are prodigious accumulators like Dr. Bill and his family.

UAWs like the Normans find it degrading to even think about shopping for a used car. To them, a used car is out of the question. Their neighbor, Dr. Bill, never felt degraded shopping for quality used cars. In fact, acquiring used "cream puffs" gives him great satisfaction. Over the years, he figures that he has saved enough buying used over new to completely fund one of his children's college and graduate school tuitions.

Where did Dr. Bill buy his latest motor vehicle, a three-year-old BMW 5 series? From Gary, a high-income, hyperconsuming sales professional employed in the high-tech field. Gary buys only new foreign motor vehicles. If Gary is like most UAWs, he firmly believes that the buyer of his old 5 series BMW is not as financially well off as he. This is one of the tell-tale symptoms of being a UAW. UAWs usually think they have more wealth than their neighbors. Many UAWs also believe that people drive the best they can afford.

Think of this situation in another way. Gary, the under accumulator of wealth, is subsidizing Dr. Bill's motor vehicle purchases. Gary takes the brunt of the three-year depreciation and then transfers title of a fine automobile to Dr.

Bill, the frugal millionaire. Also, since Gary is an employee, he cannot write off depreciation against his income tax liability. In addition, Gary has no friends, relatives, or clients in the motor vehicle business. He gets no tax write-offs, no super discounts from an uncle or aunt who owns a dealership, and no reciprocity from a client/customer who is in the automobile business. He consumes motor vehicles purely for pleasure.

What should Gary, Mr. Norman, and others of the UAW variety know? That they spend more for motor vehicles than the typical American millionaire. Gary's earned income is equal to that of many millionaires, yet Gary isn't a millionaire. Perhaps he compensates for this through his heavy consumption of status products. Is he trying to emulate the driving and buying habits of the chairman of the company that employs him? But the chairman is a millionaire and owns equity in the corporation. Unlike Gary, he never purchased an expensive automobile until after he was wealthy. Instead, he put much of his income back into the company via stock purchases. In contrast, Gary makes his expensive purchases in anticipation of becoming wealthy. But that day is unlikely to ever arrive.

ECONOMIC OUTPATIENT CARE

**THEIR PARENTS DID NOT PROVIDE
ECONOMIC OUTPATIENT CARE.**

Dear Dr. Stanley and Dr. Danko:

I just finished reading an article about your research on millionaires. My wife has an overdue trust that her parents won't release. My mother-in-law keeps putting us off with paperwork. She seems determined not ever to release the trust to my wife.

Is it possible that you have come in contact with my wife's family in your research? Her name is_____.
Or perhaps you could suggest another source that would tell us how much is in the trust.

Thank you,
Mr. L. S.

The author of this letter and his wife urgently need money. The writer (we will call him Lamar) is the husband of a woman (we will refer to her as Mary) who comes from a wealthy family. Mary receives more than $15,000 in cash gifts annually from her parents. She has received gifts of this type, as well as other forms of help, since she and Lamar got married nearly thirty years ago.

Today she and her husband are in their early fifties. They live in a splendid neighborhood in a fine home. They are country club members. Both love to play tennis and golf. Both drive imported luxury cars. They wear fine clothes and are socially involved with several nonprofit organizations. They were previously active in raising money for the private schools their children attended. Both enjoy vintage wines, gourmet foods, entertaining, high-quality jewelry, and foreign travel.

Their neighbors think Lamar and Mary are wealthy. Some are firmly convinced that they are multimillionaires. But looks can be deceiving. They are not wealthy. Do they at least earn a high income? No, neither the husband nor the wife earns a high income. Mary is a housewife. Lamar is an administrator at the local college. Never in the couple's long marriage have the two ever had an earned annual income in excess of $60,000, even though they have a lifestyle similar to those with incomes of at least twice theirs.

Some may suggest that this couple does an outstanding job of budgeting and planning. How else can they live so high with so few dollars of income? But Lamar and Mary have never put a budget plan together in all the years they've been married. They spend in excess of their income every year. They also spend all the money Mary receives from her parents. In short, Mary and Lamar are able to live so lavishly because they are the recipients of what we call economic outpatient care (EOC). Economic outpatient care refers to the substantial economic gifts and "acts of kindness" some parents give their adult children and grandchildren. This chapter will explore the implications of economic outpatient care, and how it affects the lives of those who give it and those who receive it.

EOC

Many of today's distributors of EOC demonstrated significant skill at accumulating wealth earlier in their lives. They are generally frugal with regard to their own consumption and lifestyle. But some are not nearly as frugal when it comes to providing their children and grandchildren with "acts of kindness." These parents feel compelled, even obligated, to provide economic support for their adult children and their families. What's the result of this largesse? Those parents who provide certain forms of EOC have significantly less wealth than those parents within the same age, income, and occupational cohorts whose adult children are economically independent. *And, in general, the more dollars adult children receive, the fewer they accumulate, while those who are given fewer dollars accumulate more.*

Distributors of EOC often conclude that their adult children could not maintain a middle- or upper-middle-class high-consumption lifestyle without being subsidized. Consequently, an increasing number of families headed by the sons and daughters of the affluent are playing the role of successful members of the high-income-producing upper-middle class. Yet their lifestyle is a facade.

These sons and daughters of the affluent are high-volume consumers of status products and services, from their traditional colonial homes in upscale suburbs to their imported luxury motor vehicles. From their country club affiliations to the private schools they select for their children, they are living proof of one simple rule regarding EOC: It is much easier to spend other people's money than dollars that are self-generated.

EOC is widespread in America. More than 46 percent of the affluent in America give at least $15,000 worth of EOC annually to their adult children and/or grandchildren. Nearly half the adult children of the affluent who are under thirty-five years of age receive annual cash gifts from their parents. The incidence of giving declines as adult children grow older. About one in five adult children in their mid-forties to mid-fifties receives such gifts. Please note that these estimates are based on surveys of the adult children of the affluent and that gift receivers are likely to understate both the incidence and size of their gifts. Interestingly, when surveyed, gift givers report a substantially higher incidence and dollar amount of gift giving than their adult children who are the recipients.

Much EOC is distributed in lump sums or erratic patterns. For example, affluent parents and grandparents are likely to give their children entire coin collections, stamp collections, and similar gifts in one transfer. About one in four affluent parents has already given such collections to his or her adult children or grandchildren. Similarly, payment of medical and dental expenses is often precipitated by a grandchild's need for orthodontal work or plastic surgery. About 45 percent of the affluent have provided for the medical/dental expenses of their adult children and/or grandchildren.

During the next ten years, the affluent population in America (defined as those with a net worth of $1 million or more) will increase five to seven times faster than the household population in general. Directly paralleling this growth, the affluent population will produce significantly more children and grandchildren than in the past. Economic outpatient care will increase greatly during this period. The number of estates in the $1 million or more range will increase by 246 percent during the next decade; these estates will be valued (in 1990 constant dollars) at a total of more than $2 trillion! But nearly the same amount will be distributed before millionaire parents become decedents. Much of this wealth will be distributed by so-called predecedent affluent parents and grandparents to their children/grandchildren.

The costs to provide outpatient care will also increase substantially in the future. Private school tuition, foreign luxury automobiles, homes in fashionable suburbs, cosmetic medical and dental services, law school tuition, and many other EOC items are increasing at rates that greatly exceed the general cost-of-living index.

In addition, as our population ages, more and more affluent parents and grandparents are reaching the age of estate tax realization. Widows and widowers especially are becoming more aware that the government can take 55 percent or more of their estate via estate tax mandates. Thus, as the affluent grow older, they will increase the size and incidence of their EOC in order to reduce the tax burden on their estates.

MARY AND LAMAR

How could Mary and Lamar afford the tuition to send their two children to private schools? They couldn't afford it; Mary's parents paid the bill. Unusual? On the contrary. Our survey research indicates that 43 percent of the millionaires in this country who have grandchildren pay for all or part of their private school tuition (see Table 5-1). We refer to such subsidies as third-generation educational enhancements.

We recently discussed this form of outpatient care with an audience of affluent grandmothers. We provided them with the results of our surveys. We did not endorse or criticize such behavior. After our presentation, we answered questions. The third questioner took this opportunity to make a statement:

TABLE 5-1

ECONOMIC OUTPATIENT CARE GIVEN BY AFFLUENT PARENTS TO THEIR ADULT CHILDREN AND/OR GRANDCHILDREN[1]

ECONOMIC OUTPATIENT CARE	PERCENT OF AFFLUENT
1. THIRD-GENERATION EDUCATIONAL ENHANCEMENTS	
• Funding of tuition for grandchildren's private grade school and/or private high school	43%
2. SECOND-GENERATION EDUCATIONAL ENHANCEMENTS	
• Funding of tuition for adult children's graduate school	32%
3. INTERGENERATIONAL HOME OWNERS' SUPPLEMENT	
• Payment of adult children's mortgage	17%
• Financial assistance in purchasing a home	59%
4. SUPPLEMENTAL INCOME BENEFITS	
• "Forgiveness loans" (those not to be repaid) to adult children	61%
5. GIFTS OF INCOME-PRODUCING REAL ESTATE	
• Transfers of commercial real estate to adult children	8%
6. TRANSFERS OF SECURITIES	
• Gifts of listed stock to adult children	17%
7. TRANSFERS OF PRIVATE ASSETS	
• Gift of ownership (all or part) of family business to adult children	15%

[1]The 222 affluent parents/millionaires included in this analysis all had at least one adult child, twenty-five years of age or older.

I'm as indignant as hell. What am I supposed to do with my money? My daughter's family is having a rough time making ends meet. Do you know about the problems with public school around here? I'm sending my grandchildren to private schools.

It is obvious to us that this grandmother is not completely at ease about providing economic outpatient care to her daughter's family. The real problem is not with the public schools; it is that her daughter's family is in a situation of economic dependency. Mother has difficulty with the fact that her daughter married someone who is unable to earn a high income. Daughter and grandchildren may not be able to live in an environment congruent with Mother's upper-middle-class background. So Mother is determined to enhance the environment of her daughter's family. She contributed heavily to the purchase of a home that was economically out of reach for her daughter and son-in-law. The home is in an upscale area where most of the residents send their children to private schools. The only way her children can stay in such a high-consumption residential area is with heavy doses of Mother's brand of economic outpatient care. But Mother fails to realize that such an environment has more drawbacks than does self-sufficiency, even if that means accepting a less affluent lifestyle.

Mary is much like the daughter of the grandmother in our audience. Both have received economic outpatient care. The donors in both cases made the same assumption: Economic outpatient care will "get the youngsters going" and then won't be needed anymore. Mary's mother was wrong. She has been providing her special blend of outpatient care for more than twenty-five years. Her daughter's family is economically dependent.

Lamar has also benefited from outpatient care. Shortly after he and his wife were married, Lamar quit his job to pursue a master's degree. His own parents paid all his tuition and related expenses. This is not at all unusual. In fact, 32 percent of America's millionaires pay for their adult children's graduate school education.

The couple's first child was born shortly after Lamar began his graduate studies. Mary's mother did not like the apartment that the couple initially rented near the university Lamar attended. She took it upon herself to send a cleaning crew over regularly to "freshen the place up." But in her mind this was not the ideal environment for her daughter's family. So Mother offered to help the couple buy a home.

Lamar did help to make ends meet. He received a few hundred dollars each month from the university for his part-time job as a staff assistant. Mary did not work at that time. In fact, she has been a full-time housewife throughout her marriage.

Mary's mother placed a sizable down payment on the couple's home. Nearly six in ten (59 percent) affluent parents who have adult children tell us that they have provided their children with "financial assistance in purchasing a home." Mary's mother also made the couple's mortgage payments. Note that 17 percent of the millionaires we have interviewed indicated that they have made such payments (see Table 5-1). Initially, Mary's mother was to provide these funds as an interest-free loan. But eventually the loan was converted to a more conventional type. Forgiveness loans are considered to be quite conventional among recipients of economic outpatient care. Sixty-one percent of America's affluent have provided such "loans" to their adult children. What happened when the couple traded up to a more expensive home? Mary's mother once again subsidized the purchase. Eventually the couple moved to their current residence. Once again, economic outpatient care was part of this purchase.

Lamar spent nearly four years in graduate school. During that time he received two degrees. Today Lamar is a college administrator. But given his annual salary of less than $60,000, it's still hard for Mary and him to make ends meet. Even with the $15,000 his mother-in-law provides each year, their income is not high enough to support their upper-middle-class lifestyle. What is so interesting about Mary and Lamar's $60,000 annual income level is that they are not alone. *About 30 percent of the households in America that live in homes valued at $300,000 have annual household earned incomes of $60,000 or less.* Is it because of creative budgeting, or could it be a result of widespread economic outpatient care in America? For the most part, it's because of UAWs on EOC.

According to Mary, it's not too difficult to pay for basic family necessities out of Lamar's income plus her annual cash gift from Mother. What is difficult is purchasing motor vehicles. And Mary and Lamar enjoy "foreign luxury." How do they squeeze such purchases into their budget? Do they buy used cars to reduce the "economic pain"? No, they purchase *new* cars *every three years.* Why so often? Because that's Mother's cycle. About every three years, Mary's mother gives her daughter stock from her portfolio—so do about 17 percent of America's affluent. Some adult recipients hold onto such gifts, but not Mary and Lamar. They sell the securities immediately, then purchase a new car with the proceeds!

But what will happen to Mary and Lamar after Mother is no longer alive? Obviously, this is a major concern to this couple. Unfortunately, we are not fortune tellers, so we were not able to tell them how much Mother had in trust for her daughter. We wish them good luck. It will not take long for Mary and Lamar to consume even a good-sized inheritance. They are already anticipating this economic windfall. A bigger home, a vacation home, and around-the-world travel are on the horizon.

WHAT'S WRONG WITH THIS PICTURE?

Adults who sit around waiting for the next dose of economic outpatient care typically are not very productive. Cash gifts are too often earmarked for consumption and the support of an unrealistically high lifestyle. This is precisely what happened to Mary and Lamar. Their household's annual earned income of $60,000 is the same amount a blue-collar couple in their county earned with overtime. Both the man and woman drive buses for a living. Yet they have a more realistic view of who they are and what they have achieved. Conversely, Mary and Lamar are living in fantasyland. Displaying upper-middle-class status is their socioeconomic goal in life.

Does this mean that all adult children of affluent parents are destined to become Marys and Lamars? Absolutely not. In fact, stated as a statistical probability, the more wealth parents accumulate, the more economically disciplined their adult children are likely to be. Note that America's millionaires are more than five times more likely than the average household to have a son or a daughter graduate from medical school. They are more than four times more likely to have a child who is a law school graduate.

Paying for an education is the equivalent to teaching your children how to fish. Mary's mother taught her daughter and son-in-law something else. She taught them how to spend. She taught them to look upon her as a fish-dispensing machine. There are many forms of economic outpatient care. Some have a strong positive influence on the productivity of the recipients. These include subsidizing your children's education and, more important, earmarking gifts so they can start or enhance a business. Many self-made millionaires/ entrepreneurs know this intuitively. Unlike Mary's mother, they prefer to give their offspring private stock, which cannot be readily traded in for a new foreign luxury automobile.

Conversely, what is the effect of cash gifts that are knowingly earmarked for consumption and the propping up of a certain lifestyle? *We find that the giving of such gifts is the single most significant factor that explains lack of productivity among the adult children of the affluent.* All too often such "temporary" gifts affect the recipient's psyche. Cash gifts earmarked for consumption dampen one's initiative and productivity. They become habit forming. These gifts then must be extended throughout most of the recipient's life.

The subsidized lifestyle of many adults has another consequence. Neighbors see how Mary and Lamar live. What do they conclude? Too often it is that heavy spending is an acceptable way of life. For example, off and on for several years, Mary and Lamar have been on their neighborhood's welcoming committee. Remember that the couple has also been active in fund-raising for the private school their children attended. What message do Mary and Lamar communicate to their new neighbors? Recently, a hard-charging, very successful sales manager/vice president and his family moved into the neighborhood. The sales executive was only thirty-five years old at the time. He earned nearly three times more income than Lamar. He and his wife had three school-aged children.

Within ten minutes after welcoming his new neighbors, Lamar initiated his sales pitch. He told them that the public schools in the area were inferior but that he had a solution to this problem. Lamar began to lecture his new neighbors about the benefits of the private school. The new neighbors listened attentively. Then they asked about the tuition. Lamar told them the costs were much less significant than the benefits. The annual tuition at the high school, Lamar reported, was only $9,000. Lamar tells all his incoming neighbors the same thing—that is, that $9,000 is a small price for a great education. Why, of course, Lamar loves the school. It was a real bargain for him to send his children there, since Mary's mother paid 100 percent of the tuition.

Later the sales executive and his wife did some research on the local public school system. They found that it was far better academically than Lamar had told them. They decided that all their children would attend public schools. They were pleased with the quality education provided there.

What is the value you place on a private school education, luxury automobiles, foreign travel, and a lovely home? How sensitive are you to the prices of these products and services? Lamar is quite insensitive to high prices. The sales executive is just the opposite. Lamar finds it much easier to spend other people's money than his own. The sales executive, on the other hand, never received any economic outpatient care except for some of his undergraduate college tuition. The sales executive is fully self-sustaining today. Why? Because he and his family do not receive economic outpatient care earmarked for consumption. He spends much of his time enhancing his productivity by working harder and investing wisely. Conversely, Lamar and Mary spend much of their time anticipating the receipt of stronger doses of economic outpatient care.

THE QUESTION OF QUESTIONS

You may ask, "Will I spoil my adult children if I give them cash gifts?" All the effects of cash gifts on the adult children of the affluent cannot possibly be presented in one chapter. And it is important to note that those who receive such gifts are not the "jobless dropouts" so often reported in the press. They are, in fact, likely to be well educated and to hold well-respected occupational positions. The top ten occupations of the adult children of the affluent are as follows:

1. Corporate Executive
2. Entrepreneur
3. Middle Manager
4. Physician
5. Advertising/Marketing/ Sales Professional
6. Attorney
7. Engineer/Architect/Scientist
8. Accountant
9. College/University Professor
10. High School/Elementary School Teacher

Nevertheless, it cannot be denied that adult children who receive cash gifts differ from those who do not. Let's contrast the wealth and income characteristics of adult children who do receive gifts with those who do not. Because age is highly correlated with both wealth and annual household income, it is important to attempt to hold age constant when making comparisons between gift receivers and nonreceivers. It is also useful to examine the differences in these two groups within each of ten occupational classifications, since different occupational groups tend to generate different levels of income and net worth.

Let's look at a survey of gift receivers and nonreceivers

TABLE 5-2

**RECEIVERS VS. NONRECEIVERS OF CASH GIFTS:
WHO HAS MORE WEALTH/HIGHER INCOME?**

OCCUPATIONS	HOUSEHOLD NET WORTH %	RANK	ANNUAL HOUSEHOLD INCOME %	RANK
• Accountant	57[1]	10th	78[2]	7th
• Attorney	62	9th	77	8th
• Advertising/Marketing Sales professional	63	8th	104	1st
• Entrepreneur	64	7th	94	2nd
• Senior Manager/Executive	65	6th	79	6th
• Engineer/Architect/Scientist	76	5th	74	10th
• Physician	88	4th	75	9th
• Middle Manager	91	3rd	80	5th
• College/University Professor	128	2nd	88	4th
• High School/Elementary School Teacher	185	1st	92	3rd
• All Occupations	81.1	—	91.1	—

[1]For example, households headed by accountants who receive cash gifts from their parents have 57 percent of the net worth of those in the same occupational category who do not receive gifts.

[2]For example, households headed by accountants who receive cash gifts from their parents have 78 percent of the annual household income of those in the same occupational category who do not receive gifts.

from all economic backgrounds, in their early forties to mid-fifties. Examine the numbers given in Table 5-2.

Note that in eight of the ten occupational categories, gift receivers have smaller levels of net worth (wealth) than those who do not receive gifts. For example, on average, accountants who are approximately fifty years of age and receive cash gifts from their parents have only 57 percent of the net worth of accountants in the same age group who do not receive gifts. Further, accountants who receive gifts generate only 78 percent of the annual income of accountants who don't receive gifts.

Note that cash gifts were not included in computing the annual incomes of accountants who receive gifts. When these tax-free dollar gifts are added to the incomes of gift receivers, then, on average, gift receivers have approximately 98 percent of the average annual income of nonreceivers. In spite of this, they still only have 57 percent of the net worth of accountants who do not receive gifts.

Accountants who receive gifts are not the only occupational group that has lower income and net worth characteristics. As you can see in Table 5-2, gift receivers in seven other occupational categories also have lower levels of net worth than nonreceivers, including attorneys, 62 percent; advertising/marketing/sales professionals, 63 percent; entrepreneurs, 64 percent; senior managers/executives, 65 percent; engineers/architects/scientists, 76 percent; physicians, 88 percent; and middle managers, 91 percent.

Gift receivers in only two of the ten occupational groups have higher levels of wealth than nonreceivers. In spite of having lower incomes than nonreceivers, gift receivers who are high school/elementary school teachers have higher net worths than nonreceivers. Teachers who receive gifts have 185 percent of the net worth of the average for nonreceivers, but only 92 percent of the income. College/university professors who receive gifts have 128 percent of the net worth and 88 percent of the income of nonreceivers. Affluent parents can learn a great deal from gift receivers who are teachers and professors. Teachers and professors who receive cash gifts have a much higher propensity to accumulate wealth than do gift receivers in the other eight occupational classifications. How can one explain this peculiarity? To do so it is important first to explain why most gift receivers in general have a lower propensity to accumulate wealth than do nonreceivers.

1. GIVING PRECIPITATES MORE CONSUMPTION THAN SAVING AND INVESTING.

For example, affluent parents often subsidize their children's purchase of a home. The intent may be to help their children "get started on the right foot." The parents assume that such gifts are a once-in-a-lifetime phenomenon. Some have told us that they thought "this would be the last dollar the kids would ever need." They assume that the recipients of their kindness will be able to "do it on their own" in the near future. Nearly half the time, they are wrong.

Gift receivers frequently are underachievers in generating income. All too often the income of the gift receiver does not increase at the same rate as his consumption. Remember, expensive homes are typically located in what we call high-consumption neighborhoods. Living in such neighborhoods requires more than just being able to pay the mortgage. To fit in, one needs to "look the part" in terms of one's clothing, landscaping, home maintenance, automobiles, furnishings, and so on. And don't forget to add high property taxes to all the other items.

Thus, a gift of a down payment, whether full or partial, can place a recipient on a treadmill of consumption and continued dependence on the gift giver. But the majority of these recipients' neighbors, more likely than not, receive no cash gifts from their parents. They are much more content and confident about their lifestyle than most gift receivers are. Many gift receivers in such situations become sensitive to the need for continued economic outpatient care. Their orientation may even dramatically change from a focus on self-generated economic achievement to one of hoping for and contemplating the arrival of additional gifts. Underachieving income producers in such cases find it nearly impossible to accumulate wealth.

Gifts of down payments are not the only type that precipitate more consumption. Take, for example, the affluent parents who gave their son Bill and daughter-in-law Helen a $9,000 rug that we were told contained millions of hand-tied knots. Bill is a civil engineer who works for the state. He earns less than $55,000 a year. His parents feel compelled to help him maintain a lifestyle and level of dignity congruent with someone with a graduate degree from a prestigious university. Of course, the expensive rug looked out of place in a room filled with hand-me-down furniture and inexpensive light fixtures. So Bill and Helen felt compelled to purchase expensive walnut dining room furniture, a crystal chandelier, a solid-silver service, and expensive lamps. Thus, the gift of the $9,000 rug precipitated the consumption of nearly that same amount for other "affluent artifacts."

Sometime later, Bill mentioned to his mother that the local public schools were not as good as they were when he was an elementary school student. His mother countered that she would pay for part of her grandson's and granddaughter's private school tuition. Of course, it was up to Bill and Helen to decide if they should take their children out of the public school system. Mother paid two-thirds of the tuition; Bill and Helen, the rest. In this case, a gift of $12,000 ended up costing Bill and Helen $6,000 a year.

Moreover, Bill and Helen did not contemplate the additional expenses of sending their children to private school. For example, they are often asked to make contributions to the school beyond the cost of tuition. They also felt they needed to buy a seven-passenger station wagon so they could participate in the school's car pool. Books and related fees are also costly. And their children are now exposed to other children and parents who tend to have higher-consumption lifestyles than were the case in the public school environment. In fact, their children are looking forward to traveling to Europe this summer. It's part of their education and socialization process. Gift receivers are significantly more likely than non–gift receivers to send their children to private schools. (Although there are more children of non–gift receivers in private school overall, it is because the population of non–gift receivers is much larger than its counterpart.)

2. GIFT RECEIVERS IN GENERAL NEVER FULLY DISTINGUISH BETWEEN THEIR WEALTH AND THE WEALTH OF THEIR GIFT-GIVING PARENTS.

Perhaps Tony Montage, a professional asset manager, said it best:

Gift receivers . . . the adult children of the affluent feel that their parents' wealth/capital is their income . . . income to be spent.

One of the main reasons gift receivers typically think of themselves as being financially well-off is because they receive parental subsidies. And people who think they are financially well-off tend to spend. In fact, statistically they are just as likely to view themselves as being affluent as are truly affluent non–gift receivers. This is the case in spite of earning 91 percent of the income and having 81 percent of the wealth of nonreceivers.

Look at the situation from a gift receiver's side of the equation. During each year of his adult life, William receives an annual tax-free gift of $10,000 from his parents. William is forty-eight years of age. Ten thousand dollars of tax-free income could be viewed as the product of what amount of capital? Assume an 8 percent return. This would equate to $125,000 in capital. Add this amount to his actual net worth. What is the result? William perceives himself as having $125,000 more in capital than he does.

Consider this analogy. Have you ever been confronted by an eight-year-old youngster standing in the front yard of his parents' home? If you, a stranger, attempt to walk onto the property, Billy or Janie will likely say, "You can't come into *my yard*. This is *my property*." Billy and Janie think that it is their property. At the age of eight they may be correct. After all, they are children living at home. At this age kids feel that the yard, the home, and the car are family property. But as the majority of Billys and Janies mature, they become properly socialized by their parents. They grow into independent adults, adults who can easily distinguish between what is theirs and what is not. Their parents teach them independence.

Unfortunately, a growing portion of adult children are not being taught the value of being emotionally and economically independent of their parents. How did one set of parents recently test to see if their adult son was independent? They used the "Montage Effect" as a basis for the test.

After Thanksgiving dinner at his parents' home, James and his parents had a conversation. His parents told James that they had decided to give several pieces of "their" commercial property to the local private college. His father told his son, "I know you will understand that the college really will benefit from such a gift." James's response, if written as a headline, might read:

> **Son of affluent couple screams, "That's my property, too, and the college people can't come in (to my yard)."**

James's response was predictable. He has received substantial cash gifts from his parents throughout his adult life. He needed an annual gift equivalent to about 20 percent of his income to cover his annual expenses. He viewed his parents' idea of giving their capital to the college as a threat to his future income.

Like many other gift receivers, James views himself as "self-made." In fact, about two of every three adult children who receive significant cash gifts periodically from their parents view themselves as members of the "I did it on my own" club. We are amazed when these people tell us in interviews, "We earned every dollar we have."

3. GIFT RECEIVERS ARE SIGNIFICANTLY MORE DEPENDENT ON CREDIT THAN ARE NONRECEIVERS.

Those who receive periodic gifts of cash or its equivalent are euphoric about their economic well-being. Euphoria of this type is related to their need to spend money. But much of this money is not in hand. It is tomorrow's economic outpatient care. So how do gift receivers respond to this dilemma? They use credit vehicles to smooth out their problems with cash flow. Why wait for the windfall at the end of the rainbow? Adult children who receive cash gifts are more likely than other adult children to live in anticipation of the sizable inheritance eventually coming their way.

In spite of having only about 91 percent of the total household annual income and 81 percent of the net worth of nonreceivers of gifts, gift receivers are significantly more likely to be credit-oriented. This credit is obtained for consumption, not investment, purposes. Conversely, nonreceivers of gifts borrow more for investment purposes than do gift receivers. Otherwise, in nearly every conceivable type of credit product/service category, gift receivers outpace nonreceivers. This applies both to the incidence of credit usage and to the actual dollars spent to pay the interest on outstanding balances. It applies to personal loans and to unpaid balances on credit card loans. Gift receivers and nonreceivers are not significantly different in their use of mortgage services or in the allocation of dollars for such purposes. However, a significant portion of the gift receivers were given money for sizable down payments on their homes.

4. RECEIVERS OF GIFTS INVEST MUCH LESS MONEY THAN DO NONRECEIVERS.

When surveyed, gift receivers reported that they invested less than 65 percent of what nonreceivers invested each year. Even this is a very conservative estimate, since like most heavy credit users, gift receivers overestimate the amount of money they invest. For example, they often forget to take into account major credit purchases when computing actual consumption and investing habits.

There are exceptions to this rule. Teachers and professors who receive gifts appear to remain as frugal or even more so than those who receive no gifts. They are much more likely to save and invest the money they receive as gifts than are gift receivers in other occupational categories. The issue of teachers and professors as role models is discussed more fully later in the chapter.

As we have made clear, gift receivers are hyperconsumers and credit prone. They live well above the norm for others with comparable incomes. But often people mistakenly believe that gift receivers are concerned solely with their own desires, needs, and interests. This is not the case. On average, gift receivers donate significantly more to charity than do others in the same income categories. For example, gift receivers who have annual household incomes in the $100,000 category normally donate just under 6 percent of their annual incomes to charitable causes. The general population in this income category donates only about 3 percent. Gift receivers give in proportions that are much like those of households with annual incomes in the $200,000 to $400,000 bracket. These people give approximately 6 percent of their income to noble causes.

Noble or not, gift receivers consume more, so they have significantly less money to invest. What good does it do to be well versed in investment opportunities when one has little or no money to invest? This is the situation in which a young professor of business recently found himself. He, a gift receiver, was asked to teach a course on investing for a continuing education program. His audience included many well-educated, high-income people. The professor discussed various topics, including sources of investment information and how to evaluate the stock offerings of various public corporations. The professor received high praise from his audience. He was well trained in his discipline. He held a Ph.D. in business administration with a concentration in finance. However, near the end of the course, a gentleman from the audience asked the professor a simple question:

Dr. E., may I ask about your personal portfolio? What do you invest in?

His answer surprised most of the class:

I don't have much of a portfolio at present. I'm too involved with paying two mortgages, an auto loan, tuition. . . .

Later, a member of the class told us:

It's like the fellow who wrote the book on one hundred clever things to say to attractive women. But the guy did not know any good-looking women.

Why don't the financial advisors of under accumulating gift receivers emphasize thrift in their messages? All too often financial advisors have a narrow focus. They sell investments and investment advice. They don't teach thrift and budgeting. Many find it embarrassing, even degrading, to suggest to clients that their lifestyle is too high.

In fairness, many high-income individuals as well as their advisors have no idea how much net worth someone should have, given certain income and age parameters. Additionally, financial advisors are often unaware that their clients receive sizable cash gifts each year. Relying solely on a client's earned income statement, they may likely say:

Well, Bill, for a fellow who is forty-four years of age and who earns $70,000 annually, you're doing pretty well. Pretty well in terms of your lovely home, boat, foreign luxury automobiles, donations, and even your investment portfolio.

Would the same advisor feel this way if Bill told him about the tax-free cash gift of $20,000 he receives each year from Mom and Dad?

It is important here to emphasize a point made through-

out this book. Not all adult children of the affluent become
UAWs. Those who do tend to have parents who heavily subsidize their children's standard of living. But many other
sons and daughters of affluent parents become PAWs. The
evidence suggests this happens when their parents are frugal
and well disciplined and instill these values, as well as independence, in their children.

The popular press often paints a different picture. Too
often they tout the "Abe Lincoln" stories. They dramatize
those cases in which a child from a blue-collar background
became very successful. They provide anecdotal evidence
that the discipline of being poor is a prerequisite to becoming a millionaire in America. If that were true, one would
expect there to be at least thirty-five million millionaire
households in America today. But we know that there is only
about one-tenth that number.

It is true that most millionaires are the sons and daughters
of nonmillionaire parents, since the nonmillionaire population is more than thirty times larger than its counterpart.
Only a generation ago it was more than seventy times larger. The enormous size of the nonmillionaire population has
a great deal to do with why most millionaires come from
nonmillionaire households. As a probability statement, millionaires are more likely to give birth to millionaires.
Accordingly, the odds of becoming a millionaire are lower
for individuals who are the products of nonmillionaires.

A TEACHER AND AN ATTORNEY: A CASE STUDY

Henry and Josh are brothers, but having the same parents
does not mean that these two people are similar. Henry is

forty-eight years of age; Josh is forty-six. Henry is a high school math teacher; Josh is an attorney and a partner in a modest-sized law firm.

The brothers are two of six children born to millionaires Berl and Susan, who accumulated their money by operating a successful contracting firm. The couple has always been generous with their children. Each year they have given Henry and Josh and their other son and daughters approximately $10,000 in cash. This gift giving did not stop when their sons and daughters became adults. Berl and Susan felt that such gifts would help reduce the size of their estate and thus reduce the inheritance tax their children would have to pay someday.

Berl and Susan also wanted to help their adult children get a good start in life. They felt that financial gifts would help their children ultimately become financially independent. Berl and Susan were always democratic about distributing their wealth to their children. Each adult child received the same size cash gift each year. In addition, each child was given approximately the same amount of money to help purchase a first home.

One might expect that the children in such families would become financially independent. Certainly, Berl and Susan felt this way. They always assumed that they themselves would have been even more successful if they had attended college and subsequently received cash gifts from their parents. But their parents on both sides were poor. Berl and Susan were successful because their parents gave them something other than money. Each was the product of a disciplined home life. Berl and Susan were not only well disciplined; they also taught themselves how to deal with adversity, and adversity made them what they are today—successful millionaires. Tough times in the contracting business drive out the weak

and unproductive. Berl and Susan were never weak of heart
and always ran a highly productive, low-cost operation. This
applied to both their business and their household.

Even today this couple has never owned a luxury automobile. They have never been on skis, never traveled
abroad. Nor have they ever joined a country club. But somehow they assumed that if their adult children could be
exposed to the wisdom gained from college, travel abroad,
and associating with higher-status people in general that
they would outperform their parents economically.

Berl and Susan were wrong in making such assumptions.
The children of affluent parents don't automatically perform
as well as their parents in terms of accumulating wealth.
This is not to say that the Henrys and Joshes of America will
never outpace their parents. Some do. But they are a minority among all the children of the affluent. It's important to
note that the children of affluent parents have (in today's
dollars) about a one-in-five chance of accumulating wealth
in the seven figures during their lifetimes, while the average
child in this country whose parents are not millionaires has
about a one-in-thirty chance.

Are any of the children of Berl and Susan millionaires
today? No! But one is more likely to become a member of
the seven-figure (net worth) club soon. Will it be Henry or
Josh or one of the other children? Berl and Susan's other
children are considerably younger than Henry and Josh.
Certainly age is a correlate of wealth accumulation. Young
adults are not likely to have accumulated considerable
wealth on their own. Also, the other four children have not
been receiving economic outpatient care from their parents
for the same length of time as their older brothers.

Many observers might predict that Josh would more likely accumulate a seven-figure level of net worth before his

brother. It is certainly understandable that they would feel this way. Attorneys typically generate significantly higher incomes than high school teachers. Once again, income is highly correlated with wealth accumulation. Last year Henry's total household income (not including the gift of cash from Berl and Susan) was $71,000; Josh's was $123,000. One would assume just from these figures that Josh would be much more likely to accumulate wealth. After all, his income is nearly twice that of his brother's. But observers who make such predictions overlooked the fundamental rule regarding wealth building.

Whatever your income, always live below your means.

Henry, in spite of his smaller salary, lives below his means. Josh, on the other hand, lives substantially above his income. In fact, Josh "really counts on that $10,000 from Dad and Mom to keep in balance." The $10,000 added to his $123,000 income places him in the top 4 percent of all income-producing households in America. Remember that approximately 3.5 percent of the households in America have a net worth of $1 million or more. But Josh has a net worth that even optimistically estimated is well beneath that figure. His total net worth, including the equity in his home, law partnership, pension, and other assets is $553,000.

How about Henry? In spite of his much smaller income, Henry has accumulated significantly more wealth. Stated conservatively, his net worth is $834,000. How is it possible for a teacher to have so much more wealth than an attorney with nearly twice the income?

Stated simply, Henry and his wife are frugal; Josh and his wife are heavy consumers. Much of this difference is related to their respective positions. We find that, as a group, teachers are frugal. Additionally, attorneys who receive cash gifts from their parents spend more and save and invest less than do attorneys who are comparable in age but receive no gifts. As stated earlier, attorneys who receive cash gifts from their parents have only 62 percent of the wealth and 77 percent of the income of attorneys in the same age bracket who receive no gifts (see Table 5-2).

Where do teachers who receive gifts rank along the dimensions of wealth accumulation and income? Households headed by teachers who receive cash gifts from their parents have, on average, 185 percent of the net worth and 92 percent of the annual household income of those in the same occupational and age category who do not receive cash gifts.

Teachers who receive gifts are more likely than non-receivers to teach in private schools, which generally pay their faculty lower salaries than do public schools. Perhaps unknowingly, many of the Berls and Susans in America are subsidizing private schools by giving cash gifts to their adult children. This, in turn, may encourage people like Henry to be willing to work for less money in a private school. Henry may figure that since he receives economic outpatient care, he does not need to earn a few thousand dollars more teaching in a public school. And although he teaches at a private school, Henry is quite comfortable driving his four-year-old Honda Accord or his wife's mini-van.

By contrast, Josh is in a completely different environment. In fact, the office complex where he parks his car is filled with imported luxury sedans and sports cars. Josh is responsible in part for new-business development for his firm. So even if he would like to drive a four-year-old

Honda, his clients and prospective clients might not wish to ride along with him. They might get the wrong impression.

Josh and his wife have three late-model automobiles. These include a 7 Series BMW and a seven-passenger Volvo, both leased, and a Toyota Supra. His consumption habits regarding motor vehicles are similar to those of other consumers who have significantly higher incomes. Josh spends three times more on average than Henry for motor vehicles.

Josh also spends nearly twice as much as Henry in mortgage payments. Josh lives in a larger, more luxurious home, in a so-called prestigious subdivision. Henry lives in a much more modest home in a middle-class neighborhood. Henry's neighbors are teachers, middle managers, civil servants, and store managers. Henry and his family blend in nicely in this neighborhood. The consumption habits they display are very middle class. This is true even though Henry's household has four to five times more accumulated wealth than its typical neighbor.

What about Josh's neighborhood? His primary residence (he also has a time-share in ski country) is in an upscale neighborhood. His neighbors are high-income-producing physicians, senior corporate executives, top-earning sales and marketing professionals, attorneys, and affluent entrepreneurs. Josh feels comfortable in this environment, and it is ideal for entertaining clients as well as associates. But there is something Josh does not realize: Although his income is in the third quartile compared with that of his neighbors, he is near the bottom in terms of his household net worth.

Josh and his family are playing the role of those with two, three, and even more times the net worth they have. Josh, you are not alone. At least one in five households in your neighborhood is playing the same role. They, too, are on outpatient care. They, too, spend more and invest less than others in their area.

How does Josh's budgeting system operate? How does it accommodate his propensity to spend? Josh is like many other under accumulators of wealth. He spends first. He saves and invests what is left over. What this actually means is that he saves and invests nothing beyond what happens to be injected into his pension and profit-sharing plan. More than two-thirds of his wealth is the equity in his home, his partnership, and his pension. In essence, Josh and his family invest zero dollars from their personal income. But perhaps they feel affluent anyway. Josh does receive $10,000 in cash each year. And he anticipates inheriting much more someday.

But what about Josh's children? Are they likely to receive substantial cash gifts from their father? It is very unlikely. Yet these children are growing up in a high-consumption environment. They will likely attempt to imitate their father's consumption behavior. This is a difficult act to follow, especially without the help of substantial outpatient care.

Henry's children, in contrast, may be surprised to learn that their father has accumulated a small fortune. Henry and his wife have never overextended themselves. Henry looks like a teacher, drives what teachers drive, dresses like a teacher, shops where teachers shop. He has none of the designer artifacts his brother owns. Henry has no pool, no sauna, no hot tub, no sailboat, no country club membership. He owns two suits and three sports jackets.

Henry's activities are much simpler, cost much less, and are much less status-oriented. He exercises by jogging every other day. He and his family are avid hikers and campers.

They do own two tents, several sleeping bags, and two canoes (one used). Henry reads a great deal and is active in his church and its affiliated youth group.

His simpler lifestyle translates into surplus dollars, which are saved and invested. During Henry's first year as a teacher, a senior member of the faculty advised him to enhance his investments by contributing to a 403b deferred annuity program. Henry has contributed to this program each year since he has been employed as a teacher. He has also invested most of the cash gifts his parents have given him each year.

Who will be more likely to retire in comfort someday—Henry or Josh? Their parents are now distributing their capital not only to their children but also to their grandchildren. Thus, Henry and Josh may inherit very little. At the rate Josh is consuming, he may never be able to retire in comfort. Henry will likely retire with ease. Projections are that his combined pension, deferred annuity package, and investment portfolio will be substantial by the time he reaches the age of sixty-five.

TEACH YOUR CHILDREN TO FISH

When we lecture about the relationship between cash gifts and economic achievement, people from the audience typically ask: "If not cash, then what form of gifts are more beneficial?" They are eager to learn how to enhance the economic productivity of their children. Here again, we remind them that teaching their children to be frugal is critical. Often those who are trained to be otherwise as children become adult hyperspenders, needing cash subsidies during their young and middle adult years.

What intergenerational transfers could help your children become economically productive adults? What should you give them? The affluent have a great appreciation for the value of a high-quality education. We asked millionaires if they agreed with the following statement:

◆ School/college learning is/was of little use to me in the real world of making a living.

Only 14 percent agreed; 6 percent had no opinion; and the balance, 80 percent, disagreed. That's why millionaires spend a large amount of their resources on their children's educations. What was the most frequently mentioned gift that millionaires received from their parents? Tuition!

All other economic gifts are mentioned by a significantly smaller proportion of millionaires. About one in three received some financial support in purchasing his first home; about one in five received an interest-free loan during his lifetime; only one in thirty-five ever received funds from his parents for mortgage payments.

What can you give your children to enhance the probability that they will become economically productive adults? In addition to an education, create an environment that honors independent thoughts and deeds, cherishes individual achievements, and rewards responsibility and leadership. Yes, the best things in life are often free. Teach your own to live on their own. It's much less costly financially, and, in the long run, it is in the best interests of both the children and their parents.

There are countless examples of the inverse relationship between economic productivity and the presence of substantial economic gifts. Our own data, collected over the past twenty years, repeatedly support this conclusion.

Independent of college tuition, more than two-thirds of American millionaires received no economic gifts from their parents. And this includes most of those whose parents were affluent.

WEAKENING THE WEAK

So what are affluent parents to do with their wealth? How and when should they distribute it among their children? We will detail the distribution of wealth in the next chapter. But at this point, here's some food for thought: Most affluent people have at least two children. Typically, the most economically productive one receives the smaller share of his or her parents' wealth, while the least productive receives the lion's share of both economic outpatient care and inheritance.

Consider for a moment that you are a typical affluent parent. You noted that your oldest son or daughter even at an early age was extremely independent, achievement-oriented, and well disciplined. Your instinct is to nurture these traits by not trying to control his or her decisions. Instead, you spend more time helping your less resourceful child make decisions, or you actually make decisions for him. With what result? *You strengthen the strong child and weaken the weak.*

Suppose you have a ten-year-old child who goes in for a physical checkup. The examining physician tells you that your son or daughter is underweight and underdeveloped. How would you respond to this evaluation? You would find ways to improve your child's physical health. You would likely encourage your child to exercise, take vitamins, lift weights, and perhaps play sports. Most parents would attack such a problem proactively. Wouldn't you find it odd if the parent took the opposite course? How would you respond if the parent encouraged his child to eat less and exercise less?

All too often this method of weakening the weak is applied to children who show personality-related weaknesses. In one case we know about, parents were told that their son was deficient in writing and related verbal skills. How did the parents respond to this problem? First, they transferred their child to another school. The verbal deficiency problem failed to improve, however, so the father began writing his son's papers. He still writes his son's papers today. His son is a junior in college.

In another case, an affluent couple had a twelve-year-old daughter who was very shy and rarely spoke to anyone without some prompting. Concerned about her daughter, the mother wrote a note to her daughter's teacher, asking that the child's seat be moved from the front to the back of the room, since her daughter felt more comfortable there. The mother reported that the "kids in front were too often asked questions by their teacher." The day the teacher received this request, she did not make any changes in the seating. The mother called the teacher that afternoon to protest. The teacher was unavailable, but she did return the call the next afternoon. Feeling slighted, the mother immediately transferred her daughter to another school.

In yet another case, a distinguished professor recently received a telephone call from his neighbor. The caller was irate:

Caller: Dr_____, you're in this business. I need your advice. How can I go about getting a professor fired? You probably don't know this guy. He's at the state university.

Professor: Why do you want to have him fired?

Caller: My daughter is failing his course. He says she lacks the background to do well in his class. . . . He has long hair. He never wears a suit. . . . He's a jerk! I have already spoken to his chairman. I'm getting the runaround. I want this guy fired.

Professor: Well, why doesn't your daughter just withdraw from the class?

Caller: Then she will have to go to summer school.

Professor: There are a lot worse things than summer school.

Caller: If she goes to summer school, she can't go to Europe with us. We have planned this trip for two years. Her mother won't go without her daughter. What can I do?

What have all the parents done in these cases? They have contributed to weakening the weak. If your son has a deficiency in his verbal skills, make a commitment to overcome his handicap. In one case, a father recognized that his son had an extremely high aptitude in mathematics but that his verbal skills were poor. His dad attacked the problem. Each night during dinner, Dad would ask his son to define three words taken from the SAT study guide. During hundreds of dinner sessions, Dad tutored his son. He also hired a professional tutor for him. This combination worked. Today his son is a graduate of a top Ivy League school—the one with the highest entrance requirements!

The Product of EOC

What happens when "weakened children" become adults? They typically lack initiative. More often than not, they are economic underachievers but have a high propensity to spend. That's why they need economic subsidies to maintain the standard of living they enjoyed in their parents' home. We will say it again:

> **The more dollars adult children receive,**
> **the fewer dollars they accumulate,**
> **while those who are given fewer dollars**
> **accumulate more.**

This is a statistically proven relationship. Yet many parents still think that their wealth can automatically transform their children into economically productive adults. They are wrong. Discipline and initiative can't be purchased like automobiles or clothing off a rack.

A recent case study will help illustrate our point. A wealthy couple was determined to give their daughter, Ms. BPF, every advantage. So when Ms. BPF expressed some interest in starting a business, they responded in typical fashion. They created what they thought would be the ideal environment. First, they wanted her to be debt free. So they put up all the money for their daughter to start her business. Ms. BPF put up nothing of her own. She never even applied for a commercial loan.

Second, the parents felt a strong need to provide her with substantial economic outpatient care. They felt this would enhance their daughter's chance of succeeding among the ranks of America's entrepreneurs. Ms. BPF's parents believed their adult daughter would benefit from living at home. This way Ms. BPF could put all her energy and resources into her business. She would live with her parents rent free. She would not have to allocate any time to shopping for groceries, cleaning the house, or even making her bed. This ultimate form of subsidy goes beyond economic outpatient care—call it economic inpatient care.

Is a rent-free environment ideal for a young entrepreneur? We don't think so. Nor is the gift of a business. The most successful business owners are the ones who put much of their own resources behind their ventures. Many succeed because they *have* to succeed. It's their money, their product, their reputation. They have no safety net. They have no one else to rely upon for their success or failure.

Third, the parents of Ms. BPF added yet another element to the equation. What if their daughter did not have to worry initially about generating profits from her venture? They believed that reducing this burden would enhance their daughter's probability for success. Ms. BPF became yet another member of the subsidized cluster. Her parents give her approximately $60,000 in cash and equivalents each year.

What is the result of having created this "ideal" environment? Today Ms. BPF is in her late thirties. She still lives at home. She has no commercial-related debts. Her folks financed her business and continue to do so. Last year her business earned her nearly $50,000. Her parents continue to give her $60,000 every year. They still feel that Ms. BPF will become truly independent sometime in the future. We are not as optimistic as her parents in this regard.

Most successful entrepreneurs are not like Ms. BPF. How many entrepreneurs who are still in the start-up phase of their venture would do what Ms. BPF has recently done in one year?

◆ Purchased a $45,000 automobile without shopping or negotiating the price or conditions

◆ Paid $5,000 for a watch, $2,000 for a suit, and $600 for a pair of shoes

◆ Paid more than $20,000 for clothing in general

◆ Paid more than $7,000 for interest on credit card balances and revolving retail credit

◆ Paid more than $10,000 for dues/fees at area country clubs

The answer is very few. Ms. BPF's business is not really a success. It is heavily subsidized directly and indirectly via other people's money. Actually, Ms. BPF has been short-changed by her parents. She may never know if she could make it on her own. The "ideal" conditions they provided for their daughter were an incentive for her to spend heavily on consumer goods. All the while she gave her business stepchild treatment.

Who do you think has more fears and worries—Ms. BPF or the typical unsubsidized affluent business owner? Logic might suggest that Ms. BPF should have no worries at all, since she receives intensive economic care from her parents. In fact, she has many more fears than do affluent men and women who receive no subsidies whatsoever.

Typical affluent business owners have only three major concerns (see Table 3-4 in Chapter 3). All of these are related to the federal government. They fear policies and regulations that are unfavorable to business owners and the affluent population in general.

What does Ms. BPF fear? She told us that she had twelve major fears. How is it possible that a person who is almost completely insulated from financial risk has four times more fears than the typical affluent business owner? *Because these affluent business owners have overcome most of their fears. They have inoculated themselves from many fears by becoming completely self-sufficient.* And it was the very struggle to become economically self-sufficient that helped these business owners overcome them.

What are some of Ms. BPF's major fears and concerns? Remember, these are fears that are not paramount among the self-sustaining affluent population. Ms. BPF has substantial fear of the following:

◆ Her parents' estate being heavily taxed

◆ Experiencing a significant reduction in her standard of living

◆ Her business failing

◆ Not being wealthy enough to retire in comfort

◆ Being accused by her brothers and sisters of receiving more than her fair share of financial gifts and inheritance from their parents

Who is more confident, more content, more able to deal with adversity? It's not the Ms. BPFs of America. It's those who have been brought up by parents who rewarded independent thought and behavior. It's those who don't concern themselves with other people's money, who are more concerned about succeeding than about how much is in someone else's estate. Also, if one lives below one's means, one doesn't have to be concerned with the possibility of being forced to reduce one's standard of living. The parents of Ms. BPF have failed to obtain their objective. Their goal was to have a daughter who would "never have to worry." But the method they used yielded just the opposite result. People often attempt to shelter their children from the economic realities of life. But such shelters often produce adults who are in constant fear of tomorrow.

THE PRODUCTS OF ZERO EOC

How valuable is your signature? It depends on how it is used. A signature helped Paul Orfalea start the business that bears his nickname—Kinko's.

With a $5,000 loan . . . co-signed by his father in 1969 . . . [he] rented a small garage. . . . From there he and a few friends sold about $2,000 worth [of services] . . . daily (Laurie Flynn, "Kinko's Adds Internet Services to Its Copying Business," *The New York Times*, March 19, 1996, p. C5).

It is estimated that Kinko's has annual sales in excess of $600 million. But what if Mr. Orfalea's parents had socialized their son in an environment similar to Ms. BPF's? Would he be as productive today? It's very unlikely. Mr. Orfalea has what all successful business owners possess: considerable courage. Taking financial risk is evidence of courage. But what risk has Ms. BPF ever taken? Very little.

Webster's defines *courage* as "mental or moral strength to resist opposition, danger, or hardship." It implies firmness of mind and will in the face of danger or extreme difficulty. Courage can be developed. *But it cannot be nurtured in an environment that eliminates all risks, all difficulty, all dangers.* That is precisely why Ms. BPF lacks the courage to leave home, expand her business, and wean herself from heavy doses of economic inpatient care.

It takes considerable courage to work in an environment in which one is compensated according to one's performance. Most affluent people have courage. What evidence supports this statement? Most affluent people in America are either business owners or employees who are paid on an incentive basis. Remember, whether their parents were wealthy or not, most of the affluent in America acquired their wealth on their own. They had the courage to undertake entrepreneurial and other business opportunities that were associated with considerable risk.

One of the greatest entrepreneurs and extraordinary sales professionals of all time, Ray Kroc, looked for courage in selecting potential McDonald's franchise owners and executives. Kroc actually welcomed cold-calling sales professionals. He told his secretary to "send all of them in." Why? Because it's not easy finding people who have the courage to be evaluated strictly on their own performance. He sold his first franchise outside California for $950 to Sanford and Betty Agate (see John Love, *McDonald's: Behind the Arches* [Toronto: Bantam Books, 1986], pp. 78–79, 96–97). Kroc first encountered Betty Agate while she was making cold calls on people in Chicago's financial district. Kroc's secretary asked, "What the hell is a Jew doing selling Catholic bibles?" "Making a living," was her reply. Kroc reasoned that anyone courageous enough to do what Betty Agate was doing would be a prime prospect for purchasing one of his franchises.

How many cold calls has Ms. BPF made in her life? Zero. Most of the people who buy from her are friends or business associates of her parents and relatives. Calls to these people are warm calls.

Parents often ask us how to instill courage in their children. We suggest that children be exposed to the sales profession. Encourage your children to run for class office in their elementary or high school. They will have to sell themselves to the student body. Even selling Girl Scout cookies can have a positive impact. Retail sales jobs provide another way for children to be evaluated by very objective third parties.

A WOMAN OF GREAT COURAGE

FAX TO: William D. Danko, Ph.D., Albany, NY
FROM: Thomas J. Stanley, Ph.D., Atlanta, GA
RE: A woman of great courage
DATE: Labor Day, A.M.

Guess where your colleague was at 5:30 A.M. this morning? I was boarding an early-bird flight. Although the plane had room for more than a hundred passengers, only about twenty people were on board. Soon after I sat down, we were told there was fog over the destination and that there would be another famous "short delay." As I stood up, the woman (I'll call her Laura) sitting in front of me also stood up. I mentioned to her that I was displeased about having to get up so early to make this flight. She responded that she had been flying all night and still had one more leg in her flight.

I asked Laura why she was traveling at night. She replied that it was a lot more economical to do so. What I found out shortly thereafter was that this woman did not have to fly via a highly discounted ticket. She, in fact, was affluent, but she was also very frugal. What was the purpose of Laura's travel? She was en route to a conference of real estate executives, where she was to receive the Real Estate Executive of the Year award. I then asked her how she first became involved in the real estate profession. Laura replied, "Out of necessity."

Laura told me that one morning she found a note from her husband on the kitchen table. Allow me to quote the contents:

> Dear Laura,
> I'm in love with my secretary. My attorney will fill you in on the details. Wish you and the children good luck.

How did Laura, a housewife with three small children, respond to this information? She was determined not to return to her old job as a high school teacher. Nor would she ever ask her well-to-do parents for economic support. She had grown up in an environment that nurtured independence and discipline. She wondered what she could do with undergraduate and master's degrees in English literature. She discovered that people with her educational background were in great supply and reasoned that her income from her teaching, editing, and writing jobs were not likely to be enough to support her family's current lifestyle. Thereupon, Laura discussed various employment opportunities with several enlightened business owners in the community. After these discussions, she decided to try the field of real estate sales. During her first four months, she earned more selling real estate than she did in her best year teaching English.

I know you would want to ask Laura the factors she feels contributed to her success. She told me this:

> *It's amazing what you can do when you set your mind to it. You'll be surprised how many sales calls you can make when you have no alternative except to succeed.*

As a young woman, Laura had developed an excellent foundation for her sales career. While attending school, she had convinced dozens of employers to hire her for summer jobs. She also had a variety of part-time jobs while attending high school and college. Laura was so good at finding jobs that she helped many of her friends find employment. No doubt she could have had much success in starting an executive recruiting firm. Laura was also the campaign manager for several of her friends who won student government offices in both high school and college.

It's ironic that Laura's misfortune in marrying a man who lacked integrity eventually translated into a much better life for her and her children. Because of his transgressions, Laura was able to fully utilize all her talents. The irony is that she always had more potential than her husband to excel in the business world. It's a proven fact today. She is "much better off" than her former husband. Her success is also a function of her high level of integrity, something that was lacking in her former husband.

After several banner years as a sales professional, Laura founded a highly successful real estate company. In spite of her dramatic financial success, she still flies on the red eyes and early birds. You would never think this woman had so much courage and stamina just by looking at her. I would estimate that she is barely five feet tall and weighs no more than ninety-five pounds. However, as we have often agreed, appearances are much less important than the courage, discipline, and resolve of people who are economically productive.

AFFIRMATIVE ACTION, FAMILY STYLE

THEIR ADULT CHILDREN ARE ECONOMICALLY SELF-SUFFICIENT.

Most affluent parents who have adult children want to reduce the size of their estate before they pass away. Certainly this decision makes sense, given that the alternative is to leave their children with a significant estate tax liability. The decision to share their wealth with their children is easy; the difficult decision is how to divide the capital.

Affluent parents who have younger children usually believe that the distribution of their wealth will never be a problem. They assume their assets will be distributed equally. Those parents with four children, for example, typically state that "[their] wealth will be distributed equally among [their] children—25 percent to each."

This simple distribution formula becomes more complex as the children mature. Parents of adult children are likely to find that some of their children have a greater need for substantial financial gifts than others. Who should get more? Who should get less? These are questions everyone must answer. Nonetheless, affluent parents are likely to benefit from several important research findings:

◆ Parents with nonworking adult daughters and "temporarily" unemployed adult sons have a high propensity to provide these children with heavy doses of economic outpatient care (EOC). These children are also likely to receive a disproportionately large portion of their parents' estates.

◆ The more economically successful offspring are likely to receive smaller levels of EOC and inheritance.

◆ Many of the most highly productive sons and daughters receive no wealth transfers whatsoever. Yet as we have discussed in Chapter 5, that's one reason they're wealthy!

HOUSEWIVES: A OR B?

Much of the variation in gift giving among different children can be explained by occupation (or socioeconomic status) and gender. We have found that housewives have the highest propensity of all major occupational groups to receive inheritances as well as periodic financial gifts from their parents (see Tables 6-1 and 6-2). In fact, housewives are three times more likely to receive substantial inheritances from their parents than are adult children of the affluent on average. In essence, housewives rank first in both the size of their inheritances and the incidence of inheriting wealth from their parents. They are also most likely to receive significant financial gifts on an annual basis.

We have identified two distinct types of housewife-daughters of the affluent—we'll call them Type A and Type B. Both benefit to different degrees from their parents' beliefs that nonworking women must have "money of their

TABLE 6-1

THE LIKELIHOOD OF RECEIVING A SUBSTANTIAL INHERITANCE: OCCUPATIONAL CONTRASTS AMONG THE ADULT CHILDREN OF THE AFFLUENT

LIKELIHOOD OF RECEIVING AN INHERITANCE

Significantly More Likely	Significantly Less Likely	About Average
• Housewife	• Physician	• Engineer/Architect/Scientist
• Unemployed	• Senior Manager/Executive	• Advertising/Marketing/Sales Professional
• High School/Elementary School Teacher	• Entrepreneur	
		• Attorney
• College/University Professor		• Accountant
• Craftsman/Blue-Collar Worker		• Middle Manager

own," that the economic deck is stacked against women, and that sons-in-law can never be fully trusted to provide support for their wives and children.

The Type A housewife differs significantly from her Type B counterpart. Type As tend to marry high-income-producing, successful men. They tend to take leadership roles in caring for their elderly, sometimes disabled, parents. The gifts and inheritance they tend to receive are, in part, compensation for these efforts—efforts their working brothers and sisters are more likely to shy away from. Type A housewives are well educated and tend to be the executrixes or co-executors of their parents' estates. They are likely to be leaders and volunteers in various local educational and charitable organizations.

Type A housewives are often viewed by their parents as peers and confidants rather than understudies. They are seen as intelligent, strong leaders and advisors and are frequently consulted about important family matters, such as estate and retirement planning, the sale of a family business, and the choice of professional service providers. Type As are also conversant with estate tax laws. They are likely to encourage their parents to reduce the size of their estate, and thus minimize the estate tax, by providing gifts to their children. Type A housewives receive substantial cash gifts throughout the early and middle stages of their lives, often from the time they are married. Later, gifts are associated with the purchase of a home and, in some situations, the purchase of investment real estate.

The presence of a Type A housewife is of great benefit to affluent parents as well as to their other adult children, since Type As often carry the enormous burden of providing for the emotional and medical needs of their elderly parents.

Type B housewives, in contrast, are viewed as adult children who need economic outpatient care and even emotion-

TABLE 6-2

THE LIKELIHOOD OF RECEIVING SUBSTANTIAL FINANCIAL GIFTS: OCCUPATIONAL CONTRASTS AMONG THE ADULT CHILDREN OF THE AFFLUENT

LIKELIHOOD FOR RECEIVING GIFTS

Significantly More Likely	Significantly Less Likely	About Average
• Housewife	• Craftsman/Blue-Collar Worker	• Engineer/Architect/Scientist
• Unemployed	• Entrepreneur	• Advertising/Marketing/Sales Professional
• Attorney	• Middle Manager	
• High School/Elementary School Teacher	• Senior Manager/Executive	• Physician
• College/University Professor		• Accountant

al support. They tend to be dependent on others and are unlikely to be leaders in any capacity. Type Bs tend to marry men who are not likely to produce high incomes. They tend to be less well educated than the women in the Type A category. The parents of Type B housewives often subsidize their daughter's household income in order to help their daughter's family maintain a minimum middle-class lifestyle. Type B housewives tend to live in close proximity to their parents. They often accompany their mothers on shopping trips. It's not unusual for middle-aged Type B housewives to receive clothing allowances from their affluent mothers and fathers. Parents also care for their Type B daughters via provisions in wills/estate plans. They are provided with cash gifts and inheritance because their parents believe they "really need the money." In essence, Type Bs are cared for by their parents instead of the other way around.

The parents of Type B housewives tend to hold back from distributing substantial cash gifts to their daughters out of fear that their daughters and their husbands may be poor money managers. Thus, cash gifts for Type B housewives tend to be on a need basis, such as when Type B's husband is "between jobs" or when there is a birth in the family. Gifts are often precipitated by crises and may range from direct cash payments to clothing and tuition reimbursement. Nonetheless, Type Bs receive the bulk of their parents' wealth in the form of inheritance. Often their parents' wills provide specific instructions regarding the distribution schedule and educational funds for their daughter's children. Often the family of the Type B housewife never becomes financially independent. It is not unusual for the Type B housewife in her mid-fifties to still be receiving cash subsidies from her parents.

Nor is it unusual for the husband of a Type B housewife to work for her parents' business. In some cases, the level of compensation is substantially higher than the objective labor market would indicate. In other words, the son-in-law in these situations is earning more as an employee of his in-laws' business than he would working for an objective third party. Even sons-in-law who are employed outside the family business often moonlight for the family, working part time at premium wages for the family business or doing chores or odd jobs for their in-laws.

Daughters who are not housewives but are employed in full-time positions are less likely to receive cash gifts and inheritance than their nonworking sisters. But even daughters who are employed in high-status occupations are more likely to receive cash gifts and inheritance than their economically successful brothers. Why? As stated previously, affluent parents feel rather strongly that women, even working women, must have "money of their own." They also contend that their sons-in-law "can never be fully trusted . . . to remain loyal . . . [to] support [and] protect" their daughters. Actually, the affluent are rather perceptive in this regard. Our data indicate that more than four in ten of their daughters who marry will be divorced at least once.

AFFIRMATIVE ACTION FOR WOMEN

Affluent parents understand that the income-generating opportunities facing men and women in this country are very different. These parents tend to have their own form of economic affirmative action. Consider the following facts:

◆ Women account for 46 percent of the workers in this country but represent fewer than 20 percent of the individuals who earn $100,000 or more annually. In 1980, fewer than 40,000 women had annual incomes of $100,000 or more. In 1995, approximately 400,000 women were in this income category. This translates into a tenfold increase. By the year 2000, more than 600,000 women will have incomes in the six-figure-and-higher category. But, again, as in 1995, there will still be five men for every woman in this income category.

◆ Women have made significant progress in regard to the proportion who graduate from professional schools. In 1970, for example, only 8.4 percent of medical school graduates were women. In 1995, nearly 40 percent were women. In 1970, women accounted for about 6 percent of all law school graduates; in 1995, they made up nearly 45 percent. A high-status occupational title does not automatically translate into a high income, however. A recent census headline stated: "Earnings gaps [in 1995] still apparent *even* for professional degree holders." In this regard, women employed in professional occupations in 1995 earned only 49.2 percent of what men in professional occupations earned.

◆ How do the salaries of men and women in high-income-producing occupations compare? See the results of our analysis in Table 6-3. In twenty out of twenty of the highest income-producing occupations, women on average earn significantly less than their male counterparts. For example, female physicians earn only 52 percent of what male physicians earn, female dentists earn 57.4 percent of what male dentists earn, female podiatrists earn 55 percent

TABLE 6-3

MEAN ANNUAL EARNINGS: MEN VS. WOMEN IN THE TOP TWENTY HIGH-INCOME-PRODUCING OCCUPATIONS

Job Description	Total Year-Round Full-Time	Male Year-Round Full-Time	Female Year-Round Full-Time	Difference Between Sexes	Female Income As a Percent of Male Income
Physicians	$120,867	$132,166	$68,749	$63,417	52.0
Podiatrists	$ 90,083	$ 94,180	$51,777	$42,403	55.0
Lawyers	$ 86,459	$ 94,920	$54,536	$40,384	57.5
Dentists	$ 85,084	$ 88,639	$50,919	$37,720	57.4
Medical Science Teachers	$ 82,766	$ 91,236	$48,801	$42,435	53.5
Law Teachers	$ 76,732	$ 85,376	$51,727	$33,649	60.6
Securities and Financial Services Sales Occupations	$ 67,313	$ 78,097	$37,695	$40,402	48.3
Health Diagnosing Practitioners, n.e.c.	$ 66,546	$ 76,139	$33,718	$42,421	44.3
Optometrists	$ 62,556	$ 64,988	$42,659	$22,329	65.6
Actuaries	$ 61,409	$ 71,028	$40,219	$30,809	56.6
Judges	$ 60,728	$ 65,277	$43,452	$21,825	66.6
Airplane Pilots and Navigators	$ 57,383	$ 58,123	$32,958	$25,165	56.7
Veterinarians	$ 56,451	$ 62,018	$35,959	$26,059	58.0
Petroleum Engineers	$ 55,788	$ 56,653	$43,663	$12,990	77.1
Management Analysts	$ 54,436	$ 62,588	$36,574	$26,014	58.4
Economics Teachers	$ 52,862	$ 57,220	$38,884	$18,336	68.0
Managers & Administrators, n.e.c., salaried	$ 52,187	$ 61,152	$30,378	$30,774	49.7
Physicists and Astronomers	$ 52,159	$ 53,970	$38,316	$15,654	71.0
Managers, Marketing, Advertising, and Public Relations	$ 51,879	$ 58,668	$35,227	$23,441	60.0
Nuclear Engineers	$ 50,492	$ 51,313	$36,513	$14,800	71.2

Source: Affluent Market Institute Database 1996 and 1990 U.S. Census of Occupations

of what male podiatrists earn, and female lawyers earn 57.5 of what male lawyers earn.

◆ In 1980, approximately 45 percent of the women in the six-figure-and-higher income category did not work. Conversely, 55 percent earned $100,000 or more via employment. These percentages have not changed appreciably since 1980, nor are they likely to change through the year 2005. In sharp contrast, nearly 80 percent of the men in this country who earn $100,000 or more are employed. Most of the other 20 percent are over sixty years of age and retired.

◆ The vast majority of nonworking women who have annual incomes of $100,000 or more inherited their wealth and/or received substantial financial gifts from their parents, grandparents, and/or spouses. Their income is typically generated from interest, dividends, capital gains, net rental income, and such.

◆ Women own nearly one-third of the small businesses in America. However, approximately two-thirds of these businesses have annual revenues of under $50,000.

◆ Working women are more than four times more likely to leave the workplace than are working men.

The objective data make it quite clear. In America, the odds are against women earning high incomes. Some of this variation in income can certainly be explained by biases in the economic marketplace. But biases alone do not fully explain the fact that there are five men for every one woman in the top 1 percent of the earned income distribution. Could it be that the tendency for affluent parents to subsidize their daughters is helping to perpetuate this inequality?

Daughters of wealthy couples tend not to have careers of their own. Why? In the past twenty years, the affluent population has typically been composed of one type of household: More than 80 percent have been married couples with children in which the wife did not work full time. What message did this send to the daughters of such couples? Simply stated: "Mother did not work (and the marriage survived), so perhaps I should not work." It is difficult to argue with such logic. The traditional affluent family system does, in fact, function quite well. Affluent couples have a divorce rate that is less than half the norm.

The "father works, the mother mothers and does everything else for her family" system is very often copied by the female products of such marriages. Many affluent parents actually encourage their daughters not to work, not to have their own careers, and not to be economically and psychologically independent. Affluent parents instill this "dependence" characteristic in their daughters over time with subtle cues. Thus, many affluent parents communicate messages such as the following to their daughters:

Don't worry. . . . If you don't want to have a career of your own, . . . you don't have to worry about money. We will help you out financially. . . . If you do have a career, . . . if you do become a big success . . . and become independent, you will not be receiving any major financial gifts or inheritance from us.

THE WEAK AND THE STRONG

ANN AND BETH: HOUSEWIVES AND DAUGHTERS

Ann is thirty-five years of age. She is the younger daughter of a couple we'll call Robert and Ruth Jones. Her parents are millionaires. Mr. Jones owns and operates several businesses in the distribution industry. Mrs. Jones is a traditional housewife. She never completed college and has never been employed outside the home. She is, however, active in several noble causes in her community. When her children were young, she served on the PTA.

Her daughter Ann is very candid about her relationship with her parents:

It would be so easy . . . to take money from my parents . . . for the house, . . . for private school tuition. . . . But it always comes with strings. . . . My sister [Beth, age thirty-seven] learned that. . . . She does not lead her own life. . . . She has learned that the dole comes with a price . . . do it Mother's way.

Ann understood the components of the parental control equation early on. When she was first married, she and her husband sought employment out of town. She insulated herself from her parents' influence by putting more than one thousand miles between herself and them.

Ann gave up her own career after her second child was born. But unlike her sister, Beth, Ann never accepted economic outpatient care from her parents. Ann became sensitive to the real cost of being on the dole by observing her sister's experience.

According to Ann, Beth and her family live in "subsidized housing." Mr. and Mrs. Jones made a sizable down payment on Beth's home. They also dole out thousands of dollars to Beth each year for housing and other expenses. She receives $20,000 in cash from her parents every Christmas. Beth lives less than two miles from her parents. (One of the proven ways that domineering parents control their adult children is by living close to them.) Ann reports there is some confusion about home ownership between Beth and her parents. It seems that Mother is always at Beth's—invited or not. And Mother was more involved with the choice of Beth's home than Beth was.

Beth married and became a mother before completing college. She and her husband lived with her parents for three years after they were married. This gave her husband an opportunity to complete college. Neither worked, even part time, during this period.

Beth's husband completed college and accepted an administrative position with a regional corporation, but after less than two years his position was eliminated. He then accepted a position as vice president of administration in his father-in-law's business. According to Ann, the vice president of administration was a newly titled position. The former title was office manager. But, as Ann explained, the job pays very well, and "you should get a load of the splendid fringe-benefit package."

It is difficult under such conditions for Beth and her husband to develop much self-confidence. Ann's parents, especially her father, do not show respect for Beth's husband. According to Ann, they always felt he was socially, economically, and intellectually Beth's inferior. They demonstrate much more respect for Ann's husband, who graduated with honors from a prestigious college and earned a master's degree with distinction at the age of twenty-four. Robert and

Ruth constantly tell their friends and relations of the great accomplishments of "our Ann's husband."

Robert and Ruth rolled out the red carpet for Ann's future husband the first time he paid them a visit. They were very impressed with his academic credentials. Ann reported that during this brief stay, Beth's husband, then a boarder with his in-laws, acted much like a waiter. Father-in-law Robert would direct his son-in-law to mix and serve drinks and snacks, for example. After several cocktails one evening, Robert referred to his son-in-law as a "bozo." Ann and her beau were shocked. This treatment left a lasting impression on the couple. Ann pledged that she and her husband would never become "bozos" in her parents' eyes. To date, she has kept her pledge. This is the case even though Ann's parents pressure her unrelentingly to accept economic outpatient care. In contrast, Robert and Ruth regularly ask Beth's husband to do chores for them. They treat him more like a handyman and chauffeur than the man who married their older daughter.

Why does Beth's husband tolerate this situation? Because he has been conditioned to do so. He and Beth have a high-consumption lifestyle congruent with that of his in-laws'. Yet their ability to sustain such a lifestyle is a function of their being controlled. Robert and Ruth have communicated a central message to Beth, not so much in words as in deeds:

Beth, you and your husband are not capable of generating enough income on your own to maintain your ascribed station in life. You are economically handicapped. You and your husband need our special brand of economic outpatient care.

Are Robert and Ruth correct that Beth and her husband would be unable to achieve in life without assistance? An objective third party would contend that they are. But what would the same objective third party say if he had examined this situation from its origin? He might have concluded that Robert and Ruth made a special effort to prove their hypothesis. After even just a few years of receiving aggressive and overbearing economic outpatient care, Beth and her husband have lost much of their ambition, economic self-confidence, and independence. No one will ever know if this couple could have functioned productively on its own. Beth and her husband were never given this opportunity.

The role of enlightened parents is to strengthen the weak. Robert and Ruth did just the opposite. They weakened the weak and continue to do so today. Not surprisingly, they never appreciated their role in causing much of the dependency Beth and her husband experience today. Today Ann has some resentment, even bitterness, toward her parents. She holds them responsible for creating the economic and emotional dependency that her sister and brother-in-law must deal with every day. Ann has learned much from Beth and her husband's experiences.

Ann is especially sensitive about her parents' role in usurping control of her sister's children. In them, the mistakes of the past are likely to be repeated. Ann can only wish that her parents had followed some simple rules about raising children to be independent. They can't now. But Ann can. It's not too late for her. Ann will never allow her parents to control any portion of her life or the lives of her husband and children.

CINDERELLA SARAH

Sarah is an executive in her late fifties. Her parents were affluent. Her father started his own business when she was quite young. When we interviewed her, Sarah was extremely candid about her relationship with her "Papa" and sister.

Sarah's father was a very strong-willed individual. His views about the role of women in our society were at odds with Sarah's. He felt that women should be educated in the fine arts and then marry, have children, and never work outside the home. Women, according to Papa's dictates, were not to have careers of their own. They were to be supportive—even subservient—to their husbands.

As a teenager, Sarah enjoyed debating Papa on numerous topics, including the role of liberated women in our culture. Often these debates turned into arguments centered on how Sarah would spend the rest of her life. Papa frequently threatened his defiant daughter with the loss of financial support for her college education, dowry, and so forth.

In spite of these threats, Sarah left home when she was a young woman. Her papa made good on his promise and withheld all financial support. Yet Sarah never lost her determination to become financially and emotionally independent from her parents. After leaving home, she became a proofreader for a large publishing company. During her career in the publishing industry, she rose to a very senior position. Eventually she married, but only after her own career was well established.

Sarah was distinctly different from her sister, Alice. Unlike Sarah, Alice, a Type B housewife, filled the role that Papa had assigned her. She was clearly "Papa's girl." Papa's girl married a local gentleman, a fellow from a lower social stratum who had a high propensity to spend but little propensity to earn an income. In light of this fact, Papa placed Alice, her low-income-producing husband, and their three children on his own special brand of financial outpatient care. Papa would never allow his favorite daughter to live in a home or neighborhood that was incongruent with his own upper-middle-class image. He heavily subsidized the purchase of a home and accessories for Alice and her family. Significant cash gifts and gifts of securities were bestowed upon "Papa's girl" annually.

Given these liberal subsidies, one might predict that Papa's girl would have accumulated a considerable amount of wealth. In fact, she and her husband accumulated very little money during all the years they were on outpatient care. Their budgeting system was quite simple: Spend more than you earn and more than you receive in cash gifts. The balance will be absorbed by Papa.

All during this time, Sarah, like many executives (see Table 6-4), received no outpatient care from Papa. Instead, she was punished for her audacity in violating the strict doctrines Papa had set for her.

When Papa passed away, Alice received no more annual outpatient care, although his favorite daughter did receive the bulk of what was left of his wealth. Sarah received a much smaller amount. She was surprised that she received any part of her father's estate, especially since he had told her shortly before his death that she would "receive a lot less than Sister." In his mind, his liberated and very independent daughter had much less need for an inheritance than did her sister, a Type B housewife.

It did not take many years for Alice, the favorite daughter, and her husband to spend nearly all of Papa's money. Shortly thereafter, Alice passed away. How did her children survive? Their own father did not have enough income to maintain their upper-middle-class lifestyle. Who provided for them? Who paid for their college educations? None other than their aunt, the recipient of no outpatient care, the semi-disinherited Cinderella Sarah. During all the years her father

TABLE 6-4

CORPORATE EXECUTIVE—GIFTS AND INHERITANCE: CONTRASTS AMONG THE ADULT CHILDREN OF THE AFFLUENT

PROPENSITY TO RECEIVE GIFTS/ INHERITANCE	RATIONALE FOR GIVING GIFTS/PROVIDING INHERITANCE	"POSITION" OF SON/DAUGHTER TO PARENTS	THE STAGE AT WHICH SON/DAUGHTER IS LIKELY TO RECEIVE GIFTS/INHERITANCE	FORM/TYPE OF GIFTS/ INHERITANCE
Corporate executives are significantly less likely to receive an inheritance from their parents.	Young executive types tend to demonstrate maturity earlier than others. Thus, their parents feel comfortable in not providing them with significant cash gifts.	It is unclear whether corporate executive types are any more or less "close" to their parents than other types of children of the affluent. However, limited data suggests that they tend to be somewhat distant in terms of both interaction and choice of residence.	Corporate executives tend to receive gifts, if any, early in their adulthood. But they are significantly less likely at middle/later stages to receive such gifts.	Those executives who do receive an inheritance from their parents typically receive cash/financial assets.
Their propensity to receive annual cash gifts from their parents is significantly below the average for all adult children of the affluent.	Affluent parents often feel that their middle-aged or older sons/daughters who are executives have little need for economic outpatient care/cash gifts or inheritance.			Cash gifts for the purchase of a first home often derive from a "college tuition fund" that was substantially over-funded by their parents.

had supported her sister, Sarah had never hardened or demonstrated any animosity toward Alice. Sarah never forgot to send a little gift to Alice on her birthdays. She never forgot to send Christmas and birthday presents to Alice's children. Sarah is, in fact, a very successful, independent, compassionate woman.

Today, Sarah is a self-made millionaire. She is in charge of her own family's finances and is in the process of setting up trust funds for her sister's children and future grandchildren. Sarah feels this is important. Regarding Alice's daughters, she told us: "They know nothing about money." How could they? Their role models were their parents, typical UAWs.

Sarah is a prodigious accumulator of wealth. Even today she is frugal and very well disciplined as a consumer. Her net worth is many times higher than her annual salary as an executive. Sarah told us:

People would be astonished to know how much money I have accumulated. . . . I know how to hold on to it.

Like many wealthy people, Sarah is in the process of subsidizing the incomes of others, the products of underaccumulating, overconsuming parents.

People often ask us how offspring of the same parents can differ so much when it comes to accumulating wealth. How could Sarah and her sister be so different? We are convinced that some differences exist at birth. Much of the difference, however, can be explained by variations in how parents relate to each of their children.

Papa encouraged Sarah to become a prodigious accumulator while fostering the opposite trait in her sister. In essence, he strengthened the strong daughter while weakening the weaker one. When Sarah left home, she burned her bridges. She received no outpatient subsidies. She had no choice but to learn how to "fish" for herself. And she taught herself very well. At the same time, her sister became progressively more dependent on Papa for his money.

Sarah had compassion for her parents, particularly Papa. He sacrificed much and worked extremely hard to become an affluent business owner. Papa was determined that his children would not have to work so hard and have to face the risk of "doing on their own." But the willingness and ability to work hard, take risks, and sacrifice were the qualities that made him a successful and affluent business owner. Somehow, like many of his peers, he forgot how he became wealthy.

Many parents say there is nothing wrong with providing outpatient care. This is true, perhaps, if the recipients are already well disciplined and have demonstrated that they are able to generate a decent living without other people's money. For example, what effect would accepting some outpatient care have had on Sarah once she had taught herself how to succeed, then excel at her chosen field? The answer is probably very little. She was mature enough, strong enough, to deal with money, hers or anyone else's.

The real tragedy is the helplessness of those who come to depend on outpatient care. Without Aunt Sarah's kindness, her nieces would likely be terrified of the future. Luckily for them, Sarah is helping. Wiser than Papa, she will provide trusts for these young women. Such financial support will benefit them much more in the long run than would substantial gifts of cash. Some of the funds in the trusts Aunt Sarah is setting up for her nieces are earmarked for education. The rest will not be distributed until these young women demonstrate considerable maturity. Sarah defines maturity as the proven ability to earn a good living. It is not her intention to create another generation of "weak sisters." Still, Sarah is very realistic about her sister's children. She realizes it is very difficult for teenagers to reorient themselves. It is unclear if her teenage nieces will one day become strong, independent women like their Aunt Sarah. It may be too late. They may have already been too heavily socialized in the consumption and dependent lifestyle they experienced at home. Fortunately, Sarah is a strong role model. She is confident she can have a positive impact on the behaviors and personalities of her nieces. Moreover, the compassion and love Sarah gives her nieces cannot be measured in dollars.

What did Sarah really want from her own papa? Much more than money, she wanted his love and recognition of her splendid achievements. Today Sarah has few regrets. She never dwells on the past except when speaking of her father. Although Sarah still feels she was never recognized by her father, she will tell you that she capitalized on this need. Much of Sarah's ambition and drive stem from the need to have her achievements recognized by others. So it is with many Cinderellas who turn some adversity in their early lives into lifetimes of achievement.

THE UNEMPLOYED ADULT CHILD

Like Type B housewives, unemployed adult children are significantly more likely to receive annual cash gifts from their parents than are their working siblings. In fact, our research findings regarding the incidence as well as the actual dollar amounts of gifts received are likely *understated,* since about one in four male children (twenty-five to thirty-five years of age) resides with his affluent parents, and some respondents did not perceive this living situation as gift giving/receiving. Male adult children, by the way, are more than twice as likely to live at home than female adult children.

Often the unemployed have a history of being in and out of work. Others are so-called professional students. Typically, their parents view these children as needing the money more than their brothers and sisters do, now and in the future. Thus, the unemployed are more than twice as likely as their working brothers and sisters to receive inheritances.

Often the adult child in this category has close emotional as well as economic ties to his parent. He is significantly more likely to live in close proximity to his parents—down the street, perhaps, or even in the same home. It is not unusual, especially among unemployed adult male children, for the child to act as the household handyman, assistant, or errand boy.

The unemployed adult often receives his first cash gift when he shows signs of being unable to maintain or uninterested in maintaining full-time employment. Some young adults who receive substantial cash gifts move back home upon graduation from college or graduate school. Others receive substantial cash gifts for housing, food, clothing, tuition, and transportation. The parents often pay for medical care and health insurance as well. Many of these cash gifts come from overfunded college tuition savings plans. When the adult children decide not to continue their educations, there often is a substantial amount of money that is legally theirs. This money is often used to help them maintain a comfortable lifestyle.

Unemployment during the early stages of adulthood is related to unemployment at later stages in life. Many unemployed middle-aged sons and daughters receive direct cash subsidies, often annually. Further, the incidence of unemployment is associated with larger and more frequent gifts. These adult children are also more likely than their brothers and sisters who are employed to receive inheritances in the form of personal real estate.

BEFORE AND AFTER YOU'RE GONE

For one of our focus group interviews, we asked a recruiter to supply us with eight to ten millionaires for the three-hour session. All were supposed to be PAWs and to have a minimum of $3 million in net worth. We also instructed our recruiter that the millionaires had to be sixty-five years old or older. Each was to receive $200 for participating.

Two days before the interview, nine millionaires had been recruited. But on the morning of the interview, our recruiter telephoned to tell us that one of them would not be able to participate. The recruiter said that she would likely be able to find a substitute. Just an hour before the interview, the recruiter telephoned us again to say she had found a sixty-two-year-old recruit. He was a business owner with a high income, but he did not fit the strict definition of a PAW. Nevertheless, we agreed to include him. The decision proved fortuitous.

The substitute respondent, "Mr. Andrews," was not told beforehand that the other respondents were affluent. Perhaps that was why he took the lead in bragging about how he was "very well-off financially." In reality, Mr. Andrews had a high income but a relatively small net worth. He was a classic UAW who looked and acted the part. He wore gold bracelets on each wrist and had an expensive-looking diamond-encrusted watch and several rings. When Mr. Andrews began telling the group his story, he exuded confidence. But after three hours of talking with eight wiser men, his demeanor changed. His confidence seemed to deteriorate as the interview progressed. We believe Mr. Andrews learned some important lessons that day about financial planning and the intergenerational distribution of wealth.

Mr. Andrews told us that he was already well-off and had already achieved his financial goals. But when questioned, he could not articulate his goals. A major part of his plan was to earn a high income. He always assumed that "most of the other parts" of his financial plan would "take care of themselves." We have interviewed many UAWs like Mr. Andrews. No matter how we ask them about their financial goals, their responses are predictable:

Do you know how many celebrities live in my neighborhood?

I make a lot of money.
I live two houses away from a rock star.

My daughter married a guy who earns a tremendous income.

What do UAWs such as Mr. Andrews tend to emphasize in telling us about themselves? Their income, consumption habits, and status artifacts. PAWs speak of their achievements, such as their scholarship and how they've built their businesses. You will notice that Mr. Andrews, the UAW, has a much different financial orientation than the eight PAWs who participated in our focus group interview.

Several of the more senior respondents reflected on

their experiences in unusually great detail. We don't think this information would have flowed so easily if it had not been for the initial comments made by Mr. Andrews. His views—so different from the others'—prompted an exchange that resulted in the PAWs providing valuable advice on such issues as gift giving, the role and selection of executors, conflicts among heirs, trusts, and the pros and cons of "controlling children and grandchildren from the grave."

We began our interview by asking:

Would you first tell us something about yourself?

All nine respondents briefly introduced themselves. A typical response:

I'm Martin. I am married, same wife for forty-one years. I have three children. One is a physician, one is an attorney, and one is an executive. We have seven grandchildren. I recently sold my business. I am now active in several religious organizations and two that help young people get started in business.

All the respondents currently owned and managed their own businesses or had recently retired after selling a business. All except Mr. Andrews, who was sixty-two, were in their mid-sixties to late seventies. After the respondents briefly introduced themselves, they discussed their financial goals. The first to respond was Mr. Andrews:

Being in business for myself . . . When I wake up, every day is a challenge. . . . I plan my work . . . work my plan. It's why my business is a good one.

Mr. Andrews discussed his current gift giving and how his wealth would be distributed in the future:

I have a son-in-law who is a physician. . . . Another is an attorney. They are well-off [high-income generators]. They are both in the highest tax brackets. . . . They don't need my money.

But their wives, my girls . . . my daughters, do. They are spenders. . . . Of course, I have always spoiled them rotten, and I'm paying for it now. . . . They call and ask me to pay for their kids' pianos and I buy pianos. . . . Bicycles and birthday parties . . . I pay for them, too. I enjoy giving them money.

My daughters are the beneficiaries of all my life insurance policies, more than enough to take care of all my estate's taxes and expenses. The girls are left with the balance.

After I am gone, it makes no difference to me how they dispose of my money. . . . [They] can keep it, shoot craps with it, . . . but I just want them to be happy.

"Happy" to Mr. Andrews means having money to spend. And pride is having daughters who are married to high-income generators. He spoke repeatedly about these issues.

Seated next to Mr. Andrews was Mr. Russell, a very wealthy retired gentleman who had recently sold his manufacturing business. Immediately following Mr. Andrews's admission that he spoiled his daughters, Mr. Russell moved forward in his chair and made the following statement:

*I have three daughters. . . . All have careers. All are work-
ing. . . . All are happy. All live a long way from here. They
have their own lives to live. . . . I'm not worried about paying for their futures. . . . Nor are they. We don't discuss it.
But there will be a large sum. . . . Plenty, I'm sure, left over
after I pass away.*

Another respondent, Mr. Joseph, nodded his head and
stated:

*We have two daughters, one is a vice president for a large
corporation and the other is a scientist. . . . We are very proud
of them. . . . They will be very well provided for. But as a family, we don't spend much time thinking about my estate.*

Mr. Russell and Mr. Joseph have the correct formula. *If
you are wealthy and want your children to become happy
and independent adults, minimize discussions and behavior
that center on the topic of receiving other people's money.*

Following these statements, one of the other respondents
asked Mr. Andrews about the disposition of his business.
His comments generated a series of interesting remarks
from the more senior members of the group. Mr. Andrews
stated:

*All the money I've been making in my business I dedicate to
my daughters and their children. . . . I don't need the money.
The kids can use it. I give the maximum within the bounds of
the law.*

What does Mr. Andrews plan to do about ownership of
his business? Will he eventually sell it? Will he give it to the

children to operate? Or does he have some other idea in mind?

I have an agreement with my oldest son. He is required to pay X amount of dollars each year, . . . and Billy will eventually own the business outright.

Several of the more senior respondents questioned this plan, since it clearly has the potential to create conflicts among Mr. Andrews's children. Mr. Andrews's business is in the service/distribution industry; it does not have a great deal of value unless it continues to operate under the Andrews affiliation. In other words, unless Billy Andrews keeps the business operating, there will be no business at all. Asked one respondent:

Would the business have significant value if you placed it for sale today?

Mr. Andrews admitted that it would not. Then why is he requiring his oldest son and key employee to purchase the business? Why not give it to him? Remember, Mr. Andrews gives all of the profits of the business to his daughters. He also plans to give them the revenue he receives from the sale of the business—the money his son Billy pays for the business. Moreover, Mr. Andrews's daughters already receive sizable cash gifts from their father. But not Billy. Billy, in his father's estimation, needs no subsidies. He is extremely productive in generating income. He could always "carry a great deal on his shoulders." Mr. Andrews feels that his daughters, on the other hand, do not have the ability to maintain an upper-middle-class lifestyle by themselves. But what about his high-income-producing sons-in-law?

In Mr. Andrews's mind, his sons-in-law will never generate an income high enough to support "the girls'" high-consumption habits. Also, he told us:

You can never fully trust your sons-in-law. . . . Divorce is always a possibility.

What about future outpatient care for his daughters? Billy, Mr. Andrews's surrogate, will provide the solution to this problem. Mr. Andrews's plan calls for Billy to make the payments to his sisters for years after Mr. Andrews's death. The money for these annual payments will come from the profits of "his business." Is this unusual? No. Business owners, entrepreneurs, and physicians often find themselves in similar situations (see Tables 6-5 and 6-6).

In essence, Billy will be required to heavily subsidize his sisters' lifestyle, a lifestyle predicated on conspicuous consumption. Mr. Andrews feels "fairly certain" that Billy will carry out his father's wishes. Perhaps he will. But how would you respond to this plan if you were Billy's wife? Think for a moment. Your husband is paying for his sisters' expensive clothing, luxury automobiles, vacations, and so on. Most spouses feel that charity begins at home. Note that spouses are often the initiators of family conflicts regarding inequities in the distribution of wealth.

The other participants did not criticize Mr. Andrews's plan directly. When each spoke, he looked at the group in general, not at Mr. Andrews. Yet it became increasingly clear as the discussion progressed that the other respondents rated the Andrews Plan a poor one.

One senior respondent reflected on a related situation:

TABLE 6-5

ENTREPRENEUR—GIFTS AND INHERITANCE:
CONTRASTS AMONG THE ADULT CHILDREN OF THE AFFLUENT

PROPENSITY TO RECEIVE GIFTS/ INHERITANCE	RATIONALE FOR GIVING GIFTS/PROVIDING INHERITANCE	"POSITION" OF SON/DAUGHTER TO PARENTS	THE STAGE AT WHICH SON/DAUGHTER IS LIKELY TO RECEIVE GIFTS/INHERITANCE	FORM/TYPE OF GIFTS/ INHERITANCE
Entrepreneurs are less likely than the norm for all children of the affluent to receive cash gifts or an inheritance from their parents.	Parents often provide seed money for their entrepreneurially oriented sons/daughters who wish to start a business.	Entrepreneurs are typically strong, independent types. They are less likely, both emotionally and financially, to be "tied" to their parents.	Entrepreneurs generally receive cash gifts in the early stages of their adult lives.	Entrepreneurs generally complete fewer years of college/graduate school than the norm for all children of the affluent. Often affluent parents significantly overfund entrepreneurially oriented children's college tuition funds.
Only a small minority of entrepreneurs inherit a family business. Generally, they start their own business.	Entrepreneurs are much less likely to receive any cash gifts/inheritance once they are viewed as being successful. Parents often conclude that entrepreneurs don't need economic outpatient care.	Often elderly parents are more "attached" to their entrepreneurially oriented sons and daughters than the other way around.		Gifts of cash/securities are often derived from these types of scenarios. Cash gifts are also given in the form of fully/ partially forgiven loans for seed money.
	The entrepreneurially oriented sons and/or daughters of the affluent have the highest income/ net worth characteristics of all occupational categories.			
	Some of those sons/daughters who take over their parents'/family business are often required to make long term "purchase payments" to their less productive siblings.			

TABLE 6-6

PHYSICIANS—GIFTS AND INHERITANCE:
CONTRASTS AMONG THE ADULT CHILDREN OF THE AFFLUENT

PROPENSITY TO RECEIVE GIFTS/ INHERITANCE	RATIONALE FOR GIVING GIFTS/PROVIDING INHERITANCE	"POSITION" OF SON/DAUGHTER TO PARENTS	THE STAGE AT WHICH SON/DAUGHTER IS LIKELY TO RECEIVE GIFTS/INHERITANCE	FORM/TYPE OF GIFTS/ INHERITANCE
Physicians are the least likely of all children of the affluent to receive any inheritance from their parents.	Parents often feel that the son/ daughter who is a physician has little or no need for an inheritance. In other words, they feel that physicians don't need any additional wealth since "they are already wealthy."	Physicians are among the least likely to be economically or emotionally dependent upon their parents. They are typically strong-willed in asserting their independence. Such "positioning" gives parents added evidence that "the doctor" doesn't need our money.	Physicians tend to receive cash gifts early in their adult lives. The likelihood of receiving cash gifts is greatly reduced as they approach middle age.	Gifts that are received are in the form of cash for tuition and "getting started."
Their propensity to receive annual cash gifts from their parents is about average for all adult children of the affluent.				Those who do receive an inheritance typically receive cash/ other financial assets as opposed to real estate or tangible/ collectibles.
Often parents of medical doctors expect them to give gifts of professional services and, in some cases, financial gifts to their less prosperous adult brothers and sisters.	Their brothers and sisters (non-physicians) occasionally lobby against them, encouraging their parents to "write the doctor out of the will." Some parents assume that their doctor son/daughter will provide economic support to their siblings in need.			

A son grew impatient with his father. The son wanted to take over his father's business, but he did not wish to wait for Dad to pass away. So the son opened his own business and actually competed with his father's.

Mr. Andrews quickly countered:

My son signed a noncompete contract with me. . . . Everything in a family is based on trust, isn't it?

The participants seemed to think about this statement for a moment. Perhaps Mr. Andrews was having some second thoughts about his plan.

Shortly after Mr. Andrews made this comment, he revealed that his children were the executors of his estate. Mr. Harvey then raised his hand and asked if he could respond. We were delighted. Mr. Harvey was the oldest and wealthiest respondent in the group. He began by noting the importance of facilitating harmony among one's heirs. And, according to him, the choice of executor(s) of an estate was critical in this regard. Mr. Harvey had served as executor or co-executor of several estates. He understood full well that being an executor was a difficult task and that there was often animosity among executors and the heirs of estates. For this reason, he had carefully chosen the executors of his estate:

I have two children. They are close to each other. They can settle my estate between them. . . . But they will do it along with my attorney. . . . The children and my attorney are executors of my estate. I put the attorney in just to keep the balance. . . . You know when money's involved what can happen. I want to keep good relations, . . . but good relation-

ships may deteriorate at the last moment without an experienced professional.

Mr. Andrews then spoke. He asked, with a hint of a challenge:

Are you really going to use someone from outside the family as an executor?

In response, seven of the nine participants stated that, in addition to a family member, at least one outsider would be co-executor of their estates. Mr. Ring, a retired entrepreneur and grandfather of nine grandchildren, was one such participant. Mr. Ring had served as co-executor of several estates. He knew of situations in which the heirs to a grandparent's fortune were seriously spoiled children in their late twenties and thirties who did not have the training, discipline, or ambition to support the affluent lifestyle they had been conditioned to enjoy. Several of these adults still lived at home. All had been receiving outpatient care from their grandparents. But, as Mr. Ring explained, once the "well ran dry," problems arose. When the grandparents died, the grandchildren and parents became adversaries. Each generation felt it should receive the bulk of the estate's proceeds.

These experiences had had a profound influence on Mr. Ring. He realized that long before one passes away, one should select professionals to be co-executors. Consequently, over the years, he had developed close relationships with a highly skilled estate attorney and an outstanding tax accountant. Mr. Ring sought their advice before he retired, realizing that someday these professionals would likely act on his behalf to prevent, or at least reduce, the probability that his grandchildren would battle over his estate. Through the years he had also sought their counsel on how to "give without spoiling." Mr. Ring now gives gifts to his grandchildren, but not in the form of products or social privileges. And he never gives without first gaining the approval and blessings of his grandchildren's parents.

The trusts for the grandchildren are controlled. . . . Money is distributed only when each grandchild reaches certain maturity. . . . I was a little against it. But I listened to my lawyer and tax man. . . . I don't want to reach out from the grave to control them, . . . but the way the trusts are set up, my grandchildren will have to work.

Mr. Ring's heirs will not begin to receive their inheritances until they approach their thirties. While some affluent grandparents give their grandchildren products and privileges, the Rings give them educations. Such gifts are intended to enhance their grandchildren's discipline, ambition, and independence.

Mr. Graham spoke next. He reflected on his own experiences as a co-executor, which had helped him select co-executors for his own estate.

You have to use your judgment. You have to have understanding and compassion. I was an executor of a [close friend's] estate of a substantial amount of money. I had discretionary power. . . . Every [decision] was not necessarily dictated. . . .

When the daughter [age twenty-three] was ready to marry, . . . I knew her father would have wanted her to have a nice wedding . . . so we gave her . . . the kind of wedding he would have given her.

After she married and started a family, I was still not quite sure of her maturity. So I distributed only enough money for her to buy a nice home. . . . Later I was convinced that she was able to take care of herself . . . so I approved the distribution of what was left in the trust.

The daughter received the balance of her inheritance just before her thirtieth birthday, when Mr. Graham judged her to be capable of handling her inheritance. She had demonstrated her maturity in her stable marriage, role as a mother, and career of her own.

When selecting the executors of his own estate, Mr. Graham chose an attorney who was an old friend. He discovered that "it's better for the children to be mad at the arbitrator than with each other."

Mr. Ward, yet another affluent respondent, had also served as a co-executor. He chose two attorneys as executors of his multimillion-dollar estate rather than his sons or daughters. One of the attorneys was his niece; the other, a partner in one of the top law firms in the country. Mr. Ward explained his choices:

I chose younger attorneys because I felt that they would have a better understanding of the needs of the heirs of my estate. Both have the greatest integrity and understanding, . . . and the two of them know each other professionally.

Beyond understanding, empathy, and integrity, another characteristic was critical to Mr. Ward:

The attorney who wrote [my] will was the one I selected as co-executor along with my niece. I felt that if there was a dispute between my sons and sons-in-law . . . that he would be a good one to arbitrate. That's the reason I selected him. He's been a personal friend for a long time and a very successful businessman.

Mr. Ward's comments are congruent with many of our research findings. First, most PAWs have long-term close relationships with several key professionals, such as top attorneys and accountants. Second, many people in Mr. Ward's category have relatives and/or close friends who advise them about wills, trusts, estates, and gift giving. In fact, all things being equal, estates in which the heirs, typically the sons and daughters, are professional estate attorneys tend to be taxed less. Sons and daughters who are attorneys act as formal and informal legal advisors and opinion leaders for their affluent parents. They have a significant influence over all aspects of estate plans, including the choice of the estate attorney, provisions in wills, the ultimate disposition of family assets, the choice of executor(s), the use of trust services, and the incidence and size of the financial gifts to be given to children and grandchildren.

"Attorney relatives" typically advise their affluent parents on how to minimize estate taxes via annual gift giving to the children and grandchildren. Thus, the mere presence of a son or daughter who is an attorney increases the probability that all the children in the family will receive substantial cash gifts from their parents. (Consequently, these children inherit smaller amounts than the norm for all children of the affluent, since much of the wealth in their parents' estates is distributed to the attorney and siblings prior to the death of their parents.)

What were all of these experienced respondents trying to tell Mr. Andrews? First, that his estate was complex, with many subjective provisions. He had acknowledged that his plan contained numerous verbal promises and monetary commitments. Mr. Andrews needed expert advice in how to handle these complex arrangements. He would be wise to consider having an estate attorney/arbitrator as the co-executor of his estate. Otherwise, his estate plan could very well become the cause of much conflict and animosity among his children.

But what if Mr. Andrews is like many other under accumulators of wealth we have interviewed? In that case, he is not likely to establish close and long-term working relationships with professionals such as attorneys. Remember that Mr. Andrews stated that he needed no outsiders to help him because "I trust my children. . . . It is all based on trust." But trust is not the only element in such situations.

RULES FOR AFFLUENT PARENTS AND PRODUCTIVE CHILDREN

The affluent who have successful adult children have given us much valuable information on how they raised them. Here are some of their guidelines:

1. Never tell children that their parents are wealthy.

Why is it that many of the adult children of UAWs are more likely to earn high incomes than to accumulate wealth? We believe one of the major reasons is that as children they were constantly told their parents were wealthy. Adult UAWs tend to be the product of parents who lived in ways they thought appropriate for wealthy people to act. They lived the high-status/high-consumption lifestyle so popular in America today. It's no wonder their sons and daughters attempt to emulate them. Conversely, adult PAWs whose parents were wealthy have told us time and time again:

I never knew my dad was wealthy until I became executor of his estate. He never looked it.

2. No matter how wealthy you are, teach your children discipline and frugality.

As you may recall, in Chapter 3 we profiled Dr. North, a wealthy man whose adult children live frugal, well-disciplined lives. Dr. North detailed how he and his wife raised their children. Simply stated, they taught by example. Their children were exposed to credible role models whose lives were characterized by their discipline and frugality. Dr. North said it best:

Kids are very smart. They will not follow rules that their parents themselves do not follow. We [my wife and I] were well-disciplined parents. . . . We lived the rules . . . we taught by example. . . . They [the children] learned by example.

There must be congruency between what parents tell their children to do and what we as parents do. Kids are very perceptive in pointing out inconsistencies.

Dr. North received a birthday gift from one of his daughters when she was twelve. It was a poster titled "The King's Rules." On it, his daughter wrote down the rules that her father preached to his children. Dr. North still keeps this poster in his office, prominently displayed behind his desk.

Kids are looking for discipline and rules. She honored me with the poster. Kids must be trained to take responsibility for their actions. Today all my children are well disciplined and frugal. They adhered to the rules. Why? Because their parents did. . . . Actions speak louder than rules that are just words, not actions.

What were some of the rules Dr. North's twelve-year-old daughter listed on the poster?

◆ Be tough . . . life is. In other words, there is no promise of a rose garden.

◆ Never say "poor me" . . . [or] feel sorry for yourself.

◆ Don't walk on the back of your shoes. . . . Waste not, want not. In other words, don't abuse your belongings. They will last longer.

◆ Close the front door. . . . Don't waste your parents' money letting the heat out.

◆ Always put things back where they belong.

◆ Flush.

◆ Say "yes" to those who need help before they ask.

3. Assure that your children won't realize you're affluent until after they have established a mature, disciplined, and adult lifestyle and profession.

Once again, Dr. North said it best:

I have set up trusts for my children . . . some estate tax advantages. But my plan will not distribute money to my children until they are forty years of age or older. Because in this way my money will have little effect on their way of life at that age. They will have already adopted their own lifestyle.

Dr. North also told us that he never gives his children cash gifts, not even now that they are adults.

Cash gives them too many options, . . . especially in the case of young children. Media, especially TV, controls the values of our young. Just like they try to control what we think is funny with canned laughter. . . . [There's] too much emphasis on consumption. . . . I have never just given cash for this reason. What I have always told my children [is] if you need to make a major purchase, you first must fund a good bit of it yourself.

4. Minimize discussions of the items that each child and grandchild will inherit or receive as gifts.

Never make light of verbal promises: "Billy, you will get the house; Bob, the summer cottage; Barbara, the silver," especially in a group setting, especially when consuming alcohol. You may too easily forget or confuse who gets what, but the kids are not likely to forget. They will hold you and their siblings responsible for being shorted. False promises often lead to discord and conflicts.

5. Never give cash or other significant gifts to your adult children as part of a negotiation strategy.

Give because of love, even obligation and kindness. Adult children often lose their respect and love for parents who submit to high-pressure negotiating tactics. Coercion of this type is often the product of the manner in which parents negotiate with their young children. Even preteens are taught the benefits of "Johnny got a bike so I should get a wagon." Johnny and his brother should receive symbols of love and kindness but, instead, they learn that Mom and Dad must be pushed, squeezed, and coerced into giving. The boys may begin to view each other as adversaries.

Often parents perpetuate conflicts even among their adult children. Have you ever told one of your children or grandchildren something like the following:

We helped your brother remodel his house/sent his kids to private school/paid his health insurance. We want you to have a few extra dollars. Would $5,000 be all right?

What's wrong with such offers? Often those on the receiving end view them as signs of guilt or appeasement on the part of their parents.

6. Stay out of your adult children's family matters.
Please note, parents, that your vision of the ideal lifestyle may be diametrically opposed to that of your adult son or daughter, as well as that of your son-in-law or daughter-in-law. Adult children resent interference from their parents. Let them run their own lives; ask permission even to give advice. Ask permission also when contemplating giving significant gifts to your children.

7. Don't try to compete with your children.
Never boast about how much money you have accumulated. This sends a confusing message. Often children can't compete with their parents on this basis, and do not really want to. You don't have to boast of your achievements. Your children are wise enough to appreciate what you have accom-

plished. Never start a conversation with "When I was your age, I already had . . ."

To many successful, achievement-oriented children of the affluent, accumulating money is not the superordinate goal. Instead, they want to be well educated, to be respected by their peers, and to occupy a high-status position. For many of these sons and daughters, the variations in income and wealth among occupations are much less important than they are for their parents. The typical first-generation affluent American is a business owner. He has a high net worth but often low self-esteem. The low-status, high–net worth parent often lives vicariously through his well-educated adult children who occupy high-status professions. Ask a self-made millionaire a simple question: "Mr. Ross, tell me about yourself." A prototypical multimillionaire (a high school dropout) recently answered this way:

I was just a kid, a teenager, when we got married . . . never finished high school. But I started a business. . . . Today I'm very successful, got dozens of college graduates, my managers, working for me.

By the way, did I mention that my daughter will graduate with honors from Barnard College?

This same millionaire never wanted any of his children to be entrepreneurs. And, in reality, most of the children of the affluent never do become business owners. Money is second or third on their list of goals and achievements.

8. Always remember that your children are individuals.

They differ from each other in motivation and achievement. Try as you may via economic outpatient care, inequalities will exist. Will economic outpatient care reduce these differences? It's unlikely. Subsidizing underachievers tends to enhance differences in wealth, not reduce them. This, in turn, can cause discord, since high-achieving brothers and sisters may resent such gift giving.

9. Emphasize your children's achievements, no matter how small, not their or your symbols of success.

Teach your children to achieve, not just to consume. Earning to enhance spending should not be one's ultimate goal. This is what Ken's father always taught him. Majoring in finance and marketing, Ken received an MBA with distinction. His father was a physician and a full-fledged member of the PAW group. He often told Ken:

I am not impressed with what people own. But I'm impressed with what they achieve. I'm proud to be a physician. Always strive to be the best in your field. . . . Don't chase money. If you are the best in your field, money will find you.

Ken's father lived by these beliefs. He lived well below his means and invested wisely. As Ken tells it:

My dad bought a new Buick every eight years. He lived in the same house for thirty-two years. Simple house, nice house, less than an acre. Four bedrooms for six people, two bathrooms . . . one for Mom and Dad and the other shared by four children.

What was it that Ken's father admired most about his son?

First, that I worked part time as a busboy in a pancake restaurant throughout my high school years. Second, that I never asked him for money. He volunteered to lend me a few thousand dollars to start a business—right out of undergraduate school. Third, I sold the business with enough profits to fund my graduate school education completely . . . and never had to ask for a subsidy.

Ken's focus today is on achievement. He is a key executive with a major communications and entertainment corporation. He is also an astute investor in both commercial real estate and quality public corporations. Also like his father, Ken is a prodigious accumulator of wealth. He lives in a modest home and drives used cars.

His dad was a great role model and mentor to his son. But Ken also believes that his early experience as a busboy had a big influence on him:

I got to see the masses . . . how the other people lived. I saw how hard people had to work to support their families . . . long, long hours at minimum wage just to get by. Money should not be wasted . . . no matter how much I earn.

10. Tell your children that there are a lot of things more valuable than money.

Good health, longevity, happiness, a loving family, self-reliance, fine friends . . . if you [have] five, you're a rich man. . . . Reputation, respect, integrity, honesty, and a history of achievements!

Money [is] icing on the cake of life. . . . You don't ever have to cheat or steal . . . don't have to break the law . . . [or] cheat on your taxes.

It's easier to make money honestly than [dishonestly] in this country. You will never exist in business if you rip people off! Life is the long run.

You can't hide from adversity. You can't hide your children from life's ups and downs. The ones who achieve do so by experiencing and conquering obstacles, . . . even from their childhood days. These are the ones who were never denied their right to face some struggle, some adversity. Others were, in reality, cheated. Those who attempted to shelter their children from every conceivable germ in our society . . . never really inoculated them from fear, worry, and the feeling of dependency. Not at all.

FIND YOUR NICHE

THEY ARE PROFICIENT IN TARGETING MARKET OPPORTUNITIES.

Why is it that you're not wealthy? Perhaps it's because you are not pursuing opportunities that exist in the marketplace. There are significant business opportunities for those who target the affluent, the children of the affluent, and the widows and widowers of the affluent. Very often those who supply the affluent become wealthy themselves. Conversely, many people, including business owners, self-employed professionals, sales professionals, and even some salaried workers, never produce high incomes. Perhaps it's because their clients and customers have little or no money!

But, you may say, you have told us that the affluent are often frugal. Why target those who are not "big spenders"? Why focus on people who are sensitive to the price variations in products and services? The affluent, especially the self-made affluent, *are* frugal and price-sensitive concerning many consumer products and services. But they are not nearly as price-sensitive when it comes to purchasing investment advice and services, accounting services, tax advice, legal services, medical and dental care for themselves and family members, educational products, and homes. Since the majority of the affluent are self-employed business owners and managers, they are also purchasers of industrial products and services. They are consumers of everything from office space to computer software. Also, the affluent are not at all frugal when it comes to buying products and services for their children and grandchildren. Nor are the children of the affluent frugal when it comes to spending the substantial gifts of cash that their parents and grandparents give them.

FOLLOW THE MONEY

In the next decade, there will be more wealth in this country than ever before. Opportunities to serve the wealthy will be greater than ever. Consider these facts about the American economy:

◆ In 1996, approximately 3.5 million households in America (out of a total of 100 million households) had a net worth of $1 million or more. Millionaire households accounted for nearly half of all private wealth in America.

◆ During the ten-year period from 1996 through 2005, wealth held by American households is expected to grow nearly six times faster than the household population. By the year 2005, the total net worth of American households will be $27.7 trillion, or more than 20 percent higher than in 1996.

◆ By 2005, the millionaire household population is expected to reach approximately 5.6 million. At that time, the majority of the private wealth in America ($16.3 trillion of $27.7 trillion, or approximately 59 percent) will be held by the 5.3 percent of households that have a net worth of $1 million or more.

During the period from 1996 through 2005, it is estimated that 692,493 decedents will leave estates worth $1 million or more. This translates into $2.1 trillion (in 1990 constant dollars). About one-third of this amount will be distributed to the decedents' spouses (in 80 percent of these cases, widows). Widows will receive an estimated $560.2 billion, while the children of decedents will receive nearly $400 billion (see Table 7-1). This translates into $189,484 for each of the estimated 2,077,490 children of decedents. People who receive wealth from the estates of affluent parents have a significantly higher propensity to spend than others in their income/age cohort.

Additionally, to minimize estate taxes, many affluent parents reduce the size of their estates by transferring much of their wealth to their offspring before death. During the ten-year period 1996–2005, it is forecasted that living parents/grandparents will give their adult children and grandchildren more than $1 trillion. These gifts will be in various forms, including cash, collectibles, homes, cars, commercial real estate, public securities, and mortgage payments. This $1 trillion in gifts translates into more than $600,000 (in constant 1990 dollars) for each child of the affluent. This $1 trillion figure is a very conservative estimate, since, as stated earlier, by the year 2005, households in America with a net worth of $1 million or more will account for $16.3 trillion—or 59 percent—of the personal wealth in America. The $1 trillion given to children and grandchildren thus represents a small portion (6.3 percent) of this wealth.

TABLE 7-1

**ESTIMATED ALLOCATIONS[1] OF ESTATES
VALUED AT $1 MILLION OR MORE
($ BILLIONS)**

CATEGORY ALLOCATIONS	YEARS			TOTAL FOR
	1996 N=40,921	2000 N=66,177	2005 N=100,650	1996–2005 N=692,493
Estate Tax after Credits	14.95	24.65	40.65	269.04
Bequests to Spouse	38.92	64.17	105.80	700.24
Charitable Bequests	8.56	14.12	23.28	154.07
Lifetime Transfers	21.88	36.07	59.47	393.65

[1]Estimated allocations are in 1990 dollars.

TABLE 7-2

ESTIMATED FEES[1] FOR ESTATE SERVICES ($ MILLIONS)

CATEGORY OF SERVICE	YEARS			TOTAL FOR
	1996 N=40,921	2000 N=66,177	2005 N=100,650	1996–2005 N=692,493
Attorneys' Fees	962.5	1,586.9	2,626.3	17,105.6
Executors' Fees	1,241.1	2,042.3	3,373.7	22,329.9
Administrators' Fees	938.1	1,546.7	2,550.0	16,878.1

[1]Estimated fees are in 1990 dollars.

Much of this gift giving is tax-free. Typically, parents distribute their wealth so as to limit gift tax liabilities. Each parent can give each child and grandchild up to $10,000 annually. Thus, a mother and father with three children and six grandchildren can give them $180,000 tax-free each year. Also note that gifts of tuition and medical expenses are typically not included in computations of gift tax liability.

BUSINESSES AND PROFESSIONS LIKELY TO BENEFIT FROM THE AFFLUENT

There are many. Those who are specialists in solving the problems of the affluent and their heirs should be in great demand during the next twenty years.

ATTORNEYS WHO SPECIALIZE

A father recently asked us about the ideal occupation for his son. At the time of this discussion, his son was a second-year college student with a straight-A average. How did the father respond when we suggested that his son consider becoming an attorney? He said there were too many attorneys. We replied that there were too many *law school graduates*. There is always a demand for high-grade attorneys. Attorneys who can generate new business are in even higher demand. The father asked about the areas of law that would be best suited for his son. We described three to him:

Estate Attorneys—Too Many?

The first area we recommended was estate law. During the ten-year period 1996–2005, attorneys' fees associated with settling estates in the $1 million or more category will total an estimated $17.1 billion (see Table 7-2). Many attorneys will also earn revenue by acting as executors or co-executors as well as administrators of estates. Attorneys will participate as executors or administrators for only a fraction of the estates worth $1 million and more, but even a fraction of the estimated $22.3 billion in executors' fees and $16.9 billion in administrators' fees translates into high profits for enlightened estate attorneys.

In essence, estate attorneys will likely generate more than $25 billion in revenue from servicing estates in the $1 million or more range during the 1996–2005 period. This figure is greater than the net income generated by all law partnerships for all services in 1994! Of course, this total is only a small amount compared with the nearly $270 billion that will be paid to the federal government in estate taxes during the same ten-year period (see Table 7-1).

There is more to being a successful estate attorney than just providing legal advice. The more successful ones also act as mentors and family advisors to the affluent and their heirs. These attorneys have to be especially adept at meeting the needs of the widows and widowers who are their clients. Within the affluent married-couple population, almost all husbands and wives intend to leave their estates to their spouses, since a husband or wife can inherit his or her spouse's estate without paying an estate tax.* This unlimited marital deduction essentially postpones payment of estate taxes until the death of the second spouse.

Affluent widows face a particularly difficult situation.

---

*The term *inherit* as used here does not fit the traditional definition, which relates to receiving cash or its equivalents as a right or title descendible by law from an ancestor at his or her death. Nor does a spouse fit the strict definition of an ancestor. In reality, almost all the wealth of millionaire couples is held jointly; this is the main reason it is nearly impossible to estimate the number of individual millionaires and why we substitute the number of millionaire households. Nevertheless, it is a bit misleading to use the term *inheritance* when discussing the interspousal transfer of wealth. While both spouses are alive, what is his is hers and what is hers is his.

More than half will have been married to the same spouse
for more than fifty years. Between 1996 and 2005, there are
likely to be four affluent widows created for every one affluent widower. Age is most significant in explaining this variation. Within the millionaire married-couple population, the
expected average age of a male decedent (husband) is sev-
enty-five and a half years, while the average age for a female
decedent (wife) is eighty-two years. Moreover, males in
such cases typically marry women who are on average two
years their junior. Thus, in the typical affluent-couple population, the husband who passes away at the age of seventy-
five and a half years leaves behind a widow who is two years
younger than he was at the time of death. His wife, who
became a widow at the age of seventy-three, is expected to
live until she is eighty-two. Most women in this scenario
never remarry. Therefore, most women are widowed for
nine years before their deaths.

It is estimated that during the ten-year period from 1996
to 2005, nearly 296,000 women in the millionaire married-
couple population will become widows. Their average
inheritance will be approximately $2 million (in 1990 dol-
lars). During this same period, nearly 72,000 men from this
population will become widowers. It is estimated that these
men will inherit more than $125 billion, or an average inher-
itance of approximately $1.7 million.

In what states will the demand for estate attorneys be the
strongest? We predict that demand in California, Florida,
New York, Illinois, Texas, and Pennsylvania will be especially high during the next decade (see Tables 7-3 and 7-4).

On Income and/or Wealth

Which is the number-one income-consuming category
among the affluent? Income tax. The affluent in the

TABLE 7-3

PREDICTED NUMBER AND VALUE[1] OF ESTATES OF $1 MILLION OR MORE

	Number of Estates			Total Dollar Amount of Estates		
	1996	2000	2005	1996	2000	2005
Alabama	359	563	883	952,915,427	1,571,091,934	2,590,292,690
Alaska	45	70	110	105,229,924	173,494,815	286,044,592
Arizona	508	796	1,249	1,206,636,467	1,989,407,210	3,279,977,983
Arkansas	240	376	590	97,472,127	985,065,004	1,624,097,625
California	7,621	11,952	18,744	20,784,079,307	34,267,153,645	56,496,985,101
Colorado	412	646	1,012	1,039,437,810	1,713,743,226	2,825,484,910
Connecticut	1,052	1,650	2,588	2,873,946,160	4,738,336,164	7,812,195,622
Delaware	151	237	371	349,597,194	576,388,329	950,303,699
District of Columbia	129	203	318	583,441,470	961,932,362	1,585,958,346
Florida	3,720	5,835	9,151	13,274,170,363	21,885,407,028	36,082,936,085
Georgia	731	1,147	1,799	2,057,829,634	3,392,787,490	5,593,760,901
Hawaii	259	406	637	765,840,006	1,262,656,708	2,081,768,972
Idaho	110	172	270	212,798,292	350,845,070	578,445,730
Illinois	2,002	3,140	4,925	5,688,262,029	9,378,358,600	15,462,299,309
Indiana	479	751	1,179	1,944,415,160	3,205,798,634	5,285,468,397
Iowa	502	787	1,235	933,038,664	1,538,320,691	2,536,262,045
Kansas	430	675	1,059	992,668,954	1,636,634,420	2,698,353,980
Kentucky	408	640	1,004	1,053,468,466	1,736,875,868	2,863,624,189
Louisiana	16	495	777	948,238,542	1,563,381,053	2,577,579,597
Maine	253	397	623	558,887,821	921,450,239	1,519,214,608
Maryland	766	1,201	1,884	1,936,230,610	3,192,304,592	5,263,220,484
Massachusetts	1,200	1,882	2,951	3,203,666,590	5,281,953,251	8,708,468,675
Michigan	85	1,544	2,422	2,485,764,661	4,098,333,070	6,757,008,907
Minnesota	577	904	1,418	1,403,065,660	2,313,264,197	3,813,927,887
Mississippi	231	362	568	534,334,172	880,968,115	1,452,470,870
Missouri	789	1,237	1,940	2,395,734,614	3,949,898,617	6,512,281,867
Montana	93	146	229	191,752,307	316,146,107	521,236,811
Nebraska	312	489	767	574,087,699	946,510,601	1,560,532,160
Nevada	173	271	426	411,565,927	678,557,498	1,118,752,180
New Hampshire	237	371	582	477,042,324	786,509,827	1,296,735,482
New Jersey	1,582	2,482	3,892	4,343,657,438	7,161,480,411	11,807,285,084
New Mexico	121	190	298	330,889,651	545,544,807	899,451,327
New York	3,636	5,702	8,942	12,767,897,504	21,050,704,197	34,706,743,772
North Carolina	827	1,297	2,034	2,099,921,604	3,462,185,416	5,708,178,738
North Dakota	126	198	310	192,921,528	318,073,827	524,415,084
Ohio	1,398	2,192	3,438	3,555,602,226	5,862,197,020	9,665,128,920
Oklahoma	350	549	862	1,017,222,603	1,677,116,543	2,765,097,718
Oregon	321	503	789	722,578,815	1,191,331,962	1,964,172,862
Pennsylvania	1,760	2,761	4,330	5,100,143,673	8,408,715,358	13,863,627,870
Rhode Island	214	335	525	401,042,934	661,208,016	1,090,147,721
South Carolina	482	757	1,187	952,915,427	1,571,091,934	2,590,292,690
South Dakota	81	128	200	268,920,918	443,375,638	731,002,845
Tennessee	472	740	1,160	1,556,233,661	2,565,795,539	4,230,281,681
Texas	1,922	3,014	4,727	5,849,614,580	9,644,383,983	15,900,901,016
Utah	83	131	205	377,658,507	622,653,613	1,026,582,256
Vermont	84	132	207	182,398,536	300,724,346	495,810,625
Virginia	924	1,448	2,272	2,965,145,428	4,888,698,337	8,060,100,935
Washington	697	1,093	1,714	2,015,737,665	3,323,389,564	5,479,343,064
West Virginia	126	198	310	308,674,445	508,918,123	839,064,135
Wisconsin	480	753	1,181	1,324,727,827	2,184,106,946	3,600,983,580
Wyoming	81	128	200	195,259,971	321,929,267	530,771,631
Other areas	64	101	158	275,936,246	454,941,959	750,072,484
TOTAL	40,921	64,177	100,650	117,340,719,569	193,462,140,273	318,965,145,743

[1]The value of estates is given in 1990 dollars.

TABLE 7-4

PREDICTED NUMBER OF ESTATES VALUED[1] AT $1 MILLION OR MORE RANK ORDERED BY NUMBER OF ESTATES BY STATE FOR THE YEAR 2000

STATE	NUMBER	TOTAL VALUE	AVERAGE VALUE	RANK
California	11,952	34,267,153,645	2,867,121	1
Florida	5,835	21,885,407,028	3,750,905	2
New York	5,702	21,050,704,197	3,691,901	3
Illinois	3,140	9,378,358,600	2,986,706	4
Texas	3,014	9,644,883,983	3,199,594	5
Pennsylvania	2,761	8,408,715,358	3,045,791	6
New Jersey	2,482	7,161,480,411	2,885,822	7
Ohio	2,192	5,862,197,020	2,674,136	8
Massachusetts	1,882	5,281,953,251	2,807,188	9
Connecticut	1,650	4,738,336,164	2,871,869	10
Michigan	1,544	4,098,333,070	2,654,315	11
Virginia	1,448	4,888,698,337	3,375,224	12
North Carolina	1,297	3,462,185,416	2,669,469	13
Missouri	1,237	3,949,898,617	3,192,418	14
Maryland	1,201	3,192,304,592	2,657,293	15
Georgia	1,147	3,392,787,490	2,958,510	16
Washington	1,093	3,323,389,564	3,040,937	17
Minnesota	904	2,313,264,197	2,558,322	18
Arizona	796	1,989,407,210	2,498,002	19
Iowa	787	1,538,320,691	1,953,634	20
South Carolina	757	1,571,091,934	2,076,484	21
Wisconsin	753	2,184,106,946	2,901,461	22
Indiana	751	3,205,798,634	4,265,994	23
Tennessee	740	2,565,795,539	3,467,637	24
Kansas	675	1,636,634,420	2,424,247	25
Colorado	646	1,713,743,226	2,654,536	26
Kentucky	640	1,736,875,868	2,711,934	27
Alabama	563	1,571,091,934	2,791,534	28
Oklahoma	549	1,677,116,543	3,053,025	29
Oregon	503	1,191,331,062	2,367,867	30
Louisiana	495	1,563,381,053	3,155,647	31
Nebraska	489	946,510,601	1,935,581	32
Hawaii	406	1,262,656,708	3,108,297	33
Maine	397	921,450,239	2,319,648	34
Arkansas	376	985,065,004	2,619,438	35
New Hampshire	371	786,509,827	2,120,397	36
Mississippi	362	880,968,115	2,434,008	37
Rhode Island	335	661,208,016	1,973,824	38
Nevada	271	678,557,498	2,499,696	39
Delaware	237	576,388,329	2,434,051	40
District of Columbia	203	961,932,362	4,743,494	41
West Virginia	198	508,918,123	2,574,768	42
North Dakota	198	318,073,827	1,609,230	43
New Mexico	190	545,544,807	2,871,968	44
Idaho	172	350,845,070	2,039,959	45
Montana	146	316,146,107	2,160,697	46
Vermont	132	300,724,346	2,274,795	47
Utah	131	622,653,613	4,756,169	48
South Dakota	128	443,375,638	3,471,839	49
Wyoming	128	321,929,267	2,520,857	50
Alaska	70	173,494,815	2,480,281	51
TOTAL	64,076	193,007,198,314	3,012,139	

[1] The value of estates is given in 1990 dollars.

$200,000-and-more annual realized income category account for only about 1 percent of U.S. households but pay 25 percent of the tax on personal income. They will want to become better at realizing less income in the future.

What will happen in the year 2005, when millionaire households will control 59 percent of America's personal wealth? The government will likely place increased pressure on the affluent, possibly by creating innovative ways to tax wealth in addition to income. This prospect, according to our surveys of millionaires, is foremost on the minds of the affluent. Paying increasingly higher taxes to cover government spending and reduce the federal deficit is among the greatest fears of the affluent population. Several states already have a wealth tax. Each year residents in such states must list all the financial assets they own; a tax is levied on stocks, bonds, time deposits, and so on. How difficult would it be for our federal government to tax wealth this way? Not too difficult, since it already knows how some states tax capital before it becomes realized income.

We believe that in the next twenty years, the affluent will have to use every option within the law to remain affluent. It is a segment of our economy that will be under siege by the liberal politician and his friend, the tax man. Surely the affluent will readily spend their money for legal advice that will help them withstand the siege. The tax attorney will prove to be an integral part of the defense. Thus, the second area of law we recommended to the father for his son was tax law.

For Sale: A Place in America

The third area of law we recommended was immigration law. Attorneys who specialize in immigration law are likely to benefit from predicted developments in this area. For example, it will become progressively more difficult to immigrate to this country and become a naturalized citizen. At the same time, the demand for American citizenship will increase greatly, especially among affluent foreigners. Consider how millionaire entrepreneurs and advocates of free enterprise living in Taiwan feel about their future. China also wants their capital and country. China wants the Philippines for its oil. Who can guess how the Chinese government will treat the affluent population of a country it acquires? China is a real threat to many affluent people who live within its influence. Many of these people will seek American citizenship. Immigration attorneys will surely benefit from this trend.

"People do not feel safe," said Chris Chiang of the Taiwan-based Pan Pacific Immigration Company. "They want to come to the USA. Billions of dollars have flowed out of Taiwan since mainland China held naval maneuvers off the island's coast. . . . China considers Taiwan a renegade province" (Darryl Fears, "Taiwanese Talk Deal on Blighted Area," *Atlanta Journal-Constitution*, April 27, 1996, p. 1).

The fear of affluent Taiwanese business owners is reflected in their movement of money into America. In fact, they recently invested more than $10 billion in California alone. Now they are considering investing $50 million in Atlanta (Fears, p. 1). What do they get for investing in this country?

The million-dollar investor program was created by Congress in 1990. It allows foreign nationals to attain per-

*manent U.S. residency if they invest $1 million in a U.S.
business, provided that investment creates ten jobs* (John R.
Emshwiller, "Fraud Plagues U.S. Programs That Swap
Visas for Investments," *The Wall Street Journal*, April 11,
1996, p. B1).

The need for immigration-related legal expertise is not
limited to foreigners who are affluent entrepreneurs. Many
highly skilled professionals and scientific workers are being
sought in growing numbers by American corporations.
These employees have an increasing need for the services of
attorneys who have considerable expertise and experience
with immigration statutes.

MEDICAL AND DENTAL CARE SPECIALISTS

Many specialists will benefit from the enormous number
of dollars that the affluent population will spend for health
care in the next decade. A growing number of wealthy people will pay for the medical and dental expenses of their
adult children and grandchildren. Currently, more than
four in ten millionaires (44 percent) are paying or have
paid for the medical/dental expenses of their adult offspring and/or grandchildren. We estimate that in the next
ten years, millionaires will spend in excess of $52 billion
for the medical and dental care of their adult children and
grandchildren.

Most of these medical and dental expenses are not cov-
ered by health-care insurance programs. Skilled health-
care specialists who prefer to deal directly with individual
payers and not with bureaucratic third-party organizations
will be especially important in providing these uncovered
services. A growing number of health-care professionals

are already focusing on this affluent self-payer market. Those professionals with the highest skills and corresponding reputations can most readily capitalize on this trend. Often they can demand and receive fees that are higher than any insurance company would be willing to pay. The affluent will often pay directly to the health-care professional or organization. This way they avoid the possibility of paying gift tax on such distributions. Also, many affluent people will pay for their own "elective" health-care services.

Specialists who will benefit include:

◆ **Dentists** providing cosmetic dentistry, including bleaching, bonding, veneers, invisible braces, cosmetic nasal surgery, and chin and corrective jaw surgery

◆ **Plastic surgeons** providing nose-reshaping surgery, ear-reshaping surgery, tattoo removal, facial contouring, chemical peels, and permanent hair removal

◆ **Dermatologists** providing mole removal, cosmetic surgery, acne treatment, freckle removal, and electrolysis

◆ **Allergists** providing treatment for fatigue, rashes, hives, itching, allergy-related mood swings and depression, food allergies, learning disabilities, and new house sickness

◆ **Psychologists** providing career counseling, academic and career assessment, treatments for attention deficit disorder, treatment for compulsive eating disorder, shyness and assertiveness conditioning, and intelligence and aptitude testing

◆ **Psychiatrists** providing treatment for stress and anxiety, drug and alcohol abuse, school stress, and panic disorders

◆ **Chiropractors** providing treatment for stress relief and head, neck, and lower-back pain

ASSET LIQUIDATORS, FACILITATORS, AND APPRAISERS

Not all intergenerational gifts are in the form of cash or its equivalents. Gifts to adult children and grandchildren are often in the form of private/family businesses, coin collections, stamp collections, gems and precious metals, timberland, farms, rights to oil and gas properties, personal real estate, commercial real estate, gun collections, porcelains, antiques, art, motor vehicles, furniture, and the like. Often the recipients of these items have little or no interest in them and want to transform them into cash immediately. They will need experts to advise them of the true value of the gifts or how to sell them, manage them even for short periods of time, or enhance their value.

Specialists who will benefit include:

◆ **Appraisers and auctioneers** providing valuation/appraisal services and sales of a variety of personal and other assets, such as those listed above

◆ **Coin and stamp dealers** providing appraisal services and, in some cases, instant cash for coin and stamp collections

◆ **Pawn brokers** providing services at the local level; they often promote themselves as specialists in purchasing estate jewelry, diamonds, precious metals, coins, guns, antiques, china, collectibles, expensive watches, sterling flatware, and so on

◆ **Real estate management professionals** providing property management of single/multiple family dwellings, maintenance services, rent collection, and turnkey cleanup

EDUCATIONAL INSTITUTIONS AND PROFESSIONALS

More than 40 percent of America's affluent pay for their grandchildren's private grade school and/or high school tuition. Coupled with the rapid growth of the affluent population, this translates into several million students whose tuition to attend private school will be subsidized within the next ten years. Given these facts, the demand for private school facilities and private school teachers, counselors, and tutors will likely accelerate. At the same time, tuition and related expenses should increase significantly. Why? Because affluent grandparents are bidding up the cost of private school tuition. Since many of their adult children do not have to pay for the services from which their children benefit, the parents are relatively insensitive to the escalating cost of a private school education.

Organizations and specialists who will benefit include:

◆ **Proprietors and teachers** at private schools that provide tuition-based education at the preschool, kindergarten, elementary, and high school levels

◆ **Proprietors and teachers** in specialized areas such as music, drama, the arts, special education/learning disability programs, career counseling, and tutorials for SAT and other types of entrance/aptitude tests

PROFESSIONAL SERVICES SPECIALISTS

As stated previously, attorneys play a pivotal role in the transfer of wealth between generations. Accountants are also important in this regard. These professionals often serve as key advisors to the affluent. Advice in this context extends beyond the normal core of accounting and legal services. These professionals are relied on for their insights into how best to distribute substantial financial and other gifts to children and grandchildren. Clients often view these accountants as their first line of defense against paying substantial gift and estate taxes. They are often called upon to be co-executors of the estates of their affluent clients. It is not unusual for co-executors in these situations to receive a percentage of the estates of their clients. This is one way the affluent reward these trusted advisors for a lifetime of sage advice.

Specialists who will benefit include:

◆ **Accountants** providing tax-planning strategies; estate, trust, and gift tax solutions; fiduciary services; business/asset valuation; and retirement planning

HOUSING SPECIALISTS/DWELLING PRODUCTS/SERVICES

More than half the affluent population will provide their offspring with financial assistance in purchasing a home. This figure actually understates the incidence of such outpatient care because often other substantial financial gifts not earmarked for specific use are used for home purchases and related expenses. Those who receive "home-acquisition subsidies" from their relatives are often less sensitive to the variations in home prices than the nonsubsidized. (As always, our data suggest that it is easier to spend other people's money.) This trend should benefit many of those who are employed in the residential housing and mortgage-lending businesses.

Home-acquisition subsidies typically do not negate the need for credit. Actually, parents who provide part of the purchase price of a home often precipitate the purchase of more expensive homes and larger mortgages on the part of their sons and daughters.

Specialists who will benefit include:

◆ **Home building contractors**

◆ **Mortgage lenders**

◆ **Remodeling contractors**

◆ **Renovation contractors**

◆ **Residential real estate developers**

◆ **Residential real estate agents**

◆ **Retailers of paint, wall coverings, and decorating products**

◆ **Marketers of alarm and security systems and security consultation services**

◆ **Providers of interior design and decorating services**

TABLE 7-5

ESTIMATED NUMBER OF MILLIONAIRE HOUSEHOLDS IN THE YEAR 2005

	TOTAL	PER 100,000 HH	RELATIVE CONCENTRATION
United States	5,625,408	5,239	100
Alabama	66,315	3,844	73
Alaska	19,216	7,148	136
Arizona	76,805	4,501	86
Arkansas	32,008	3,228	62
California	773,213	5,762	110
Colorado	92,677	5,936	113
Connecticut	109,481	8,702	166
Delaware	18,237	6,247	119
District of Columbia	14,076	6,815	130
Florida	289,231	4,911	94
Georgia	146,064	4,973	95
Hawaii	30,857	6,046	115
Idaho	19,264	3,883	74
Illinois	283,329	6,054	116
Indiana	108,679	4,674	89
Iowa	46,202	4,100	78
Kansas	49,784	4,755	91
Kentucky	56,271	3,668	70
Louisiana	62,193	3,611	69
Maine	18,537	3,887	74
Maryland	149,085	7,283	139
Massachusetts	154,390	6,746	129
Michigan	202,929	5,406	103
Minnesota	102,662	5,533	106
Mississippi	30,045	2,841	54
Missouri	92,665	4,431	85
Montana	12,954	3,661	70
Nebraska	28,026	4,276	82
Nevada	36,272	5,577	106
New Hampshire	26,941	6,013	115
New Jersey	258,917	8,275	158
New Mexico	26,352	3,758	72
New York	431,607	6,153	117
North Carolina	130,362	4,450	85
North Dakota	9,559	3,865	74
Ohio	197,554	4,485	86
Oklahoma	46,734	3,593	69
Oregon	62,776	4,795	92
Pennsylvania	238,010	5,033	96
Rhode Island	19,672	5,125	98
South Carolina	58,479	3,867	74
South Dakota	10,613	3,584	68
Tennessee	91,263	4,285	82
Texas	365,034	4,736	90
Utah	33,850	4,097	78
Vermont	10,035	4,407	84
Virginia	171,516	6,327	121
Washington	134,570	5,764	110
West Virginia	21,774	3,077	59
Wisconsin	100,421	4,852	93
Wyoming	9,021	4,493	86
Other Areas	41,239	3,640	69

FUND-RAISING COUNSELORS

Specialists who will benefit include:

◆ **Professionals who conduct philanthropic research, develop targeting strategies, and counsel foundations and educational institutions**

TRAVEL AGENTS AND BUREAUS AND TRAVEL CONSULTANTS

The affluent enjoy vacationing with their children and grandchildren, and many of the affluent spend considerable amounts doing so. About 55 percent recently spent more than $5,000 for a vacation. About one in six spent in excess of $10,000.

Specialists who will benefit include:

◆ **Marketers of family-oriented vacation resorts**

◆ **Marketers of cruises, tours, worldwide vacations, and treks and safaris**

WHERE ARE THE OPPORTUNITIES LIKELY TO BE?

People who are interested in targeting the wealthy need to know the geographic distribution of the opportunities available. Note that earlier in this chapter we provided estimates by state of the number and total dollar value of estates in the $1-million-or-more category (see Tables 7-3 and 7-4). But keep in mind that for every estate in the $1 million or more category, there are about forty millionaires who are still alive. Thus, for many people who wish to market to the affluent, living millionaires are the more important of the two groups.

With this in mind, we have estimated how many U.S. households will have a net worth of $1 million or more in the year 2005. We have also estimated how many of these households there will be in each of the fifty states, the District of Columbia, and among Americans living outside the U.S. (see Table 7-5). Note that California has the largest millionaire household population. In terms of concentration per 100,000 households, however, Connecticut ranks first.

JOBS: MILLIONAIRES
VERSUS HEIRS

THEY CHOSE THE RIGHT OCCUPATION.

A bout ten years ago, a reporter from a national news magazine called. She asked the question we are most frequently asked:

Who are the affluent?

By now you probably can predict the answer. Most of the affluent in America are business owners, including self-employed professionals. Twenty percent of the affluent households in America are headed by retirees. Of the remaining 80 percent, more than two-thirds are headed by self-employed owners of businesses. In America, fewer than one in five households, or about 18 percent, is headed by a self-employed business owner or professional. *But these self-employed people are four times more likely to be millionaires than those who work for others.*

The reporter followed with the next logical question:

What types of businesses do millionaires own?

Our answer was the same one we give everyone:

**You can't predict if someone is a millionaire
by the type of business he's in.**

After twenty years of studying millionaires across a wide spectrum of industries, we have concluded that *the character of the business owner is more important in predicting his level of wealth than the classification of his business.*

But no matter how hard we try to make our point, reporters want to keep things simple. What a great story, what a great headline, it would make if they could tell readers:

Here are ten businesses millionaires own!

We have gone out of our way to emphasize that there are no sure steps one can take to become wealthy. Too often reporters ignore the facts. They sensationalize and twist our research findings. Yes, you are more likely to become affluent if you're self-employed. But what some of these reporters don't tell you is that most business owners are not millionaires and will never come close to becoming wealthy.

We do tell reporters that some industries tend to be more profitable than others. Thus, those who own businesses in the more profitable industries tend, by definition, to realize more income. But just because you're in a profitable industry does not guarantee that your business will be highly productive. And even if your business is highly productive, you may never become wealthy. Why? Because even if you earn big profits, you may spend even bigger amounts on nonbusiness-related consumer goods and services. You may have been divorced three times or have a habit of gambling on the horses. You may not have a pension plan or own any shares in quality, publicly traded corporations. Perhaps you feel little need to accumulate wealth. Money, in your mind, may be the most easily renewable resource. If you think it is, you may be a spender and never an investor.

But what if you're frugal and a conscientious investor and you own a business that is profitable? In this case, you're likely to become wealthy.

It is easier to earn higher profits in some industries than others. We identify several of these profitable industries in this chapter. But again, we caution readers not to oversimplify our findings and suggestions. Too often people want a "sound-bite" answer to the question of how to become wealthy in America. Even worse are those who distort our data-based findings. Consider, along these lines, the message that was recently left for us by a business broker:

I thought you would like to know that someone has printed a brochure stating that you are a professor at Stanford University and that you found that 20 percent of the millionaires in America are dry cleaners. . . . Is this true?

First, neither one of us ever taught at Stanford. Second, neither of us has ever stated that one in five millionaires is at this moment pressing shirts. We did find in the mid-1980s that dry cleaning was a profitable small-business industry. But again, profits don't automatically translate into affluence or accumulated wealth. This is like those sons of ours and perhaps yours who thought they would make the varsity basketball team because they bought a pair of Air Jordan shoes. A label does not make a varsity player. Nor does an industry label make the business owner wealthy. It takes talent and discipline to generate profits and ultimately wealth.

That is why we are offended by people who tell the American public:

Just buy my educational/study-at-home kit and your new business venture will be a success. Start your own business today—you will be wealthy tomorrow. I did it in this industry. You can do it, too! It's so easy!

Again, it's not the kit, not the idea, not the industry. For example, the profitability data for hardware/lumber retail establishments twenty-five years ago never got us excited. They didn't convince us to invest in a business of this type. But think what the founders of the highly profitable Home Depot did. They reinvented the industry. They did not allow industry standards for profits, sales volume, or overhead to dictate how they operated their business and invested their money. These founders had tremendous talent, discipline, and courage. They became wealthy and helped make a lot of their employees and other investors financially independent. Most people who make it big in business set their own very high standards.

ONLY CHANGE IS PREDICTABLE

Things do change, even in the so-called owner/manager business environment. Take, for example, the industry we mentioned previously—dry cleaning. (In fact, the appropriate title is laundries, dry cleaning, and garment services.) With regard to this industry, Tom Stanley reported in 1988:

In 1984 there were 6,940 partnerships; 91.9 percent have net income, while the average return on receipts (net profit as a percent of receipts) was 23.4 percent (Thomas J. Stanley, *Marketing to the Affluent* [Homewood, Ill.: Irwin, 1988, p. 190]).

What about the profitability of this industry in the 1990s? We analyzed the IRS's federal income tax return data. In 1992, we determined that there were 4,615 partnerships; only 50.5 percent had any net income, while the average return on receipts was 13 percent. Also in 1992, there were 24,186 sole-proprietorship dry cleaners in America. What was their average net income? On average, it was $5,360. This placed dry cleaners 116th out of 171 sole proprietorships based on average net income criteria. The industry at that time ranked 119th in return on receipts, which equaled 8.1 percent. What percentage of dry cleaners generated a net income? Nearly three in four, or 74.1 percent, made at least one dollar of net income. In this regard, dry cleaning ranked 92 out of 171 industries analyzed.

What a difference eight short years can make. But the dry cleaning industry is not the only one to encounter such changes. The data in Table 8-1 contrast selected industries. You will notice that several have experienced significant changes in profitability over the years. The number of men's and boys' clothing and furnishings stores, for example, more than doubled from 1984 to 1992. In 1984, all of the sole proprietorships in that industry made a profit. But in 1992, only 82.7 percent were profitable. Its rank in this regard dropped from first to fifty-seventh among the 171 sole proprietorships studied. The highway and street construction contractors industry moved from a ranking of 8 to 138, while coal mining moved from 14 to 165.

Many external and often uncontrollable factors influ-

TABLE 8-1

RANKINGS OF SELECTED CATEGORIES OF SOLE PROPRIETORSHIPS ACCORDING TO THE PERCENTAGE WITH NET INCOME[1]: 1984 VS. 1992

Category	Total Number of Businesses	1984 Percent with Net Income	Rank	Total Number of Businesses	1992 Percent with Net Income	Rank	Average Net Income ($000's)
Men's and boys' clothing and furnishings stores	1,645	100.0	1	3,410	82.7	57	8.2
Offices of osteopathic physicians	1,001	100.0	3	10,598	96.3	13	7.76
Mobile-home dealers	4,718	95.4	7	6,844	92.3	23	10.1
Highway and street construction contractors	6,812	92.5	8	8,641	56.0	138	12.7
Carpentry and flooring contractors	312,832	92.0	9	497,631	92.0	25	8.9
Offices of chiropractors	18,928	91.5	10	32,501	85.1	49	47.5
Roofing and sheet metal contracting	53,539	91.4	11	98,235	86.9	42	9.1
Drug stores and proprietary stores	14,128	90.9	12	8,324	82.2	60	45.5
Coal mining	717	90.7	14	76	34.2	165	196.6
Drapery, curtain, and upholstery stores	17,508	90.3	15	29,827	79.2	74	6.2
Agriculture/veterinary	16,367	89.7	16	19,622	92.5	22	41.7
Taxicabs/passenger transportation	42,975	89.5	17	38,907	97.1	11	7.0
Other local and interurban passenger transportation	16,945	89.4	18	30,666	93.6	20	8.8
Dental laboratories	15,246	89.4	19	28,101	96.0	15	15.2
Primary metal manufacturing	4,972	89.2	20	3,460	100.0	1	26.1
Painting, paper-hanging, and decorating contractors	180,209	88.8	21	235,599	91.1	28	7.6
Offices of dentists	77,439	88.2	22	96,746	94.9	16	73.1
Bowling alleys	1,456	88.1	23	1,547	91.3	27	57.4
Offices of optometrists	16,919	86.9	25	12,576	96.1	14	60.1

[1]Net income was computed from the IRS's federal income tax data for 1984 and 1992.

ence the profitability of industries and firms within those industries. Often the presence of high numbers of profitable firms within an industry attracts more and more people to the industry, which can have a dampening effect on profits. Changes in consumer preferences can also affect profits. So can the actions of our government. If it had an energy policy that favored the use of coal, perhaps the number of sole-proprietorship coal mining businesses would not have dropped from 717 to 76 in just eight years. Note that only 34.2 percent of the 76 coal mining businesses made a net profit. But in spite of this, sole proprietors in this business earned an average net income of $196,618. Obviously a minority of coal mining operations owners ignore industry trends and standards, and many of these people have been rewarded for their tenacity and contrary beliefs about the coal industry. Many successful business owners have told us that they enjoy "short periods of rough times" in their chosen industries because they weed out much of the competition. This seems to be the case in the coal mining industry. The 34.2 percent of the businesses in the industry that were profitable had a net income of approximately $600,000.

Many people ask us, "Should I go into business for myself?" Most people have no business ever working for themselves. The average net income for the more than fifteen million sole proprietorships in America is only $6,200! About 25 percent of sole proprietorships do not make one cent of profit during a typical year. It's even worse for partnerships. Forty-two percent, on average, make no profits in a year. What about corporations? Only 55 percent have any taxable income during a typical twelve-month period.

SELF-EMPLOYED PROFESSIONALS VERSUS OTHER BUSINESS OWNERS

Fewer than one in five millionaire business owners turns his business over to his children to own and operate. Why? Give credit to wealthy parents. They know the odds of succeeding in business. They understand that most businesses are highly susceptible to competition, counter consumer trends, high overhead, and other uncontrollable variables.

So what do these millionaires advise their children to do? They encourage their children to become self-employed professionals, such as physicians, attorneys, engineers, architects, accountants, and dentists. As stated earlier, millionaire couples with children are five times more likely to send their children to medical school than other parents in America and about four times more likely to send them to law school.

The affluent know the risks and the odds of succeeding or failing in business. They also seem to understand that only a small minority of self-employed professionals fail to make a profit in any given year, and that the profitability of most professional service firms is substantially higher than the average for small businesses in general. We will elaborate on these issues with hard numbers. But first let's discuss the other attributes associated with being a self-employed professional.

For a moment assume you are Mr. Carl Johnson, the sole proprietor of Johnson Coal. You're the owner of one of the twenty-six coal mining businesses that made a profit last year out of the seventy-six in the industry. Not long ago, 717 sole proprietors were still in your industry. More than nine of every ten made a profit. Now the industry has been reduced in number by 90 percent. But you're tough, you're resourceful, and you're intelligent. In spite of the withdrawal of most of the other operators, you hung in there. Now you're reaping the benefits. You made a net profit of $600,000 last year. And you're doing well this year. Now you have two children in college who are outstanding students. You begin to ask yourself some questions:

◆ Should I encourage my David and Christy to become involved in the coal mining business?

◆ Should I encourage them to eventually take over my parents' coal mine?

◆ Is coal mining the best place for my children?

Most of the millionaire business owners we have interviewed would not encourage their children to take over such a business. This is especially true in cases in which the children are outstanding students. They would suggest that David and Christy, the young scholars, consider other avenues.

Most businesses today require some investment in land, equipment, and buildings. The Johnson Coal Mining business owns mountains that contain coal. It owns millions of dollars' worth of equipment. It employs many miners and must constantly upgrade the safety of its operation. It must conform to OSHA's mandates. It must deal with the uncontrollable price the market places on a ton of coal. It must constantly be vigilant about competitors who are trying to steal its customers. It must keep a careful watch on changes in America's energy policy. It also must keep its workers happy and safe. It must constantly deal with the possibility of a mine cave-in and halted production. Finally, the operation is in a fixed location. Mountains can't be moved to a warmer climate or closer to a more efficient railroad operation. What happens if there is a prolonged railroad strike?

Ask yourself these questions. If you do, you will soon realize you're in a precarious position. So what if you run a superior operation? The uncontrollable factors outlined above can kill your business. Given these considerations, that $600,000 you earned last year seems smaller. How many $600,000 years are in your future? What if the uncontrollable factors drive you bankrupt next year? Can you use your skills to teach coal mining at the technical university? Probably not. Your skills are more hands-on, not intellectual.

We once asked an affluent business owner who had fled Europe because of the Holocaust why all his adult children were self-employed professionals. His response:

They can take your business, but they can't take your intellect!

What does this mean? A government and/or a creditor can confiscate a business composed of land, machinery, coal pits, buildings, and so on. It can't confiscate your intellect. What do professionals sell? Not coal, not paint, not even pizza. What they sell most of all is their intellect.

Physicians, for example, can take their intellect anywhere in America. Their resources are quite portable. The same is true for dentists, attorneys, accountants, engineers, architects, veterinarians, and chiropractors. These are the occupations held by a disproportionate number of the sons and daughters of affluent couples throughout America.

What about the income characteristics of professionals as compared with the Johnson Coal Mining operation? Only a minority of self-employed professionals have ever made as

TABLE 8-2

THE TOP TEN MOST PROFITABLE¹ SOLE-PROPRIETORSHIP BUSINESSES

TYPE OF BUSINESS	NUMBER OF BUSINESSES	AVERAGE NET INCOME ($000'S)	RANK ACCORDING TO AVERAGE NET INCOME	PERCENT WITH NET INCOME	AVERAGE RETURN ON RECEIPTS	AVERAGE RECEIPTS REQUIRED TO GENERATE AVERAGE NET INCOME ($000'S)	AVERAGE RECEIPTS REQUIRED TO GENERATE THE AVERAGE NET OF COAL MINING ($000'S)
Coal Mining	76	196.6	1	34.2	8.2	2,397.6	2,397.6
Offices of Physicians	192,545	87.0	2	87.2	56.2	154.8	349.8
Offices of Osteopathic Physicians	10,598	77.6	3	96.3	57.8	134.3	340.1
Offices of Dentists	96,746	73.1	4	94.9	34.2	201.9	543.1
Offices of Optometrists	12,576	60.1	5	96.1	30.7	195.8	640.4
Bowling Centers	1,547	57.4	6	91.3	31.0	185.2	634.2
Offices of Chiropractors	32,501	47.5	7	85.1	39.3	120.9	500.3
Drug Stores	8,324	45.5	8	82.2	8.7	523.0	2,259.8
Veterinarian Services	19,622	41.7	9	92.5	22.5	185.3	873.8
Legal Services	280,946	39.8	10	86.6	47.4	84.0	414.8

¹Net income was computed from the IRS's federal income tax data for 1992. At that time, there were more than 15 million sole proprietorships in 171 classifications in the U.S.

much as $600,000 profit in a single year. And most self-employed professionals spend many years in training, which is costly both in dollars and time. Nevertheless, most affluent parents believe that the lifetime benefits associated with being a professional greatly outweigh the costs. Remember, most of these parents pay all or a significant portion of their sons' and daughters' tuition and fees for training. Their vote is with their hard-earned money.

How will you vote? Notice that coal mining, on average, produced a higher net income ($196,600) than any of the sole proprietorships listed in Table 8-2. But what proportion of coal mining operations made any net income during the same period of time? Only about one in three (34.2 percent). This is in sharp contrast with the percentages of profitable businesses in each of the professional service categories listed in Table 8-2. What percentages were profitable? About 87.2 percent of the offices of physicians, 94.9 percent of the offices of dentists, 92.5 percent of the offices of veterinarians, and 86.6 percent of the offices providing legal services.

Also examine the average return on receipts. On average, it would take $2.4 million in receipts for a coal mining operation on average to generate a net income of $196,600 (approximately 8.2 percent of $2.4 million in receipts). What about physicians? The average net income of a physician's office is $87,000—that's 56.2 percent of the $154,804 receipts generated. With that kind of return on receipts, how many dollars in receipts would a physician's office have to generate to earn the same average net income that coal mining businesses earned ($196,600)? Only $349,800, a far cry from the $2.4 million required of coal mining operations. The figure's even lower for osteopathic physicians; on average, they require receipts of $340,138 to earn the expected $196,600 in net income.

Legal service providers, on average, would need to generate $414,800 in sales to earn what the average coal mine operation earned in net income.

What will you advise David and Christy to do? If you're like most successful business owners, you will advise them to become professionals. So it is with the affluent in America. The first-generation affluent are typically entrepreneurs. They beat the odds. Their businesses succeed, and they become affluent. Much of their success depends on their living a frugal existence while building their businesses. Luck is often involved. And most who succeed understand that circumstances could have gone against them.

Their children will have it better. They will not have to take significant risks. They will be well educated. They will become physicians, attorneys, and accountants. Their capital is their intellect. But unlike their parents, they will postpone entering the job market until they are in their late twenties or even their early thirties. And most likely they will adopt an upper-middle-class lifestyle as soon as they start working, a much different lifestyle then their frugal parents had when they started their businesses.

Often their children are not frugal. How could they be? They have high-status positions that require higher levels of consumption and thus lower levels of investing. As a consequence, they may require economic outpatient care. In spite of earning high incomes, as most professionals do, they are obligated to spend. Thus, because there are corresponding high levels of household spending requirements for many high-income-producing categories of business, it is difficult to predict levels of wealth based on the income characteristics of various types of businesses.

"DULL-NORMAL" BUSINESSES AND THE AFFLUENT

A recent article in *Forbes* had an interesting lead:

Dull companies with steady earnings growth may not make for stimulating cocktail party chatter, but over the long term they make the best investments (Fleming Meeks and David S. Fomdiller, "Dare to Be Dull," *Forbes*, Nov. 6, 1995, p. 228).

Later in the same article, the authors mention that in the long run high-tech companies can and often do fall down on the performance scale. Typically, it's the companies in what we call the "dull-normal" industries that consistently perform well for their owners. *Forbes* lists several top-performing small businesses that have had great endurance for the past ten years. Some of the industries represented include wall-board manufacturing, building material manufacturing, electronics stores, prefab housing, and automobile parts.

No, these industries don't sound very exciting. But typically it's these mundane categories of businesses that produce wealth for their owners. Often dull-normal industries don't attract a great deal of competition, and demand for their offerings is not usually subject to rapid downturns. We recently developed our own list of businesses that are owned by millionaires (see Appendix 3). We would like to list just a sample at this juncture (see Table 8-3). What businesses do the affluent own? A wide variety of dull-normals.

RISK—OR FREEDOM?

Why do people operate their own businesses? First, most successful business owners will tell you that they have tremendous freedom. They are their own bosses. Also, they tell us that self-employment is less risky than working for others.

A professor once asked a group of sixty MBA students who were executives of public corporations this question.

What is risk?

One student replied:

Being an entrepreneur!

His fellow students agreed. Then the professor answered his own question with a quote from an entrepreneur:

What is risk? Having one source of income. Employees are at risk. . . . They have a single source of income. What about

TABLE 8-3

SELECTED BUSINESSES/OCCUPATIONS OF SELF-EMPLOYED MILLIONAIRES

Advertising Specialty Distributors	Human Resources Consulting Services
Ambulance Service	Industrial Chemicals-Cleaning/Sanitation Manufacturer
Apparel Manufacturer-Ready-to-Wear	Janitorial Services-Contractor
Auctioneer/Appraiser	Job Training/Vocational Tech School Owner
Cafeteria Owner	Long-Term Care Facilities
Citrus Fruits Farmer	Meat Processor
Coin and Stamp Dealership	Mobile-Home Park Owner
Consulting Geologist	Newsletter Publisher
Cotton Ginning	Office Temp Recruiting Service
Diesel Engine Rebuilder/Distributor	Pest Control Services
Donut Maker Machine Manufacturer	Physicist-Inventor
Engineering/Design	Public Relations/Lobbyist
Fund Raiser	Rice Farmer
Heat Transfer Equipment Manufacturer	Sand Blasting Contractor

the entrepreneur who sells janitorial services to your employers? He has hundreds and hundreds of customers . . . hundreds and hundreds of sources of income.

Actually, there is considerable financial risk in being a business owner. But business owners have a set of beliefs that helps them reduce their risk or at least their perceived risk:

♦ I'm in control of my own destiny.

♦ Risk is working for a ruthless employer.

♦ I can solve any problem.

♦ The only way to become a CEO is to own the company.

♦ There are no limits on the amount of income I can make.

♦ I get stronger and wiser every day by facing risk and adversity.

To be a business owner also requires that you have the desire to be self-employed. If you hate the thought of being outside the corporate environment, entrepreneurship may not be your calling. The most successful business owners we have interviewed have one characteristic in common: They all enjoy what they do. They all take pride in "going it alone."

Consider what a multimillionaire once told us about being self-employed:

There are more people [employees] today working at jobs that they don't like. I'll tell you honestly that the successful man is a guy who works at a job, who likes his work, who can't wait to get up in the morning to get down to the office, and that's my criteria. And I've always been that way. I can't wait to get up and get down to the office and get my job under way.

For this fellow (a widower without children), it's not the money. In fact, his estate plan calls for all his wealth to go to the undergraduate scholarship fund at his alma mater.

How did this fellow and others like him select the businesses they wanted to start? He was well trained in college by engineering and science professors, many of whom were also entrepreneurs. These professors were his role models. Most successful business owners had some knowledge or experience with their chosen industry before they ever opened their own businesses. Larry, for example, worked for more than a dozen years selling printing services. He was the top performer for his employer. But after growing tired of the constant fear that his employer would go bankrupt, he considered opening his own printing company. He sought our advice in this regard.

We asked Larry a simple question: "What's the number-one thing that printing companies need?" He immediately responded, "More business, more revenue, more customers." Thus, Larry answered his own question. He did start his own business, but not his own printing company. He became a self-employed broker of printing services. He now represents several outstanding printing firms and receives a commission on every sale he makes. His business has little overhead.

Before starting his own business, Larry told us he did not have the courage to be an entrepreneur. He told us that every time he even thought about "going it alone" he encountered fear. Larry believed that the self-employed were fearless, that fear never entered their minds.

We had to help Larry adjust his thinking. We began by explaining that his definition of courage was wrong. How do we define courage? Courage is behaving in a way that conjures up fear. Yes, Larry, courageous people, entrepreneurs, recognize the fear in what they are doing. But they deal with it. They overcome their fears. That's why they are successful.

We have spent a considerable amount of time studying courageous people. Certainly Ray Kroc had enormous courage to think he could market food to the world. Remember that he was an ambulance driver on the front lines in World War I. So was Walt Disney. Lee Iacocca had to have enormous courage to tell Congress and the world that Chrysler would come back "big time." He does not fit the strict definition of an entrepreneur, but in our minds he has entrepreneurial blood in his veins.

Fear abounds in America. But, according to our research, who has less fear and worry? Would you guess it's the person with the $5-million trust account, or the self-made entrepreneur worth several million dollars? Typically, it's the entrepreneur, the person who deals with risk every day, who tests his or her courage every day. In this way, he learns to conquer fear.

* * *

We saved the following case study for last, because in our minds it encapsulates the differences between PAWs and UAWs. Throughout this book, we have stressed that the members of these two groups have distinctly different needs. PAWs need to achieve, to create wealth, to become financially independent, to build something from scratch. UAWs more often need to display a high-status lifestyle. What happens when members of these two groups attempt to occupy the same space at the same time? As the following case study demonstrates, the likely result is conflict.

Mr. W. is a self-made millionaire with a net worth conservatively estimated to be over $30 million. A typical PAW, Mr. W. is the owner of several companies that produce industrial equipment, testing instruments, and specialty gauges. He is also involved in many other entrepreneurial activities, including real estate ventures.

Mr. W. lives in a middle-class neighborhood surrounded by people who have only a small fraction of the wealth he has accumulated. He and his wife drive full-sized General Motors sedans. His living and consuming habits are quite middle class. He never wears a tie or suit to work.

Mr. W. enjoys venturing into, as he calls it, luxury real estate:

I make money outside of the [equipment] business ... in real estate. ... God continues to make more people, but he doesn't make any more land. ... You will make money if you're smart and you're choosy where you pick the spot.

Mr. W. is very picky indeed. He buys property outright or in partnership only when the price is right. He typically purchases property or a part ownership from an owner and/or a developer who is in great need of financial assistance.

Recently he uncovered yet another "superior investment opportunity in sun country":

Some poor guy was putting together a luxury high-rise condominium. ... For a builder to build, he had to have 50 per-

*cent of the units sold. . . . So I went in and made a deal with
him. . . . [I] bought all of the units of the same style . . . floor
plan . . . with a lot of leverage, and he got his money. And
he built. Because I bought all the one style, . . . anybody
[who] wanted to buy that style had to see me. . . . Like
monopoly, nobody else competes with me. . . . I sell 'em all
right out, all but one.*

But Mr. W. does not even keep the one remaining unit for
very long. He and his family use it for a short vacation or
two. Occasionally, he invites his close friends to use it.
Otherwise, he rents the remaining unit until it is sold. Why
doesn't Mr. W. maintain a more permanent presence in these
condominium complexes? It's not his style.

Most of the people who buy Mr. W.'s vacation condominiums are upper-middle-class UAWs. Mr. W. and many
of the buyers of his condominium units have had a number
of disagreements. In several of the complexes where Mr. W.
previously bought units, his buyers passed so many restrictive covenants that Mr. W. was uncomfortable even spending vacation time in his condominiums. Thus, he felt compelled to sell that "one remaining unit" in each of these complexes.

*I have a dog. . . . Call him the six-figure doggie. . . . I have
sold several condominiums because . . . the people passed
dog laws. [They told me,] "You know, you've got to get rid
of the dog. . . ." I'll sell an entire building before I get rid of
my dog.*

Mr. W. anticipated that the status-conscious buyers of
his latest venture would also be insensitive to his desire to
have a dog. So before construction on the complex was

even started, he listed his dog in the building's declaration. It stated that Mr. W. and his family would have the right to have a dog with them when they were in residence.

All the buyers, according to Mr. W., were given copies of the declaration. Thus, they were all aware of Mr. W.'s right to have a dog in the complex. Not one owner objected at the time they purchased property. But shortly after the complex was completely sold out, excluding Mr. W.'s "last available unit," the owners banded together and formed an action committee. Its purpose was to develop and enforce an expanded list of restrictive covenants. Certainly these new covenants would not restrict the rights of Mr. W. and his dog? After all, these rights were specified in the original declaration.

The action committee passed a dog law. It sidestepped the original declaration concerning dogs and stated that dogs would be allowed on the complex, with certain restrictions, if they weighed less than fifteen pounds. So much for doggie rights and original declarations. Mr. W. felt that this was a subterfuge to encourage him to sell out. His six-figure doggie weighed thirty pounds. He felt that even if the dog dieted, it could not come into compliance. Mr. W. was particularly disturbed that he was never allowed to cast a vote for or against the dog-related covenant. Nonetheless, he was determined to keep his dog in spite of the covenant. After all, he had been a major investor in the building before construction even began.

They [the action committee] wrote me a letter [and] stated that I had to get rid of the dog because it was over fifteen pounds. . . . So I went to one of their meetings. . . . I complained about their voting system. . . . I had no representation.

Just prior to leaving the meeting, Mr. W. addressed the committee:

How do you know he's over fifteen pounds? . . . How do you know? He could be hollow. . . . I won't get rid of the dog.

A few days after the meeting, the head of the action committee cornered Mrs. W. while she was walking her dog. He told her in a legalese tone: "Get rid of the dog. You're in violation of our covenant." Later that afternoon, Mrs. W. told her husband what had transpired. She was noticeably upset about the encounter. He advised her to stay calm.

Several weeks later, Mr. W. received a letter that demanded that he remove his dog. It also stated that legal action would be initiated if he did not comply with the dog-related covenant. Two more letters followed. Each contained statements that were even more threatening than the first.

Mr. W. was not impressed with these requests. The author of the letters was the chairman of the action committee. He was also an attorney. But as Mr. W. discovered, the chairman was not licensed to practice law in the state where the complex was located. Thus, Mr. W. "promptly ignored" each of the action committee's demands.

However, Mr. W. and his family began to feel that they were out of place even just vacationing at this condominium complex. Was the action committee using the dog as leverage to evict his entire family? Mr. W. was convinced this was the real issue. He and his family were not what some would consider to be "beautiful people." In contrast, the complex was filled with (in Mr. W.'s parlance) the best-scrubbed condominium owners one could ever imagine.

Mr. W. was growing increasingly angry with the members of the action committee. He felt that its members were going out of their way to be rude to him. He was especially annoyed that the chairman of the committee had embarrassed his wife in front of several other condominium owners. Mr. W. devised a plan.

At a meeting of the condominium owners, at which all the members of the action committee were present, Mr. W. stood up and introduced himself.

I'm the guy that you have been sending letters to . . . about our dog. . . . I have given your proposal some careful consideration. . . . I've decided I'm not going to get rid of my dog, nor am I going to sell my condominium.

This statement drew anticipated boos and hisses from the audience. After gaining the undivided attention of his targeted audience, he outlined his counterproposal: to turn his condominium unit over to his company's profit-sharing and pension plan and allow assembly-line employees to use the unit as a vacation resort fifty-two weeks a year. He asked his audience: "Would that be okay with all of you folks?"

Numerous members of the audience moaned. They were undoubtedly envisioning Mr. W.'s blue-collar employees invading their space fifty-two weeks a year! Some attendees shouted out, "Keep the dog, keep the dog!" The chairman of the action committee proposed that a committee meeting be held immediately in the adjoining conference room. Five minutes after this behind-closed-doors meeting, the committee members filed back into the room. The chairman told the audience of condominium owners that the action committee had made a decision.

"After reviewing all the elements of this situation, the action committee recommends that the W.s be allowed to

keep their dog. I ask that the covenant be so amended. All in favor . . ."

Not long after this brilliant victory, the W.s sold their condominium unit. They did so because, as Mr. W. observed:

I don't want to live in a building with people who don't like dogs.

According to Mr. W., his dog was very important to him and his family. So much so that they sold the unit at a bargain price. They have sold other units in other complexes in which people were hostile to their dog. So how much is that doggie in the condominium worth? To the W.s, it's worth several hundreds of thousands of dollars. That's how much he estimates he lost in selling his units at below-true-market value. A hostile environment, even in an atmosphere of beautiful people, is not a good place for dogs—or for prodigious accumulators of wealth.

ACKNOWLEDGMENTS

The cornerstone for *The Millionaire Next Door* was put in place in 1973, when I undertook my first study of the affluent population. This book reflects the knowledge and insights that were gained from that initial study and from many studies of the affluent that followed. Most recently, my coauthor, Bill Danko, and I conducted a survey from May 1995 through January 1996 that we consider to be most revealing. We underwrote the study ourselves. This allowed us to have complete control in focusing on the factors that explain how people become affluent in America.

Along the road of gathering intelligence abut the wealthy, I have been assisted by truly extraordinary people. Bill has been my most important and valuable "wing man" since the beginning of this research. No one could ask for a better coauthor than Dr. Bill Danko.

I am indebted to my wife, Janet, for her guidance, patience, and assistance in the development of the early forms of the manuscript. A very special thank-you is accorded Ruth Tiller for her outstanding job in questionnaire formatting, interview transcription, editing, and word processing. I owe a deep debt of gratitude to Suzanne De Galan for her extraordinary work in editing the manuscript. I also wish to acknowledge the contribution of my children, Sarah and Brad, for their assistance as student interns on this project.

Finally, I would like to acknowledge the thousands of people who have contributed to our work through their candor, willingness, and interest in telling "their story." They are truly the millionaires next door!

Thomas J. Stanley, Ph.D.
Atlanta, Georgia

Many people fostered my career. I am particularly grateful to my core set of supporters from the University at Albany, State University of New York. Professors Bill Holstein, Hugh Farley, Don Bourque, Sal Belardo, and others have consistently contributed to an atmosphere of collegiality at the University that allowed this work to come to fruition. And, for certain, if it weren't for Bill and Don bringing Tom Stanley to teach at the University in the early 1970s, this book and other fruitful efforts by the Stanley/Danko team would never have come about.

The laborious tasks associated with much of the empirical research necessary to complete the book were cheerfully completed under my direction by my three children, Christy, Todd, and David. Their diligence and attention to detail could not have been and was not motivated by a "fee for service." They executed their tasks as if they had a true equity stake in the project. I trust that this exposure to marketing research will make them informed consumers when shaping their careers.

Finally, I must recognize and applaud my mother, who instilled in me discipline and faith. Through her living example of hard work in spite of adversity, she taught me how to live an honorable life of perseverance and courage guided by God.

William D. Danko, Ph.D.
Albany, New York

APPENDIX 1

HOW WE FIND MILLIONAIRES

How do we go about finding millionaires to survey? A "C" student of ours once tried to answer this question in a marketing research course. He suggested that we merely obtain a list of people who drive luxury cars. As readers know by now, however, most millionaires do not drive luxury cars. Most luxury car drivers are not millionaires. No, this method will not work!

TARGETING BY NEIGHBORHOOD

The method used in our most recent study, as well as many others we have conducted, was developed by our friend Jon Robbin, the inventor of geocoding. Mr. Robbin was the first to classify—or code—each of the more than 300,000 neighborhoods in America. Using this system, one can code more than 90 percent of America's 100 million households.

Mr. Robbin coded these neighborhoods first according to the average income for each. Next, he estimated the average net worth of each neighborhood by first determining the average interest income, net rental income, et al., generated by households in each neighborhood. Then, using his mathematical "capitalization model," he estimated the average net worth that would be required to generate such incomes. Once he had determined the estimated average net worth for each neighborhood, he assigned each a code. A code of one was assigned to the neighborhood with the highest estimated average net worth; a two was assigned to the neighborhood with the next highest average net worth, and so on. (Also see Thomas J. Stanley and

Murphy A. Sewall, "The Response of Affluent Consumers to Mail Surveys," *Journal of Advertising Research* [June/July 1986], pp. 55–58.)

We use this estimated net-worth scale to help us find millionaires to survey. First, we select sample neighborhoods that rank significantly higher than average along the estimated net-worth scale. A commercial mailing list company calculates the number of households in each of our chosen high–net worth neighborhoods. Next, the list company randomly selects heads of households within the selected neighborhoods. These are the people we survey.

In our most recent national study, conducted from June 1995 through January 1996, we selected 3,000 heads of households. Each received an eight-page questionnaire, a form letter asking for his participation and guaranteeing the anonymity and confidentiality of the data we collected, and a dollar bill as a token of our appreciation, along with a business reply envelope in which to return the completed questionnaire. A total of 1,115 surveys were completed in time to be included in our analysis. An additional 322 surveys could also be accounted for: 156 address unknown, 122 incomplete, and 44 otherwise usable surveys returned after data analysis had commenced. Overall, the response rate was 45 percent. Out of the 1,115 respondents, 385, or 34.5 percent of the total, had a household net worth of $1 million or more.

TARGETING BY OCCUPATION

We supplemented this survey with alternative surveys. Often we employ what is called the *ad hoc* method, in which we survey a narrowly defined population segment, as opposed to people who live within affluent neighborhoods in general. These population segments include affluent farmers, senior corporate executives, middle managers, engineers/architects, health-care professionals, accountants, attorneys, teachers, professors, auctioneers, entrepreneurs, and others. *Ad hoc* surveys are useful because even the best geocoding methods typically ignore affluent people who live in rural areas.

APPENDIX 2

1996 MOTOR VEHICLES: ESTIMATED PRICE PER POUND

MAKE AND MODEL	APPROXIMATE LIST/ RETAIL PRICE	WEIGHT IN POUNDS	COST PER POUND	RELATIVE COST INDEX (AVERAGE = 100)
Dodge Ram	$17,196	4,785	$3.59	52
Hyundai Accent	$ 8,790	2,290	$3.84	56
Isuzu Hombre	$11,531	2,850	$4.05	59
Chevrolet S-Series	$14,643	3,560	$4.11	60
Dodge Dakota	$15,394	3,740	$4.12	60
Ford Ranger	$15,223	3,680	$4.14	60
Mazda B-Series	$15,320	3,680	$4.16	61
Ford Aspire	$ 9,098	2,140	$4.25	62
Dodge Neon	$11,098	2,600	$4.27	62
Plymouth Neon	$11,098	2,600	$4.27	62
GMC Sonoma	$15,213	3,560	$4.27	62
Geo Metro	$ 9,055	2,065	$4.38	64
Ford Escort	$11,635	2,565	$4.54	66
GMC Sierra C/K	$17,394	3,829	$4.54	66
Hyundai Elantra	$12,349	2,700	$4.57	67
Ford F-Series	$20,143	4,400	$4.58	67
Plymouth Voyager	$18,703	3,985	$4.69	68
Plymouth Grand Voyager	$18,958	4,035	$4.70	68
Mercury Cougar	$17,430	3,705	$4.70	69
Ford Thunderbird	$17,485	3,705	$4.72	69
Pontiac Grand Am	$14,499	3,035	$4.78	70
Mitsubishi Mirage	$11,420	2,390	$4.78	70
Plymouth Breeze	$14,060	2,930	$4.80	70
Mercury Mystique	$15,018	3,110	$4.83	70
Saturn	$11,695	2,405	$4.86	71
Nissan Truck	$15,274	3,125	$4.89	71
Ford Aerostar	$20,633	4,220	$4.89	71
Eagle Summit	$11,712	2,390	$4.90	71
Chevrolet Astro	$22,169	4,520	$4.90	71
Jeep Wrangler	$15,869	3,210	$4.94	72

MAKE AND MODEL	APPROXIMATE LIST/ RETAIL PRICE	WEIGHT IN POUNDS	COST PER POUND	RELATIVE COST INDEX (AVERAGE = 100)
Dodge Stratus	$15,285	3,085	$4.95	72
Eagle Summit Wagon	$15,437	3,100	$4.98	73
Oldsmobile Ciera	$15,455	3,100	$4.99	73
Pontiac Trans Sport	$19,394	3,890	$4.99	73
GMC Safari	$22,562	4,520	$4.99	73
Chevrolet C/K	$19,150	3,829	$5.00	73
Suzuki Swift	$ 9,250	1,845	$5.01	73
Mazda Protegé	$13,195	2,630	$5.02	73
Chevrolet Cavalier	$14,000	2,765	$5.06	74
Dodge Avenger	$16,081	3,175	$5.06	74
Chevrolet Lumina	$17,205	3,395	$5.07	74
Mercury Tracer	$12,878	2,535	$5.08	74
GMC Yukon	$27,225	5,343	$5.10	74
Geo Prizm	$12,820	2,510	$5.11	74
Chevrolet Lumina Van	$19,890	3,890	$5.11	75
GMC Suburban	$28,855	5,640	$5.12	75
Ford Bronco	$25,628	5,005	$5.12	75
Hyundai Sonata	$15,849	3,095	$5.12	75
Toyota Tercel	$11,128	2,165	$5.14	75
Dodge Caravan	$20,505	3,985	$5.15	75
Ford Contour	$14,978	2,910	$5.15	75
Oldsmobile Achieva	$14,995	2,905	$5.16	75
Chevrolet Corsica	$14,385	2,785	$5.17	75
Ford Probe	$15,190	2,900	$5.24	76
Saturn SC	$12,745	2,420	$5.27	77
Chevrolet Caprice	$22,155	4,205	$5.27	77
Pontiac Sunfire	$14,619	2,765	$5.29	77
Dodge Grand Caravan	$21,375	4,035	$5.30	77
Eagle Talon	$17,165	3,235	$5.31	77
Chevrolet Monte Carlo	$18,355	3,450	$5.32	78
Nissan Sentra	$13,364	2,500	$5.35	78
Pontiac Grand Prix	$18,970	3,535	$5.37	78
Chevrolet Suburban	$30,340	5,640	$5.38	78

MAKE AND MODEL	APPROXIMATE LIST/ RETAIL PRICE	WEIGHT IN POUNDS	COST PER POUND	RELATIVE COST INDEX (AVERAGE = 100)
Jeep Cherokee	$18,411	3,420	$5.38	78
Chevrolet Beretta	$15,090	2,785	$5.42	79
Buick Skylark	$16,598	3,055	$5.43	79
Ford Crown Victoria	$21,815	4,010	$5.44	79
Isuzu Rodeo	$22,225	4,080	$5.45	79
GMC Jimmy	$23,876	4,380	$5.45	79
Chevrolet Tahoe	$29,337	5,343	$5.49	80
Honda Civic	$13,415	2,443	$5.49	80
Toyota T100	$19,013	3,460	$5.50	80
Ford Windstar	$21,675	3,940	$5.50	80
Toyota RAV 4	$15,998	2,905	$5.51	80
Oldsmobile Cutlass Supreme	$18,808	3,410	$5.52	80
Suzuki Esteem	$12,649	2,290	$5.52	81
Nissan 200SX	$14,259	2,580	$5.53	81
Toyota Corolla	$14,143	2,540	$5.57	81
Ford Mustang	$19,338	3,450	$5.61	82
Toyota Tacoma	$17,078	3,040	$5.62	82
Honda Passport	$22,935	4,080	$5.62	82
Mercury Grand Marquis	$22,680	4,010	$5.66	82
Oldsmobile Silhouette	$22,005	3,890	$5.66	82
Suzuki Sidekick	$15,949	2,805	$5.69	83
Ford Taurus	$19,998	3,516	$5.69	83
Suzuki X90	$14,249	2,495	$5.71	83
Geo Tracker	$14,340	2,500	$5.74	84
Chevrolet Blazer	$23,995	4,180	$5.74	84
Chrysler Sebring	$18,296	3,175	$5.76	84
Buick Century	$18,063	3,100	$5.83	85
Mitsubishi Galant	$17,644	3,025	$5.83	85
Chrysler Cirrus	$18,525	3,145	$5.89	86
Chevrolet Camaro	$19,740	3,350	$5.89	86
Volkswagen Jetta	$17,430	2,955	$5.90	86
Mazda MPV	$24,510	4,150	$5.91	86
Dodge Intrepid	$20,353	3,435	$5.93	86

MAKE AND MODEL	APPROXIMATE LIST/ RETAIL PRICE	WEIGHT IN POUNDS	COST PER POUND	RELATIVE COST INDEX (AVERAGE = 100)
Toyota Paseo	$13,038	2,200	$5.93	86
Mercury Villager	$23,165	3,900	$5.94	87
Buick Regal	$20,623	3,455	$5.97	87
Nissan Quest	$23,299	3,900	$5.97	87
Ford Explorer	$26,558	4,440	$5.98	87
Nissan Altima	$18,324	3,050	$6.01	88
Chrysler Concorde	$21,410	3,550	$6.03	88
Mercury Sable	$20,675	3,415	$6.05	88
Pontiac Firebird	$21,489	3,545	$6.06	88
Eagle Vision	$21,540	3,550	$6.07	88
Mitsubishi Eclipse	$19,713	3,235	$6.09	89
Honda Accord	$20,100	3,255	$6.18	90
Volkswagen Golf	$16,563	2,635	$6.29	92
Subaru Impreza	$15,345	2,425	$6.33	92
Buick Roadmaster	$26,568	4,195	$6.33	92
Volkswagen Passat	$20,375	3,180	$6.41	93
Toyota Camry	$20,753	3,230	$6.43	94
Pontiac Bonneville	$23,697	3,665	$6.47	94
Chrysler Sebring Convertible	$22,068	3,350	$6.59	96
Nissan Pathfinder	$27,264	4,090	$6.67	97
Toyota 4Runner	$26,238	3,930	$6.68	97
Oldsmobile 88	$23,208	3,470	$6.69	97
Mazda 626	$19,145	2,860	$6.69	98
Chrysler Town & Country	$27,385	4,035	$6.79	99
AVERAGE	**$23,992**	**3,450**	**$6.86**	**100**
Buick Le Sabre	$23,730	3,450	$6.88	100
Toyota Previa	$28,258	4,105	$6.88	100
Subaru Legacy	$20,995	3,040	$6.91	101
Acura Integra	$18,720	2,665	$7.02	102
Oldsmobile Bravada	$29,505	4,200	$7.03	102
Nissan 240SX	$20,304	2,880	$7.05	103

MAKE AND MODEL	APPROXIMATE LIST/ RETAIL PRICE	WEIGHT IN POUNDS	COST PER POUND	RELATIVE COST INDEX (AVERAGE = 100)
Honda Odyssey	$24,555	3,480	$7.06	103
Mitsubishi Montero	$31,437	4,445	$7.07	103
Jeep Grand Cherokee	$28,980	4,090	$7.09	103
Isuzu Oasis	$24,743	3,480	$7.11	104
Mazda MX-6	$20,372	2,865	$7.11	104
Honda Civic del Sol	$17,165	2,410	$7.12	104
Isuzu Trooper	$31,657	4,365	$7.26	106
Land Rover Discovery	$33,363	4,535	$7.36	107
BMW 318ti	$20,560	2,790	$7.37	107
Toyota Celica	$20,568	2,720	$7.56	110
Toyota Avalon	$25,453	3,320	$7.67	112
Nissan Maxima	$23,639	3,070	$7.70	112
Acura SLX	$33,900	4,365	$7.77	113
Toyota Land Cruiser	$40,258	5,150	$7.82	114
Buick Riviera	$29,475	3,770	$7.82	114
Oldsmobile 98	$28,710	3,640	$7.89	115
Honda Prelude	$22,920	2,865	$8.00	117
Audi A4	$26,500	3,222	$8.22	120
Cadillac Fleetwood	$36,995	4,480	$8.26	120
Acura CL	$25,500	3,065	$8.32	121
Buick Park Avenue	$30,513	3,640	$8.38	122
Chrysler LHS	$30,255	3,605	$8.39	122
Oldsmobile Aurora	$34,860	3,995	$8.73	127
Infiniti G20	$25,150	2,865	$8.78	128
Mazda MX-5 Miata	$20,990	2,335	$8.99	131
Subaru SVX	$32,745	3,610	$9.07	132
Volvo 850	$30,038	3,285	$9.14	133
Lexus LX450	$47,500	5,150	$9.22	134
Mazda Millenia	$31,560	3,415	$9.24	135
Mitsubishi Diamante	$35,250	3,730	$9.45	138
Lexus ES300	$32,400	3,400	$9.53	139
Cadillac De Ville	$38,245	3,985	$9.60	140
Mercedes-Benz C-Class	$32,575	3,370	$9.67	141

MAKE AND MODEL	APPROXIMATE LIST/ RETAIL PRICE	WEIGHT IN POUNDS	COST PER POUND	RELATIVE COST INDEX (AVERAGE = 100)
Acura TL	$31,700	3,278	$9.67	141
Lincoln Town Car	$39,435	4,055	$9.73	142
Audi A6	$33,150	3,405	$9.74	142
Infiniti I30	$31,300	3,195	$9.80	143
Volvo 960	$34,610	3,485	$9.93	145
BMW 3-Series	$33,670	3,250	$10.36	151
Lincoln Mark VIII	$39,650	3,810	$10.41	152
Lincoln Continental	$41,800	3,975	$10.52	153
Saab 900	$33,245	3,145	$10.57	154
BMW Z3	$28,750	2,690	$10.69	156
Cadillac Eldorado	$41,295	3,840	$10.75	157
Saab 9000	$36,195	3,275	$11.05	161
Toyota Supra	$39,850	3,555	$11.21	163
Infiniti J30	$40,460	3,535	$11.45	167
Cadillac Seville	$45,245	3,935	$11.50	168
Nissan 300ZX	$41,059	3,565	$11.52	168
BMW 5-Series	$43,900	3,675	$11.95	174
Range Rover	$58,500	4,875	$12.00	175
Lexus GS300	$45,700	3,765	$12.14	177
Acura RL	$45,000	3,700	$12.16	177
Chevrolet Corvette	$41,143	3,380	$12.17	177
Mitsubishi 3000 GT	$47,345	3,805	$12.44	181
Mercedes-Benz E-Class	$44,900	3,585	$12.52	183
Lexus SC400/SC300	$47,900	3,710	$12.91	188
Mazda RX-7	$37,800	2,895	$13.06	190
Infiniti Q45	$56,260	4,250	$13.24	193
Lexus LS400	$52,900	3,800	$13.92	203
BMW 740iL	$62,490	4,145	$15.08	220
Jaguar XJ6	$61,295	4,040	$15.17	221

APPENDIX 3

BUSINESSES/OCCUPATIONS OF SELF-EMPLOYED MILLIONAIRES

Accountant
Accounting/Auditing Services
Advertising Agency
Advertising Specialty Distributor
Advertising/Marketing Advisor
Aerospace Consultant
Agriculture
Ambulance Service
Antique Sales
Apartment Complex Owner/Manager
Apparel Manufacturer-Sportswear
Apparel Manufacturer-Infant Wear
Apparel Manufacturer-Ready-to-Wear
Apparel Retailer/Wholesaler-Ladies'
    Fashions
Artist-Commercial
Attorney
Attorney-Entertainment Industry
Attorney-Real Estate
Auctioneer
Auctioneer/Appraiser
Audio/Video Reproduction
Author-Fiction
Author-Textbooks/Training Manuals
Automotive Leasing
Baked Goods Producer
Beauty Salon(s) Owner-Manager
Beer Wholesaler
Beverage Machinery Manufacturer
Bovine Semen Distributor
Brokerage/Sales
Builder

Builder/Real Estate Developer
Business/Real Estate Broker/Investor
Cafeteria Owner
Candy/Tobacco Wholesaler
Caps/Hats Manufacturer
Carpet Manufacturer
Citrus Fruits Farmer
Civil Engineer and Surveyor
Clergyman-Lecturer
Clinical Psychologist
Coin and Stamp Dealer
Commercial Laundry
Commercial Real Estate Management
    Company
Commercial Laboratory
Commercial Property Management
    Company
Commodity Brokerage Company-Owner
Computer Consultant
Computer Applications Consultant
Construction
Construction Equipment Dealer
Construction Equipment Manufacturing
Construction-Mechanical/Electrical
Construction Performance Insurance
Consultant
Consulting Geologist
Contract Feeding
Contractor
Convenience Food Stores Owner
Cotton Gin Operator
Cotton Farmer

Cotton Ginning Owner/Manager
CPA/Broker
CPA/Financial Planner
Curtain Manufacturer
Dairy Farmer
Dairy Products Manufacturer
Data Services
Dentist
Dentist-Orthodontist
Department Store Owner
Design/Engineering/Builder
Developer/Construction
Diesel Engine Rebuilder/Distributor
Direct Mail Services
Direct Marketing
Direct Marketing Service Organization
Display and Fixture Manufacturer
Donut Maker Machine Manufacturer
Electrical Supply Wholesaler
Employment Agency Owner/Manager
Energy Production Engineer/Consultant
Energy Consultant
Engineer/Architect
Excavation Contractor
Excavation/Foundation Contracting
Executive Transportation/Bodyguard Service
Farmer
Fast Food Restaurants
Financial Consultant
Florist Retailer/Wholesaler
Freight Agent
Fruit and Vegetable Distributor
Fuel Oil Dealer
Fuel Oil Distributor
Fund Raiser/Consultant
Funeral Home Operator
Furniture Manufacturing
General Agent Insurance Agency

General Contractor
Grading Contractor
Grocery Wholesaler
Grocery Store Retailer
Heat Transfer Equipment Manufacturer
Home Health Care Service
Home Builder/Developer
Home Repair/Painting
Home Furnishings
Horse Breeder
Human Resources Consulting Services
Import-Export
Independent Investment Manager
Independent Insurance Agency
Industrial Laundry/Dry Cleaning Plant
Industrial Chemicals-Cleaning/Sanitation
    Manufacturer
Information Services
Installations Contractor
Insurance Agent
Insurance Agency Owner
Insurance Adjusters
Investment Management
Irrigated Farmland Realtor-Lessee
Janitorial Services Contractor
Janitorial Supply-Wholesaler Distributor
Janitorial Contractor
Jewelry Retailer/Wholesaler
Job Training/Vocational Tech School Owner
Kaolin Mining, Processing, Sales
Kitchen and Bath Distributor
Labor Arbitrator
Labor Negotiator
Laminated and Coated Paper Manufacturer
Land Planning, Designing, Engineering
Lawyer-Personal Injury
Lecturer
Liquor Wholesaler

Loan Broker
Long-Term Care Facilities
Machine Design
Machine Tool Manufacturing
Managed Care Facilities Owner
Management Consulting
Manufactured Housing
Manufacturer-Women's Foundation Wear
Marina Owner/Repair Service
Marketing/Sales Professional
Marketing Services
Marketing Consultant
Mattress/Foundation Manufacturer
Meat Processor
Mechanical Contractor
Medical Research
Merchant
Micro-Electronics
Mobile-Home Park Owner
Mobile-Home Dealer
Motion Picture Production
Motor Sports Promoter
Moving and Storage
Newsletter Publisher
Non-Profit Trade Association Management
Nursing Home
Office Furnishings
Office Temp Recruiting Service
Office Park Developer
Office Supply Wholesaler
Office Machines Wholesaler
Oil/Gas Investment Company Owner
Orthopedic Surgeon
Oversize Vehicle Escort Service
Owner/College President
Paint Removal/Metal Cleaning
Patent Owner/Inventor
Paving Contractor

Pest Control Services
Petroleum Engineering Consulting Services
Pharmaceuticals
Pharmacist
Physical and Speech Therapy Company
Physician
Physician-Anesthesiologist
Physician-Dermatologist
Physicist-Inventor
Pizza Restaurant Chain Owner
Plastic Surgeon
Poultry Farmer
President/Owner Mutual Fund
Printing, Self Storage, Farming
Printing
Private Schooling
Property Owner/Developer
Public Relations/Lobbyist
Publisher of Newsletters
Publishing
Race Track/Speedway Operator
Radiologist
Rancher
Real Estate Agency Owner
Real Estate Broker
Real Estate Developer
Real Estate Investment Trust-Manager
Real Estate-Broker/Developer/Financier
Real Estate Auctioneer
Real Estate
Restaurant Owner
Retail Jeweler
Retail Chain-Women's Ready-to-Wear
Retail Store/Personnel Service
Rice Farmer
Sales Agent
Sales Representative Agency
Salvage Merchandiser

Sand Blasting Contractor
Sand and Gravel
Scrap Metal Dealer
Seafood Distributor
Seafood Wholesaler
Service Station Chain Owner
Ship Repair-Dry Dock
Sign Manufacturer
Soft Drink Bottler
Software Development
Specialty Steel Manufacturer
Specialty Oil Food Importer/Distributor
Specialty Tools Manufacturer
Specialty Fabric Manufacturer
Speculator in Distressed Real Estate
Stock Broker
Store Owner
Tax Consultant/Attorney
Technical Consultant/Scientific Worker
Technical/Scientific Worker
Textile Engineering Services

Timber Farmer
Tool Engineer
Tradesman
Trading Company
Transportation/Freight Management
Travel Agency Owner/Manager
Travel Agency Owner
Truck Stop(s) Owner
Trustee Advisor
Tug (Boat) Services Owner
Vegetables Farmer
Vehicle Engines & Parts Wholesaler
Water Supply Contracting
Welding Contracting
Welding Supply Distributor
Wholesale Distribution
Wholesale/Distributor
Wholesale Grocery
Wholesale Produce
Wholesale Photo Franchiser
Xerox Sales/Service

Visit
❖ **Pocket Books** ❖
online at

....

www.SimonSays.com

....

Keep up on the latest new
releases from your favorite
authors, as well as author
appearances, news, chats,
special offers and more.

SIMON & SCHUSTER
A VIACOM COMPANY
www.SimonSays.com

Pocket
Books

2381-01